BOMBAY
AFTER
AYODHYA

Praise for *Bombay after Ayodhya*

'Mumbai has been the City of Dreams for multitudinous generations. Jitendra Dixit's book takes me down memory lane as I have been witness to many of the events enumerated therein. Jitendra's elucidation of Mumbai is honest, stark and gripping, capturing the key events speckled on the city's landscape. A pure-bred Mumbaikar, Jitendra is the most able and qualified to pen this treatise.'

—Rakesh Maria, former commissioner of police, Mumbai

'The first big terrorist attack in the world on a mega city happened in March 1993. The serial blasts and the two riots preceding them have changed the *mayanagri* (magic city) Mumbai forever. As a Bombayite and a journalist, Jitendra Dixit has closely witnessed those events that have shaped present-day Mumbai. I commend his attempt to chronicle those unprecedented events, and no one who loves Mumbai should miss reading this book.'

—D. Sivanandhan, former director general of Maharashtra Police and joint director, CBI

'Jitendra Dixit's *Bombay after Ayodhya: A City in Flux* is a fascinating read of how religious matters and identities are used for electoral gains. Dixit is an ace chronicler in documenting how the quest for power makes man constantly seek to change the face of God by force.'

—Rasheed Kidwai, senior journalist and author

'Having lived and worked in Mumbai, it's clear to me that the Ayodhya incident deeply affected the city. Ayodhya was not just the turning point of Indian politics but also of Mumbai. An outstanding journalist, Jitendra Dixit delves deep into this impact and the changes in my favourite city.'

—Abhigyan Prakash, author and TV journalist

BOMBAY AFTER AYODHYA

A CITY IN FLUX

JITENDRA DIXIT

HarperCollins *Publishers* India

First published in India by HarperCollins *Publishers* 2022
4th Floor, Tower A, Building No. 10, Phase II, DLF Cyber City,
Gurugram, Haryana – 122002
www.harpercollins.co.in

2 4 6 8 10 9 7 5 3 1

P-ISBN: 978-93-5629-411-0
E-ISBN: 978-93-5629-412-7

Typeset in 11.5/15 Bembo Std
Manipal Technologies Limited, Manipal

Printed and bound at
Thomson Press (India) Ltd

MIX
Paper
FSC FSC® C010615

This book is produced from independently certified FSC® paper to ensure responsible forest management.

For my paternal grandfather, Umadutt Dixit (Dada), and my maternal grandfather, Ramkumar Shukla (Nana)

Contents

Author's Note ix

1. Bombay before Ayodhya 1
2. The Rush+Die Riot of 1989 14
3. 1990: The Rath Reaches Bombay 24
4. December 1992 Riots 32
5. January 1993 Riots 44
6. 12 March 1993: A Blood-Soaked Bombay 60
7. Reign of the Underworld 76
8. Bitter Pill: The End of Underworld? 104
9. Tears of Khaki 134
10. A New Politics 152
11. Pramod Mahajan: The Man, His Murder and His Politics 174
12. Terror Returns 184
13. 26/11: The Lessons Not Learnt 194
14. Nature's Revenge 208

15. Unglamorous Bollywood 219
16. Lalbaugcha Raja 235
17. Dance Bars: Playing Hide-and-Seek with the Law 245
18. Heroes and Villains of the Financial Market 260
19. Landscape to Skyline 279
20. All That Glitters … Is Going Away from Mumbai? 291

Notes 303
Index 319
Acknowledgements 341
About the Author 345

Author's Note

Bombay was renamed as Mumbai in 1996.

The author has called the city Bombay while referring to the events preceding 1996, and Mumbai for events since that year.

It is also worth mentioning here that even before the official naming of the city in 1996, the Marathi and Gujarati population referred to it as 'Mumbai'. The Hindi-speaking people called it 'Bambai'.

The residents of Mumbai have been referred to as 'Bombayites' and 'Mumbaikars'.

1

Bombay before Ayodhya

THE STRAINER EMERGED FROM A LARGE BLACK wok of boiling palm oil and struck Yeshwant on his buttocks. He screamed in agony; the hot, oil-laced strainer had burnt not only his pants but also the skin of his posterior. Yeshwant's two accomplices fled after they saw him lying in such an awful state on the street. A crowd gathered to see the commotion. Shopkeepers closed their shutters in fear. Nobody ever thought that Yeshwant, whose name had become synonymous with terror for street-side stall owners, would be dealt with in such an audacious manner. People feared that now Umadutt, who had dared to take on this goon, would have to face an imminent brutal backlash.

It was the early 1970s, and the newly born political party Shiv Sena was making its presence felt in the city. The party was expanding with the support of youngsters and was rapidly turning into a cadre-based organization that didn't hesitate to deploy violence to pursue its agenda. It had the implicit support of the incumbent Congress Party, which needed to counter the growing clout of the Communist political outfits in the city. Some people attempted to capitalize on the fear and aggression that the Shiv Sena reflected by falsely claiming to be its office-bearers. Yeshwant was one of them. He operated in south Bombay's Kalbadevi and Zaveri Bazaar areas, which were known for the business of textiles and gold jewellery, extorted money from small shopkeepers and roughed up whoever refused to pay. He carried a Rampuri knife with him and had stabbed two people who were reluctant to meet his demands. The local businessmen avoided any confrontations with him, and seldom filed a complaint with the police. Power proliferates rapidly in the absence of challengers, and Yeshwant was a fine example of this. No one had ever dared to confront him until this day.

An obese and bald Umadutt, who wore the traditional north Indian dhoti–kurta, had set up a street-food stall at Zaveri Bazaar, where he sold vada-pao, samosas and *bhajiya*s. Every afternoon, Umadutt went home at 2 p.m. for lunch and returned by 5 p.m. after a siesta, leaving his helpers to manage the stall. It was during this time that Yeshwant would arrive with his cronies, eat at the stall and leave without paying.

Once, as the regular helper was absent, a youngster called Munna was employed as a substitute. As always, Yeshwant arrived at the stall with two of his cronies and gorged on the hot eatables. The two unhooked upper buttons of his shirt prominently displayed his thick gold chain. Oblivious to Yeshwant's abrasive reputation, Munna asked him for payment. Yeshwant abruptly slapped Munna and threw his empty plate at him. Showering him with expletives, Yeshwant threatened that if Munna ever asked for money again, he would shut the stall.

When Umadutt reached the stall that evening, he found a miserable Munna pleading to quit the job. Astounded at learning the events of the day, Umadutt calmed him down. Being a *pehelwaan*, Umadutt's conscience didn't allow him to be so easily bullied.

The next day, Umadutt didn't go home for lunch in the afternoon and stayed back at the stall. A fresh batch of batata vadas was placed in boiling oil. One of the last remnants of Portuguese rule in the city, batata vada-pao was a prominent meal for mill workers and manual labourers.

As the yellow vadas gurgled in the black wok, Yeshwant appeared at the stall with his cronies. After devouring many servings of batata vadas, he ordered a cup of chai from an adjacent tea stall. As he finished eating and prepared to leave, Umadutt shouted at him, '*Aye, paisa kaun dega* (Aye, who will pay the money)?'

'*Apne baap se paisa mangta hai? Ye le* (Are you asking your father to pay? Here, take this)!'

Yeshwant threw the glass teacup at Umadutt's face, causing his forehead to bleed. Umadutt responded with a punch to the goon's nose. Yeshwant's cronies rushed to attack Umadutt, but the stall owner's helpers had stepped forward. Yeshwant was shocked at Umadutt's audacity. In a fit of rage, Yeshwant whipped out his Rampuri knife, but before he could attack, Umadutt picked up a strainer straight from the bubbling, hot oil in the wok and struck Yeshwant on his buttocks with all his strength. Yeshwant fell to the ground, crying in pain while his companions ran away.

Umadutt then called the police and, while handing Yeshwant over to them, bribed them handsomely with a request that he must be booked under strict penal sections and 'treated well' in the lock-up. That day onwards, Yeshwant and his cronies were never seen in the area again. Although Umadutt's well-wishers warned that there could be retribution from Yeshwant, that never happened. Umadutt emerged as a hero overnight, one who had fought the villain away. He was now a people's man, admired and appreciated by one and all. Locals turned to him with hopes of settling petty disputes. Nobody now dared to mess with Umadutt. As is the way of the world, people worship those who perform miracles, and ending Yeshwant's frightful reign meant nothing less to the people of Zaveri Bazaar and Kalbadevi.

Dealing with goons like Yeshwant was one of the initial struggles that migrants like Umadutt had to encounter. Some lived in conformity with the circumstances, while others gave up and returned. For Umadutt, the harshness of the city was outweighed by the opportunities Bombay offered to those who worked hard and were willing to struggle. Those who intend to become residents of Bombay must first qualify in the city's 'entrance test', and only a select few are rewarded with the city's embrace for the long haul.

Umadutt Dixit was my paternal grandfather, who had arrived in Bombay with my maternal grandfather, Ramkumar, as teenagers in the early 1950s. It was a time when Bombay was being introduced to the world through black-and-white cinema, trams still ran on the roads, a few trains were still hauled by steam engines, roads were washed every day, local trains had nine bogies only, the police uniforms were blue, horse carts called 'Victorias' were a popular mode of short-distance transport, and going from south Bombay's Victoria Terminus to suburbs like Andheri was equivalent to travelling to a distant city.

Migrants: From the Portuguese to Purabias

Both my grandfathers hailed from a village in the Barabanki district of Uttar Pradesh. Their families owned ancestral farmlands close to the village, and agriculture was the only source of livelihood. They employed people from the village to work as labourers and shared the agricultural produce with them. The crops comprised wheat, peppermint, mustard and lentils. A substantial amount of the produce was sold, while some was kept for consumption at home. However, a major chunk of their land was acquired by the British government in the early twentieth century for constructing a branch of the ambitious Sharada Canal Project, the lengthiest canal in Uttar Pradesh, stretching over several thousand kilometres. The compensation given to farmers was measly, and both families had to look for other means of livelihood. And even as the sizes of the families grew, the land remained limited. Employment opportunities in north India were scarce, and many villagers who lost land to the project migrated to different cities of undivided India. At first, only male members of the families travelled to these cities and, once they got jobs, secured enough money and shelter, the rest of the family followed.

Almost all the urban centres across the globe have evolved because of migration, and the same holds true for Bombay. Scattered over seven islands, Bombay was originally inhabited by peasants of the Aagri community and fishers belonging to the Koli community. The first Europeans to lay hands on these islands were the Portuguese, who developed the archipelago as their naval base and port. However, major geographical, demographic and infrastructural changes began to occur in Bombay when the seven islands were handed over to England as dowry after a Portuguese princess married the king of England in 1661. Around 200 years later, these islands were merged into a single landmass through reclamation projects. The early migrants to arrive in the city were from land routes and came from modern-day Gujarat, Goa and Rajasthan. The beginning of India's first passenger train service in 1853 acted as a catalyst for migration and transformed the demography of the city. Over the years, people from north India, south India, Bengal, Sindh and Afghanistan began arriving in Bombay in large numbers. By the early 1940s, commercial international flight operations began at the Santacruz airport, which helped to develop Bombay as an international city.

The north Indian population, which migrated to Bombay, came from different regions. There were Biharis and Purabias (eastern Uttar Pradesh) who spoke Bhojpuri and Maithili. Many came from the Awadh region of Uttar Pradesh and spoke Awadhi. My grandfathers took pride in having their roots in the Awadh region, which is considered the kingdom of Lord Rama. His birthplace, Ayodhya, is hardly a hundred kilometres from my native village. My grandfather and his friends often cycled this distance from the village, and returned the next day after taking Rama Lala's darshan and a dip in the river Sarayu, on whose banks Ayodhya is settled. Several religious ceremonies in our family are conducted in Ayodhya till date. It is imperative for the men in the family to participate in the *mundan* ceremony and get our heads shaved at least once on the banks of the Sarayu. The family is still devoted to Lord Rama, and be it any auspicious event—a wedding, childbirth or professional success—an Akhand Ramayan Paath is organized. The said *paath* is a continuous recitation of '*Sriramcharitmanas*', an Awadhi-language adaptation of the Ramayana by the sixteenth-century poet Goswami Tulsidas. Many people participate in this relay recitation, which takes around twenty-four hours to complete.

The community of people from Uttar Pradesh and Bihar in the city presents a paradoxical picture of itself. On the one hand, a large number of bureaucrats belonging to the Indian Administrative Service (IAS) and the Indian Police Service (IPS) are natives of these two states, who rule the city with the power bestowed on them.[1,2] It was a dream commonly shared by several middle-class north Indian families to see their children become top-rank government officials, move around in red-beaconed Ambassador cars, live in spacious houses, and have several household staff catering to their needs and comforts. A government job not only assured financial security but also brought with it power, prestige and perks. Hence, it was common for youngsters to begin preparing for these competitive exams much before they'd become eligible candidates. On the other hand, many people from these states led very lowly lives in the city and struggled to make ends meet. They generally accepted labour-oriented jobs, like being loaders at the ports, mill workers, coolies and handcart pullers, or worked as watchmen, housekeeping staff, hawkers and delivery boys. Those who were slightly educated got clerical jobs or became assistants to businesspeople and merchants.

Life in a Chawl

After reaching Bombay, my grandfathers stayed with a few relatives who had arrived in the city earlier, and began their hunt for jobs. After wandering in the city for a few days, my maternal grandfather, Ramkumar, took on a job as an office caretaker in a charitable trust. The trust was named after a Gujarati philanthropist Keshavji Jadhavji, who had donated his property for public welfare. The trust owned properties across Bombay, including a charitable homoeopathic clinic and gaushala in south Bombay's Masjid Bunder. The primary source of income for the trust was rent money, which came from an auditorium, a wedding hall and many shops leased in the buildings owned by the trust.

Ramkumar was made a custodian of the office at Masjid Bunder, and was also given keys to the auditorium and the wedding hall. Since he was a Brahmin, he was also asked to perform the daily pujas of the small Ganpati idols and Lord Giriraj's picture placed in the trust's office. He was given a small room as official accommodation on the premises of the trust building, where he was soon joined by my paternal grandfather, Umadutt.

Umadutt began as a newspaper seller in Zaveri Bazaar. Those days, the Gujarati newspapers, *Janmabhoomi* and *Mumbai Samachar*, gave considerable space to the stock market and business-related news. In his free time, Umadutt also tried reading these papers and, within a few years, was well-versed in Gujarati. While interacting with his clientele for over five years in his newspaper business, he observed that most Gujaratis and Marwaris were foodies, and yearned for variety and taste, which led to the idea of setting up the snack stall. As he had projected, the food stall did well.

Soon, Umadutt bought a house in a chawl in Masjid Bunder. Chawls are one- or two-storey buildings, with around eight to ten single rooms made sequentially. These rooms serve as the kitchen, bathroom, living room and bedroom for its occupants. Many residents had partitioned their rooms vertically by making mezzanines that were used for keeping possessions or for children. There were common toilets on each floor, and people had to carry water in small buckets for washing and flushing purposes. Since the rooms were small, the common passage area was encroached upon by each household, who kept items such as drums, buckets, brooms, cycles, and chairs outdoors. A typical chawl had a roof covered with red Mangalorean tiles, and, before every monsoon, the broken tiles were layered with asphalt to prevent leakage. Most of the residents in the chawl were lower-middle-class Gujaratis. Some worked at stockbroking firms, some sold audio cassettes—which had just arrived in the Indian market—at roadside stalls, some repaired electronic gadgets for a living and some sold eatables at a nearby street food junction. The place where this chawl, auditorium and wedding hall were located was known as Wadi, which loosely translates into English as a 'compound'. The entrance of Wadi had an enormous gate that resembled prison gates. One of the two doors of the gate had a smaller portal for pedestrians. For the entry of vehicles, both the bigger doors were required to be opened. The Wadi gate opened on to a road named after Yusuf Meherali, a freedom fighter based in Bombay. Meherali was the man who coined the iconic slogans of the Independence movement, 'Quit India' and 'Simon Go Back!'.

The Road That Connects Masjid to Mandir

The Yusuf Meherali Road connects to Masjid railway station on the Central railway line and is, hence, also famously known as Masjid Bunder Road. This name comes from two of its landmarks – the Juni Masjid, a synagogue built in the mid-nineteenth century, and a port, which is called 'bunder' in Marathi. The two-kilometre-long Yusuf Meherali Road passes through two well-known religious structures in the city. One is the temple of Mumbadevi, the presiding deity of the city, and another is Zakariya Masjid, a prominent place of worship for Muslims. The road is lined with hundreds of small stalls on both sides, which sell items ranging from shoes to household gadgets, fruits to cutlery. Most of these stalls were owned by local Muslims, who changed the wares of their stalls as per the festive season. Before Diwali, they would be filled with crackers and decorative items, while around Holi there would be a display of colours and water guns all around. In one of the bylanes of Yusuf Meherali Road, industrialist Dhirubhai Ambani began his journey of success in business. Circa 1960, Ambani set up a small office from where he traded in spices such as black pepper, cardamom and turmeric. He stayed in a chawl in nearby Bhuleshwar.

Yusuf Meherali Road also divides the settlements of two different communities. Muslim-dominated areas such as Khadak, Utraan and Dongri are on the northern side of this road, while Hindu-majority areas such as Vadgadi, Daryasthan, Koliwada and Katha Bazaar are towards the south. The area around the

Masjid Station used to be populated by Hindus on both sides. The Wadi—where both my grandfathers stayed—was one of the very few premises in the northern side where the owners and residents were all Hindus. The Wadi seemed like an island, surrounded by buildings owned by Muslims on three sides, with the fourth side being a road. The road remained heavily crowded throughout the day with thousands of pedestrians, handcarts, trucks and taxis. Due to its high density, Bombay Electricity Supply and Transport (BEST) ran just one double-decker bus service on this road.

After spending a few years in the city and arranging accommodation for themselves, my grandfathers invited their respective families over. Ramkumar's wife, Vidya, shifted to Bombay with their two sons, Ramakant and Shashikant. While my parents, Ram and Prema, moved in with Umadutt, my grandmother felt more comfortable residing away from the hubbub of this big city. Uncles Ramakant and Shashikant, and my father, were soon employed by different Marwari jewellers to help them in their business. As each of them understood the city and the crowd better, they penetrated into the market with independent businesses over the years. Ramakant opened a calculator and watch repair shop, while Shashikant and my father set up a small stall at Zaveri Bazaar to sell imported items, such as perfumes, electronic gadgets, toys, cosmetics and stationery.

I was born in July 1979 at Laxmibai Maternity Home, across the Wadi road in the Hindu settlement of Vadgadi. I am the first person in my family to be born in Bombay. My name, Jitendra, means the one who has won over his senses and is credited to my family's strong devotion to Lord Hanuman. My father had set his heart on making me an IAS officer since the day I was born. He had completed his education in the Hindi medium but believed that English education would be advantageous for me to compete in the civil services examination. There were just two English-medium schools within walking distance from our residence—Dawood Fazal High School and Khoja Khan High School. Most Khoja Muslims living in the city speak Gujarati, and are believed to be accepting and progressive. I was admitted to Khoja Khan High School situated two lanes away on Samuel Street. My grandparents were wary of sending me to a school run by Muslims, as they feared that it would influence my religious beliefs and lifestyle choices. In my family, consuming eggs, fish or meat was forbidden. My grandparents relented after being convinced that most of the teachers in the school were Hindus and that all the Hindu-owned, English-medium schools were far away.

By the time I reached Class VIII, my friend, Hu Shih Foong, a Buddhist of Chinese origin, and I were the only non-Muslims left in a class of forty. His parents ran their dental clinic at Dongri. Most of the students in the school came from middle-class Muslim families living in adjacent Dongri, Bhendi Bazaar, Pydhonie and Imamwada. A few students were distant relatives of members of the dreaded Pathan gang run by underworld don Karim Lala.

It was believed that with enrolment in the Road Safety Patrol (RSP), a student became more disciplined and confident. The RSP cadet had to wear a maroon uniform. However, one of my elderly neighbours, Kunjbihari Sharma, wished to see me in a different uniform—khaki shorts, a white shirt and a black cap, the uniform of the Rashtriya Swayamsevak Sangh (RSS). One of the RSS *shakha*s was set up at Kalbadevi Road, around 2 kilometres away from my house, and Kunjbihari convinced my parents to enrol me there. The elderly and religious Kunjbihari organized *kirtan*s every Saturday night, which was attended by many north Indian neighbours. The coordinated beats of the *dholak* and *ghanti* are still fresh in my ears as I write this book so many years later. The chorus amplified the decibel sound levels even without any loudspeakers.

Nobody in the neighbouring Muslim buildings ever objected to the singing that at times continued till 4 a.m.

Like many others in our neighbourhood, Kunjbihari was appreciative of the RSS and its political offshoot, the Bharatiya Janata Party (BJP), and firmly believed it to be a truly nationalist organization. My parents, however, had my poor performance at school in mind and preferred sending me to two-hour-long mathematics tuitions instead. I never wore those khaki shorts.

Indira's Assassination and Changing Loyalties

Till 1984, my family staunchly supported the Congress in general and Indira Gandhi in particular. Like her cult followers, they recounted with great pride how India defeated Pakistan in 1971 and created Bangladesh under Indira Gandhi's leadership, how she forged a friendship with the Soviet Union when the USA took on a pro-Pakistan posture, how she conducted nuclear tests and made India a nuclear power, and how she dealt with the Khalistani militants of Punjab. She meant no less than a living goddess to my family. Every time she addressed the rallies in Bombay's Azad Maidan, my family members and all the men in the neighbourhood enthusiastically went to listen to her, adorning badges with her picture and waving Congress flags. What she said at these public meetings used to be a matter of serious discussion for the days that followed. Her excesses during the Emergency were forgiven and forgotten by holding her son Sanjay responsible for them.

With Indira Gandhi's demise, support for the Congress slowly began to fade. Driven by sympathy votes, the Congress won by 404 seats in the following Parliamentary polls. Later, Rajiv Gandhi's action on the Shah Bano case and the subsequent ban on Salman Rushdie's book *The Satanic Verses* was capitalized on by the BJP and used against the Congress to label the party as a 'pseudo-secular', Muslim-appeasing party. In the next Lok Sabha elections held in 1989, the Congress Party was ousted from power. Its number of seats dwindled from 404 in 1984 to 197, while the BJP skyrocketed from just two seats in 1984 to eighty-five seats this time. However, it was a hung Parliament, and V.P. Singh of the Janata Dal, with the support of smaller parties under the banner of the National Front and outside support of the BJP, became the prime minister.

It was in 1989 that the BJP adopted Hindutva as its ideology. For the BJP, Hindutva was not just a religious concept but an expression of cultural nationalism that represented the Indian identity. In Bombay, the BJP found a partner with the same ideology in the Shiv Sena—a political partnership that continued for almost the next three decades.

2

The Rush+Die Riot of 1989

IT WAS A PLEASANT FEBRUARY AFTERNOON IN 1989, AND I was heading back from school when I saw a commotion on Mohammed Ali Road. A mob of thousands of people swarmed behind a police van: a few policemen were already stationed on the sidewalks with lathis in their hands. Confused and curious, I started moving along with the crowd on the sidewalks. The mob blazed with anger and shouted slogans: 'Salman Rushdie Haay Haay', 'Salman Rushdie Murdabad', 'Naara-E-Takbeer ... Allah Ho Akbar.' They also carried placards with text in both English and Urdu.

Oblivious to the politics of *The Satanic Verses* by Salman Rushdie, I gathered my share of information by overhearing conversations at home. I knew the book had hurt Muslims' sentiments. I marched with the crowd for about a kilometre when the thought of returning home struck me. The Bombay Police had barricaded the junction at Crawford Market and restrained the crowd from moving further. This led to a verbal confrontation between the men who appeared to be leading the mob and the cops. Out of nowhere, some people began hurling stones and glass bottles at the police, which resulted in a prompt backlash. A lathi charge was ordered, and the cops, who were till then silently moving ahead with the crowd, pounced on the protesters. It led to a stampede on the road.

In an attempt to escape being hit by the police, a man ran towards the sidewalk and inadvertently pushed me. The cops chasing the man managed to surround him nonetheless and rained their lathis down on him. As I lay on the ground, I saw him being beaten mercilessly, with blood oozing out of his head. 'Do you want to die? What are you doing here?' I turned towards the voice. He was an elderly Bohri Muslim. He wore a white kurta and an embroidered topi. Words failed me as I shivered in panic. He realized my plight and took me to his office nearby, filled with hardware supplies on the first floor of a building. He calmed me down, offered me some water and asked one of his helpers to apply an antiseptic cream on my bruises. Once he assured me that I was safe there, he enquired about my whereabouts.

'Hmm … You should not have followed that crowd. Although you stay nearby, it is very difficult to take you there now. The police are firing, and it is impossible to go out. Your parents might be anxious. Do you have a phone at home so that we can inform them you are safe?' Though we had filed an application for a telephone connection, in those days, it took aeons to get one. Those with political connections were recommended for a priority connection, but my parents couldn't pull any such strings. There was one number of a neighbouring stationery shop that my parents had given to our relatives to contact us in emergencies, but I didn't have that number.

'I can imagine what thoughts might come to your parents. The situation outside is terrible. Many people might have died, I fear,' he sighed.

Battleground Mohammed Ali Road

The sound emanating from the violence outside—the expletives casually being thrown about, the smashing of tube lights and glass bottles, and the pops of gunshots—could be heard clearly inside the building. Many vehicles had been burnt and smoke filled the air. Through a half-opened window, we saw a policeman ruthlessly battering any and everybody who came in his way. I was fretful about how long this was going to continue. I longed to be home, which was merely a kilometre away but felt like worlds apart now. Everyone sympathized with me and was thinking of ways to help me out.

Nobody had expected that the anger against an author would culminate in such bloodshed. Salman Rushdie was born and raised in Bombay, but later moved to Britain and then to the USA. Although he had become a celebrated name in the literary world when his novel *Midnight's Children* won the Booker Prize in 1981, barely anybody in this part of the city knew who he was. His controversial novel *The Satanic Verses* was published in 1988, but it was only a year later, when the Iranian leader Ayatollah Khomeini admonished him and passed a fatwa for his assassination, that he became known all over the world. A bounty was placed on his head. The novel was seen as blasphemous, anti-Islam and as an insult to the Prophet. It led to outrage by Muslims across various parts of the world, and many countries banned the book. Many bookstores were vandalized, copies were burnt, and people associated with the novel's publishing, editing and translation were attacked. Considering the widespread backlash against the book, the Congress government at the Centre banned it in India in November 1988. Salman Rushdie then wrote an emotional letter to then Prime Minister Rajiv Gandhi to revoke the ban. However, it failed to alter the government's stance.

The ban wasn't enough to placate angry Muslim organizations, and they decided to augment their protest by surrounding the British mission in Bombay. Their ire was not directed towards Indian authorities, but against Salman Rushdie and the British government that ensured his security. Advertisements were published in Urdu newspapers such as *Inqilab* and *Urdu Times*, announcing the protests. The organizers had to publish paid advertisements because the newspapers refused to publish the content as news, which sounded provocative and justified the death sentence against Rushdie. Several Muslim organizations were named in the advertisement as the organizers of the protest. It included groups like Tanzeem-e-Allah-Ho-Akbar, the Muslim Integration Council and a retired underworld don who had just floated a political party.[1]

The date for the protest was set for 24 February, which was about ten days after Khomeini had announced the fatwa against Rushdie. Mastan Talao, the open ground in south Bombay's Muslim-dominated Nagpada, was fixed as the location[2] from where protesters would gather and march towards the British Consulate. It was announced that in Muslim localities, a bandh would be observed, and all shops and offices would be shut. Protesters were supposed to meet after the Friday namaaz. The Bombay Police had refused to give permission for the protest march and invoked Section 144 of the Criminal Procedure Code (CrPC) in the city, which prohibited any assembly of four or more people and deemed such an assembly as unlawful. Various law-enforcing authorities across India invoke this section of the code whenever they anticipate trouble that could endanger life and property. The police arrested most of the organizers and took them to lockups in Mulund, a distant suburb in north Bombay.

A Leaderless March

Despite its leaders being detained, the members of their organizations began pouring into Mastan Talao in trucks with banners, placards and black flags. The texts on such banners and placards screamed 'I am ready to kill Rushdie' and 'Rushdie–Rush+Die'. By 2 p.m., over 2,000 protesters had reached the ground. The Bombay Police, along with the State Reserved Police Force, cordoned off the ground and detained the youngsters by pushing them into their vans. Several protesters still managed to head towards the British mission via Mohammed Ali Road. As per reports, protesters had arrived from various Muslim-dominated localities of the city, and their number surged to around 2,000.[3]

The cops were unprepared to meet such a situation. They thought that after the arrest of protesters at Mastan Talao, the matter would end. However, a large number of protesters managed to reach Crawford Market, which was just a few kilometres away from the British Consulate. The situation became explosive. An additional commissioner-rank officer of the Bombay Police offered that a delegation be allowed to meet the officials at the British Consulate and submit a memorandum of protest. Some protesters agreed to be part of the delegation and were taken aside by the cops. However, others were adamant that they wanted to protest outside the consulate. The rabble was not willing to listen to anybody, neither to the cops nor to those with whom the police were negotiating to defuse the situation. The police had blocked the road with barricades at Crawford Market junction.

Even as the police officers argued with the protesters, some of them began throwing stones, glass bottles and bricks. The cops lost their cool. Their first response was a lathi charge. Whoever came in sight was beaten up mercilessly. It led to a stampede, and the crowd dispersed into the by-lanes. However, the protesters soon surfaced again in small groups and attacked the cops. It was at this point that I got stuck and was pulled by the elderly man into the building for safety.

The situation only got worse, and the cops enhanced their response by not only hitting the protesters with lathis, but also using tear-gas shells. However, such a response failed to contain the situation, and the cops resorted to firing. Eleven people were killed and over forty were injured. Among those killed were both protesters and innocent bystanders and pedestrians, who had nothing to do with the protests. In the list of dead were two young men from Kerala, who were set to leave for Saudi Arabia for Umrah, a short pilgrimage to Mecca. They were looking at the mayhem below from the balcony of their building and were hit by stray police bullets. Twenty-four-year-old Zuber Lakdawala ran a timber shop in Kazi Mohalla along with his two brothers. Sensing the tension in the area, they closed the shop and began heading home. When they were about to reach their house, the arson started. To save themselves from getting caught in the confrontation, the brothers hid behind a truck. A stray bullet pierced Zuber's head, and he fell down in front of his brothers. They rushed him to Sir J.J. Hospital, but he died four days later. Over sixty rounds of bullets were fired by the cops. Almost all the people killed in the firing were between the ages of eighteen to twenty-five. Three policemen also got injured in the violence and were hospitalized.[4]

It took almost three hours for the situation to be brought under control. A grave silence enveloped the deserted streets, and the fire brigade was busy extinguishing the blaze from burnt vehicles. A police van siren penetrated the deathly tranquillity with its frequent tours. The elderly man asked people from neighbouring offices, who had gathered in the passageway, if any of them could drop me home. Nobody wanted to take the risk of stepping outside to the bloody streets. The situation was still tense, and cops could beat up and detain any person seen on the road.

The elderly man's appeal evoked no response. He held my hand and led me towards the stairs. As we began to descend, someone said, 'Chacha, please don't bother. I will drop the child.' We saw a tall man, Anwar, with a thumb-sized beard, wearing a white kurta and topi, approaching us. He was a garment seller with an office next to the elderly man's. He reasoned that he would walk me through the by-lanes, avoiding the more dangerous main road. 'Go with this uncle. He will take you home,' the elderly man told me with a smile.

Holding my hand, Anwar started walking briskly. We had walked just a few metres down the narrow lane when I screamed in pain. A shard of broken glass lying on the street had pierced my left foot, and it was bleeding profusely. In my hurry to avoid the police, I was oblivious to the fact that my feet were without shoes and the street was full of broken glass splinters, suggesting that the riots had also spilt into the by-lanes of Mohammed Ali Road. Anwar removed the glass from my bleeding feet, but I could barely put my feet back on the ground. He took out his handkerchief and tied it to my feet without delay.

While passing through Chakla Street junction, I saw an old police picket that had turned to ash. The wooden picket was used as a changing room, a place to relax and have lunch and tea for the cops who were deployed in the area. It also served as a temporary detention room for pickpockets and petty criminals before they were taken to the police station.

As Anwar dropped me at the entrance of Wadi, I saw my mother standing there crying uncontrollably and the women from the neighbourhood consoling her. She came rushing towards me and slapped me, shouting hysterically, 'If something had happened to you today, how I would have survived? Where the hell were you?'

Considering the history of communal tension in the area, it was a matter of great astonishment for many in the neighbourhood to see a Muslim man safely bring a Hindu boy home.

A few hours later, a neighbour who had gone to J.J. Hospital to see an ailing relative informed us of chaos at the hospital. It wasn't prepared to deal with so many patients in a trice. Relatives of the dead and injured moved frantically on the hospital premises. The situation was chaotic. Some abused the doctors who informed them of a person's death. Others moaned in pain and pleaded with the doctors before succumbing to their fate. In the absence of any senior police officer, the constables proved to be incapable of handling the chaos. Some ministers and local politicians attempted to enter the hospital, but they were mobbed and roughed up as soon as they were spotted by the angry crowd and were forced to flee.

The newspapers the next day were full of reports describing various aspects of the events. Some newspapers, quoting 'intelligence sources', said that the violence was sponsored by foreign forces. A few reports claimed that the violence was pre-planned, as the protesters had carried sharp weapons and firearms with them. Some tried to give the violence a communal colour by spreading a rumour that vehicles and shops of Hindus were targeted in the mayhem. The police justified the firing and said that it was in retaliation, after being fired upon by protesters. The chief minister also supported the police and reasoned that such an action was imperative to bring the situation under control. It was also discovered that the organizers of the protest had claimed to have the backing of several Muslim groups without seeking their permission.

The Indictment of the Police

A few days later, a fact-finding team was set up by a non-governmental organization named the Committee for Protection of Democratic Rights (CPDR). The team comprised prominent lawyers, teachers, journalists and rights activists. It scrutinized the role of organizers, the police, the participants of morcha and the politicians. They interviewed Vasant Saraf, then police commissioner of Bombay; families of the dead and injured; and the organizers. The fact-finding team, in its report, made several observations and concluded that such a bloodbath could have been avoided. The report indicted the Bombay Police for how it dealt with the situation. It pointed out that the decision of the police to disallow the morcha and arrest its organizers had proved counterproductive. The report noticed that the firing on protesters was in excess, and the actions of the police only aggravated the situation.

This violence provides a background to the 1992-93 post-Babri Masjid demolition riots. It led to widespread animosity towards the police and administration among the Muslim population. It was suggested that the police were biased against Muslims, as another morcha of Dalit organizations was given permission the same day to march down on the same route. But the question remained as to why the police disallowed the Muslims to protest. The march was neither against the government nor the Hindu community, but to vent anger against Rushdie and the British government. After the riots, an IPS officer made statements to a newspaper, which included lines like, 'If they go after our blood, we will draw more' and 'They will not look at a police van for another six months', all of which added to the hostility towards the police.[5]

Several lumpens rose to become religious leaders in the city. They reacted to issues at full tilt and announced rigorous protests, but lacked the leadership acumen to execute peaceful processions or manage mobs. The fatal episode also brought to light the vulnerabilities of the middle class, lower-middle class and the poor to religious provocation. Relatives of at least six youngsters out of the eleven who were killed in the police firing that day told the fact-finding committee that they had gone to take part in the march because they felt Rushdie had insulted Islam and it was necessary to protest.

3

1990: The Rath Reaches Bombay

THAT SEPTEMBER EVENING, THE USUAL HUBBUB filled Bombay's Kalbadevi area as people rushed in all directions, vehicles honked their impatience as they slowly made their way through the crowded street, fruit and vegetable vendors screamed their prices in a musical crescendo, and customers were busy bargaining with shopkeepers. And yet, despite the commotion all around, the message on the RSS blackboard—installed at the Cotton Exchange Junction—was still the loudest of all.

It was nothing less than a right winger's Twitter account of the pre-internet age. A major link of communication between the RSS and the people, the board regularly updated messages—ideas ranging from the formation of a Hindu Rashtra to the sacrality of cows, from threats surrounding Hindus, the appeasement of Muslims by the Opposition party, calls for abrogation of Article 370 in Jammu and Kashmir to a Uniform Civil Code, and their philosophy of Akhand Bharat.

That day, while returning from my tuition classes, on the blackboard, I saw a picture of a bald, bespectacled man with a grey moustache, beaming through the saffron poster placed over the board. His name, Lal Krishna Advani, flashed in a bold font, and the text below announced his upcoming visit to the city in a rath—a chariot.

Those were the days when Doordarshan telecast Ramanand Sagar's *Ramayan* (1987) and B.R. Chopra's *Mahabharata* (1988), in which characters appeared to be fighting with each other while standing on chariots. Though the period-specific prop of the chariot appealed to me, as a ten-year-old, I could not help but wonder why anyone would use such a primitive vehicle to travel across cities.

After this first poster appeared in Kalbadevi, Advani's rath yatra became the talk of the town. Hundreds of banners and posters were printed with pictures of Advani and Lord Rama, assuming an aggressive posture, holding a bow in his hand. Every day, newspaper reports about the progress of the rath yatra galvanized everyone even further.

Just a year ago, in June 1989, the BJP, in its Palampur convention, had adopted Ram Mandir as its agenda, and the rath yatra was its first on-ground manifestation. At the convention, it was resolved that the BJP would take up the Vishwa Hindu Parishad's (VHP) demand for constructing the Rama temple at Ayodhya as a political issue. The resolution was based on the premise that, in 1528, the Mughal emperor, Babur, had invaded Ayodhya and demolished the temple that stood, marking the place where Lord Rama was born. A mosque was constructed in that location, which was named Babri Masjid. It was alleged that the incumbent Congress Party didn't care for the sentiments of Hindus. After adopting Hindutva as an ideology, the BJP's clout skyrocketed. The party emerged as a major political force in the 1989 Lok Sabha elections that happened five months after the Palampur convention. With eighty-five seats in the election, the BJP was now the third-largest party in the country after the Congress, with 197 seats, and the Janata Dal, with 143 seats.

The next step was to launch a movement on the ground to implement the resolution passed at Palampur's Rotary Bhavan. Thus, the rath yatra commenced at Gujarat's Somnath temple on 25 September 1990. Somnath is one of the twelve *jyotirlingas* of Lord Shiva and, like the Babri mosque, was considered a reminder of foreign invasion. The Turkish ruler Mahmud Gazni was the first one to attack the temple in the eleventh century, followed by other Muslim rulers in later centuries. It was destroyed and rebuilt several times. The present temple was restored after India attained Independence. Crossing a distance of over 10,000 kilometres via different states, the rath would eventually reach Ayodhya, where *karsevaks* would seize the mosque and start constructing the Rama temple. With a target of covering approximately 300 kilometres a day, Advani was now headed towards Bombay. He addressed five to six public meetings every day, while heading towards the destination. With the rath yatra being an expression of cultural nationalism and militant Hinduism, the reported stray incidents of violence en route came as no surprise.

Bombay: A Theatre of Conflicts

The centre stage of the film and television industry, Bombay, had by now also become a theatre of communal conflicts. From 1893 to 1990, the city witnessed seven major Hindu–Muslim riots.[1]

As per recorded history, the first clash between the two communities happened on 11 August 1893, over the issue of cow slaughter. To control the violence, the British summoned the army that opened fire in the Grant Road area. Eighty people were killed in the riots that raged for over three days. In 1929, a rumour spread among mill workers that members of a particular community were abducting children, which led to a rampage in the city. This time, too, the army was called, and the death toll was 149 people. In 1932, Bombay once again came under the grip of violence, when a place of worship was demolished in the C.P. Tank area. Ninety-six people were killed in the riots that ensued for five days.[2]

Four years later, in 1936, a major riot broke out in the Byculla area, and the army had to be called in once again. The issue was that one community's place of worship had encroached upon the other community's. Sixty people were killed in that uproar. The next year, in 1937, riots began when a wedding procession with a music band was passing in front of a place of worship belonging to one community. When devotees asked to stop the music, a bloody conflict ensued. In 1938, the two communities clashed for a trifling reason—a dispute during gambling, which soon took on a communal colour. That violence claimed eighty lives and eighty-six people were injured.[3]

Similarly, in 1941, members of the two communities fought over an inconsequential reason, which resulted in twenty-four deaths. Apart from Hindu–Muslim riots, Bombay had also witnessed three Parsee–Muslim clashes and sectarian violence between Shias and Sunnis during Moharram.[4] The history of communal clashes in Bombay presents a contradictory picture of the city, which is seen as having a cosmopolitan and modern character. And Advani, with his rath, was slowly advancing towards this city where communal tensions were always ready to flare.

Advani in Bombay

A public rally had been arranged at Borivali on 29 September 1990 to welcome the rath yatra in Bombay. An enthusiastic crowd waited patiently for the rath slated to arrive by 5 p.m. Sweaty attendees squeezed through the limited seating area as the entrance of the rath kept getting delayed. Those who had come with children struggled to find ways to keep them occupied. The local vendors selling beverages and snacks sold out faster that evening than on other days. Despite the exhaustion, the crowd kept multiplying in numbers as the hours went by.

North Bombay BJP unit's then vice-president, R.U. Singh, recounts the heavy attendance at Advani's meeting. Finally, around 9 p.m., a Toyota truck redesigned as a chariot—studded with saffron flags, garlands, speakers and banners—carried the energetic Advani to the stage as the deafening mob shouted party eulogies. Advani was accompanied by politician Pramod Mahajan and Madhya Pradesh's chief minister, Sundarlal Patwa. The local member of Parliament, Ram Naik, welcomed the rath. After garlanding a statue of Swami Vivekananda, Advani began his address, emphasizing the futility of the nation's freedom and on its failure at liberating Rama's birthplace. He claimed that people had sacrificed their lives for this land for over 450 years, and now was the time to seek vengeance. Further, Pramod Mahajan mentioned in his speech how he wasn't against any religion, but one must demolish the property constructed by an invader despite the challenges it posed.[5]

It was ironic that the driver of the truck used in the rath yatra, whose subtle agenda was anti-Muslim, was from the Khoja Muslim community; his name was Salim Makani. A resident of Dombivli, a town close to Bombay, Makani's father was a member of the Jan Sangh, the predecessor of the BJP, and ran a transport business. The responsibility of coordinating the rath's complete journey was given to the BJP's Maharashtra unit, which had to arrange everything from spare batteries for the rath to tyre repairs, mechanics, food and venues for press conferences.

Raghunath Kulkarni, secretary of the Maharashtra BJP, was the coordinator for the rath yatra in Bombay. His amazement at Advani's vigour is reflected in his words, 'Even if he slept at 3 a.m., he was ready at 7 a.m. Whenever the rath moved into the city, he used to stand for hours on top of the vehicle. We requested him to move inside and rest for some time, but he always declined by saying that people had come to see him and it was wrong to stay inside.'[6]

On the second day of the arrival of the rath in Bombay, public meetings were called in the Khetwadi and Colaba areas of south Bombay. That evening, Advani and Shiv Sena supremo Bal Thackeray addressed a joint meeting at Dadar. The Shiv Sena had politically adopted Hindutva as a plank in 1987, although its anti-Muslim stance became evident earlier during the Bhiwandi riots of 1984, when the *sainik*s indulged in large-scale violence. Together, the BJP and the Shiv Sena formed an alliance using Hindutva as an adhesive. While Thackeray sought opportunities to expand his party beyond the Bombay, Thane and Konkan region, the BJP needed some local partners to strengthen its wing in Maharashtra. Pramod Mahajan engineered the alliance between the two parties. They fought the 1984 and 1989 Lok Sabha elections and the 1990 Vidhan Sabha polls together.

Although the following day's newspapers carried pictures of Advani and Thackeray seated together on the stage at Dadar, the press expressed concern over the absence of Thackeray's lieutenant, Chhagan Bhujbal, at such an important event. Bhujbal was disappointed when fellow politician Manohar Joshi was announced to be the leader of the Opposition in the Maharashtra Vidhan Sabha instead of him, and his non-attendance made his displeasure clear. The following year, Bhujbal joined the Congress Party, taking his supporters with him. His defection was engineered by Sharad Pawar, Bal Thackeray's close friends but his political nemesis at the same time.

The meeting at Dadar was followed by another one at Ghatkopar. The area swarmed with visitors from all around, leading to a traffic deadlock in the neighbouring areas. As Bollywood actor Shatrughan Sinha struggled to reach the venue, the BJP workers arranged an ambulance with a blaring siren for him to swiftly make his way to the meeting.

The rath yatra brought another BJP leader into the spotlight: The forty-year-old RSS member Pramod Mahajan. It is believed that Advani had earlier proposed a *pad yatra*, but it was Mahajan who suggested using a motorized vehicle instead, pointing out the distance and duration. He also planned the route and coordinated the entire yatra at different locations. Raghunath Kulkarni remembers how Mahajan was by Advani's side throughout the journey and even got arrested with him at Samastipur in Bihar.

Tense Days for Bombay Police

After a series of communal riots in the preceding years, the arrival of the rath yatra caused anxiety for the Bombay Police. The risk of communal violence kept cops on their toes, and extensive security arrangements were made throughout the city. The two-day yatra proceeded with impunity and no untoward incidents took place. While writing this book, to acquaint myself with the undercurrents felt among Muslims, I interviewed a few residents from the Muslim neighbourhoods of the city.

Atique-ur-Rehman, who stays near the Minara Masjid, feels that people didn't take the rath yatra very seriously. Sayeed Noori, who runs an organization called Raza Academy, observed that, initially, the Muslims of Bombay considered the yatra as nothing but a political gimmick. The outlook changed when riots broke out in Uttar Pradesh. Eventually, Advani was arrested on 23 October at Samastipur in Bihar, but Bombay remained peaceful. Although the rath yatra passed from Bombay creating no trouble, its residual effects were highlighted and came to the fore in the city in the years that followed.

Post the rath yatra, Advani emerged as the face of abrasive Hindu cultural nationalism in India and, since then, the celebrated cartoonist R.K. Laxman always caricatured this avatar with a trident in Advani's hand and a crown on his head.[7]

4

December 1992 Riots

'FETCH ME THE GARLANDS FROM THE BASKET. OHO, get the marigold ones.' It was difficult to comprehend who was calling out these instructions in all the commotion. It was my cousin Mahesh's ear-piercing ceremony, and our *kholi* was brimming with guests throughout the day. Amid the repeated rounds of samosas and soft drinks, we were oblivious to what was happening in Ayodhya that day—6 December 1992.

By the time the ceremony was over and my aunt had cleared the puja arrangements, it was already midnight. We were laying the beddings across the floor when our neighbours received a call from my uncle's friend, Deepnarayan. He had left from our place about an hour ago and had anxiously rung to inform us of the threatening state of affairs all around.

The Carnage Begins

As Deepnarayan's taxi reached the Minara Masjid junction, he realized that a mob of around 400–500 people had blocked the entire road. By the time he could get a sense of what was happening around, some rioters began brandishing swords, sticks and rods over those stuck at the junction. Deepnarayan's driver promptly reversed the taxi, grazing other vehicles stuck in this tumult, and somehow managed to get him home safely via a different route. He was certain that numerous innocents would have been slaughtered by then.

The TV flashed news reports about the karsevaks demolishing the disputed structure in Ayodhya, and Deepnarayan's call was an alarm to what had to follow. Being surrounded by Muslim communities from three ends, our Wadi was prone to easy damage. While the children were unaware, the elders in the chawl grew truly concerned.

A sudden flash of light and a deafening explosion broke through the dire silence suddenly. Everybody in the chawl rushed out and saw the labourer Madhav writhing in pain as his right leg burnt steadily. A petrol bomb had been flung, and his leg had got caught in it. People immediately doused him with water. No one in the Wadi owned a car nor were there any transportation facilities available at the moment—given that it was the middle of the night. Someone called the cops and Madhav was taken to the hospital in a police van. Some of his co-workers accompanied him, as his entire family stayed far away in a distant village.

By now, riots had escalated in different parts of the city. We heard firing and sirens throughout the night, and saw the city glowing alternately red and black through our window. A group of rioters, in their twenties and thirties, gathered, hurling stones and expletives at the police vehicles. As some cops aimed rifles at the rioters, they vanished into thin air.

After admitting Madhav to St. George Hospital, his co-workers returned, intimidated by the bloodbath they'd seen in the city. The casualty ward of the hospital was congested with victims of the riots. Hospitals all around the city faced a shortage of beds and emergency supplies.

The city rose rather early the next morning, with newspaper vendors making much more earnings than usual. My uncle bought three different newspapers that day to get a clearer picture of the Babri Masjid's demolition, and the subsequent aftermath. The newspapers were filled with reports of violence that rocked the city. Since we had been busy with the family function, we only now learnt what Bombay had witnessed that day. The city witnessed tensions since the morning of 6 December.

The VHP and the BJP had organized meetings of karsevaks at various locations. A grand gathering of over 400 people was held at the Shiva temple in Dadar. By noon, when the news of the demolition of the disputed structure broke, the Shiv Sena had organized a bicycle rally from Dharavi junction. The rally passed through many communally sensitive locations and culminated in a meeting at Kala Killa, where provocative speeches were delivered. The city saw celebrations all around, and by evening, the movement expanded into the Muslim-dominated areas. Muslims were obviously enraged over what had happened. Not only had the government disappointed them in securing the Babri Masjid, but the extravagant celebrations by the Hindutva groups also mocked their religious sentiments.

By the end of the day, people assembled in areas such as Bhendi Bazaar, Imamwada, Pydhonie and Mohammed Ali Road. One such group gathered at Minara Masjid too, where Deepnarayan had gotten stuck. The mob attacked the cops, and the police fired in retaliation. The Minara Masjid junction, which was a gastronomic heaven every year during Ramadan and attracted gourmets across faiths, now stood as an ironic site of communal strife.

A curfew was imposed in the city, and the police actively patrolled the area, making necessary announcements over loudspeakers.

Despite the strict precautions, 7 December proved to be the most disastrous day for cops. In Deonar, the rioters killed two police constables with swords and threw one of their bodies into the garbage. Another policeman was butchered in south Mumbai's Byculla the same day. An inspector in Jogeshwari died of bullet injuries. Rioters from both communities were more organized and better equipped than the previous night. They clashed face to face, using stones, glass bottles and tube lights. Many temples, mosques and madrasas were demolished or razed to the ground. Several buses of BEST parked at Bombay Central Depot were damaged.

That day, ninety-two people were reported dead and over 150 injured. The police machinery was overwhelmed too. For a population of around 1.4 crore, there were just 40,000 policemen in the city. The police force, which was once compared to Scotland Yard for its swift crime detection, was failing in its duty of maintaining law and order in the city.[1]

Most of the Gujarati families of Wadi fled to suburbs such as Ghatkopar, Mulund, Vile Parle and Santacruz. Daryasthan Street's wedding banquet hall was converted into a relief camp, where some other families moved in with their essential belongings and valuables. We were among the remaining few families in the Wadi now.

Escaping the Fire

A neighbouring building that housed godowns of edible oils and asafoetida was set on fire the following day. The entire area reeked of asafoetida. The helpline numbers were constantly engaged. Finally, a fire brigade arrived with four firefighters. They aimed their hoses and began dousing the fire. Meanwhile, the elders in my family made arrangements for us and my *mamis* (maternal aunts) to shift to a safer location. While my mamis hurriedly gathered our clothes and essentials, I packed my school books and comics. We were ferried to Vadgadi, where Premshanker Sharma, an acquaintance of my grandfather, lived.

While crossing the road, we saw scared firefighters rushing towards their vehicle after a group of rioters brandished guns at them. I briefly caught a glimpse of the rioters, whose faces were covered with handkerchiefs. At many locations across Bombay, firefighters were intimidated and restrained from discharging their duty.

A wooden staircase led us to the fourth floor of the fifty-year-old building. Most buildings in this area were old and were built in a similar fashion. The floors numbered anywhere from three to seven, but only a few buildings had manually operated elevators. These buildings were in a dilapidated condition and needed repairs to survive another monsoon. Premshanker's house was spread over an area of around 750 square feet, with two rooms and a spacious hall. The eight-member family welcomed us with great warmth. We were informed that there was enough food to sustain us for the next few days, but, if the curfew continued, the situation might become tighter. Since Premshanker ran an ice-cream factory nearby, we had a substantial stock of milk in reserve.

Rioters with Firearms

The street opposite Premshanker's Shri Ram Ice Cream Factory connected Vadgadi to the Muslim-dominated Chakla Street. Just a few minutes after we reached Premshanker's residence, a communal clash broke out in front of his factory. Though the shutter was down, there were several workers inside. What first began as stone pelting soon turned into heavy firing. Two bullets pierced the shutter of the shop, injuring one of the workers, Sundariya, in the chest. On learning this news, Premshanker immediately rushed to help

Sundariya. Premshanker's wife Devmala knew how Premshanker was a guardian figure to all the workers, but she kept weeping, seeing her husband leave home to step out into a burning city. Sundariya bled heavily and had to be taken to St. George Hospital on a local train.

Minutes after Premshanker left for the hospital, we heard gunshots again. In a few moments, we saw a middle-aged man being brought on a handcart down the street. He quivered as blood gushed out of his forehead. This was Paresh Joshi, who was throwing stones all this while and had got hit by a bullet in front of the shop. Though he needed immediate hospitalization, there was no means to carry him to one. His grief-stricken friends and wailing wife anxiously waited for the police to take him to the hospital. Paresh worked at a bookstall in Matunga. He was an introvert who rarely interacted with the neighbours. No one could really understand what made him join the stone pelters that day. His companions explained how Paresh was fearful of the rioters entering their locality and harming his family. Many innocents like him had resorted to violence because of the deadly cocktail of fear and hatred. A police van finally came to his rescue. But he died a few hours later in hospital.

Your Identity Decides Your Survival

Our new premises gave us a bird's-eye view of the happenings in the locality. A group of youngsters looted the shops of the opponent community, while one of their mates kept an eye out for the police. In case a police van was seen approaching, he whistled as a signal, and everybody swiftly dispersed in the narrow by-lanes. Scrap dealer Babbu Batliwala's godown served as an arsenal for the rioters looking for empty glass bottles. After being looted, the godown was set on fire. The entire area was engulfed in smoke.

These youngsters asked every passer-by to strip, to ascertain their religious identity.

Premshanker encountered one such group as he returned home after getting Sundariya admitted to the hospital. He had a long beard like an ascetic and wore a *pathani* kurta. Looking at Premshanker's appearance, some Muslim youngsters near the Masjid Station mistook him for a Muslim and warned him against proceeding towards the Hindu area. But when Premshanker ignored their warnings and kept walking, they threw stones at him from behind.

The Police and Politics

Although we were safe, my uncle and grandparents were still in the Wadi, susceptible to violence. The sirens of police vans and ambulances kept us awake all night. The carnage in Bombay continued the following day as well. To disperse violent mobs, the police had to open fire at forty-three locations in which fifty-two people were killed. The rioters had damaged many temples, mosques, madrasas and shrines. It was on this day that the police appeared to be strictest since the riots broke out. Although there were casualties from both communities in the firings, it was alleged that the police were more ruthless while dealing with Muslims.

The chief minister of Maharashtra, Sudhakarrao Naik, who represented the Congress Party, was under pressure to instruct the police to be less harsh. He ordered the police commissioner to avoid firing and try to control the mobs by using tear-gas shells and lathis instead. The police now had to rely on lathis to deal with the rioters equipped with swords, choppers, rods and petrol bombs. Some rioters carried firearms, which was evident from the fact that since the night of 6 December, there were many incidents of private firings. The brutality continued the next day. The rioting became so extreme that the cops had to fire frequently, defying the orders of the CM. Seventeen people from both communities died from bullet injuries.

The police's stern approach had an impact on the city. By 10 December, the riots were confined to the areas of Dharavi and Mahim. The cops fired here too, but nobody was killed. Peace was restored at last in these areas—by 11 December. It appeared that the city was returning to normalcy. The police relaxed the curfew as well. We finally returned to the Wadi, where a van of the State Reserved Police (SRP) was stationed right outside the gate. The violence had ceased, but we feared that the Friday namaaz might trigger the rioters once again. Since there was no traffic on the road, we could clearly hear the sermons at Zakariya Masjid. We thought that the gathering would be provoked, but that didn't happen. The imam of Zakariya Masjid was Maulana Hamid Ashraf, who was a soft-spoken man and a pacifist. He had already disallowed namaaz outside Zakariya Masjid when the Shiv Sena had raised the issue of prohibiting namaaz on the street. Although the incident at Ayodhya was condemned, people were asked to maintain peace. After some time, a white flag was installed at the entrance of Kambekar Street next to the mosque.

Meanwhile, another incident in south Bombay's Azad Maidan reignited tensions in the city when two bikers fired at a group of boys playing cricket. One youngster died, while the other four were critically injured. The next day, on 12 December, there were a few incidents of violence in the Ghatkopar, Bhandup and Dindoshi areas. Rioters had killed eight people by stabbing them. The victims were from both communities. But, before the brutality could escalate, the police controlled the situation. From that day onwards, the incidents of violence saw a sharp downward trend.

A Brief Retreat to Normalcy

Despite being battered with a thousand wounds, Mumbai has the knack of regaining normalcy rather swiftly. The Monday morning of 14 December saw life resume. The roadside shops reopened. The BEST bus on route number 102, which passed through Yusuf Meherali Road, became operational again. The pedestrians at the Masjid railway station reappeared, to head towards Zaveri Bazaar and the Mumbadevi temple. Gujarati families that had left the Wadi returned. The banality of this morning made it difficult for us to believe that it was the same city that had raged in the fire of communal hatred the previous week, killing over 300 people.

The personnel of the SRP and the Central Reserved Police Force (CRPF) were still deployed on the road at various locations. Some social workers took out a rally to collect relief material for the riot-affected families. Through a loudspeaker, they appealed to people to donate money, clothes and other essentials. An arrangement was made on Daryasthan Street to feed the poor. They were provided with a wholesome meal at the cost of Re 1. There was a long queue of people at the food counter. Throughout the city, many Good Samaritans came out to provide relief to the distressed.

My uncle was apprehensive about sending me back to the Muslim-led school. After being assured of the police van stationed outside the school, he sighed with relief. On my way to school on Tuesday morning, I walked past the street next to the Wadi, where the rioters had set a godown on fire on 8 December. The two-storey building had turned into a heap of ash. The pungent smell of asafoetida still emanated and remained in my nose till I reached school. The class was almost in full attendance. Everybody had a story of the riots to tell. Students were impatient to share what they saw and how they escaped.

From my Muslim classmates, I got to know what transpired in their areas during the riots. My classmate Salim Kazi narrated how he could not move out of his home since 6 December. He abstained from playing in the street and praying in the mosque. Salim added how he had heard the gunshots and shouts of violent crowds at his home. Rizwan's family just about managed to escape becoming a victim of the riots, as the Umarkhadi area, where they lived, was dominated by Marathi Hindus. Rizwan's family had cordial relations with their neighbours, but one evening, some drunk men turned up outside their area saying that they should not be spared. Neighbours advised Rizwan's parents to temporarily shift to a safe place, sensing the volatile situation. His parents found it prudent to leave their home, and took refuge in a school that was temporarily converted into a relief camp. A week later, they returned to an unlocked home with broken doors.

Some students also alleged that the police were biased towards Hindus. They firmly believed that the cops were sterner in the Muslim areas. A Pathan classmate even approached me, saying in an intimidating tone, 'It was just that the cops were with you people, otherwise ...'

I also heard about what transpired on 6 December from a friend of mine, Aslam Malkani. He stayed near my place, in the Char Null area of Dongri, and studied in Class VI at Dawood Fazal High School. On the evening of 6 December, he attended a wedding reception in Bhisti Mohalla, where a mob of about fifty people broke in with sticks and swords. They were resentful of any celebrations taking place after news of the Babri Masjid demolition had come. They threatened everyone and asked them to leave.

Aslam also mentioned how the people gathered at Bhendi Bazaar the next day in protest, which soon turned into violent riots. Some of the first victims of the rampage were the BMC sweepers on duty. The BEST buses passing through the junction were also targeted, and their drivers and conductors were attacked. The workers of the Mandvi Telephone Exchange also became victims of the violence. Aslam recalled the looting of an audio cassette shop called 'Aakashwani' near his home. Criminals associated with Dawood Ibrahim and Pathan gangs were at the forefront of the killings and lootings, and they were instigating more people to join in the carnage. These were the same people who used firearms during the riots and attacked the police. Overhearing the discussions of elders in the locality, Aslam gathered that the rioters could easily buy swords from Null Bazaar, which was a market for metal products. They stole petrol from parked vehicles, and filled it in glass bottles to use as petrol bombs.[2]

'We' and 'They'

After witnessing a week-long carnage, the city appeared calm on the outside, but fear, hatred and distrust boiled within. Bombay was now polarized into 'our people' and 'their people'. Hindus and Muslims avoided entering areas dominated by the other community. This fear gradually faded in the coming weeks, since the businesses and daily lives of both communities were so intertwined that it was unviable to stay apart. Retail Hindu garment sellers had to buy their wares from wholesale dealers in the Muslim-dominated Chakla Street. Similarly, many bakeries situated in Muslim localities had their distributors in Hindu-dominated areas. Many owners whose shops were looted decided to sell them, while others refilled their shops with fresh stocks. With the passage of time, police presence waned, even in the sensitive areas. The SRP van posted at the Wadi gate was withdrawn by the end of December.

While several incidents of stabbing were reported in the city, none were communal in nature. In the last week of December, the Shiv Sena launched a campaign against the offering of namaaz outside mosques on the road. Shiv Sena's mouthpiece, *Saamana,* published Islamophobic editorials every other day. Although the editor of *Saamana* was Bal Thackeray, it was the recently appointed twenty-eight-year-old executive editor, Sanjay Raut, who wrote the daily editorials and decided what appeared in print.

To counter namaaz prayers being held on the road, the Shiv Sena launched maha-artis. Most maha-artis were organized in temples that were at the periphery of areas dominated by the two communities—like Kalbadevi temple and Gol Deval temple. These hour-long maha-artis were attended by hundreds of devotees, and yet appeared less like events of devotion and more like acts of aggression. The maha-artis called for Hindu unity and asserted the idea of the nation having only one religion, using slogans of 'Jai Shri Ram' and 'Bharat Mata Ki Jai'.

5

January 1993 Riots

PRINCIPAL ZAMIRUL KHAN STORMED INTO THE classroom in the middle of algebra class and took our teacher aside. They whispered together for a while before announcing that school was over for the day and we must all leave immediately. Our teacher hastily packed his bag and warned us to head home directly. It was 11 a.m., and we were being asked to leave already! No maths test today! We were thrilled.

The day was 6 January 1993.

However, on my way home, the joy soon gave way to anxiety when I saw shopkeepers hurriedly shutting down their shops and leaving. The fear of getting caught in a tumultuous riot resurfaced, and I rushed home as fast as I could.

Bombay Burns Again

The night before, two Mathadi workers had been murdered near our school in Chinch Bunder. Most Mathadi workers hail from western Maharashtra—from districts such as Satara, Sangli and

Pune—and are engaged by godowns to help load cargo. Their union is powerful, and whenever they go on strike, all business activities come to a standstill. This is what happened after the union discovered the two bodies, and the city shivered as the news spread.

My classmate Zahid[1] Momin's brother, Jaseem, was arrested for the murders. The previous night, Jaseem was at home, watching TV, when a report was telecast highlighting the atrocities committed against Muslims in Surat. This infuriated Jaseem. He immediately contacted his friends, Lala and Firoze Konkani, both of whom were associated with the underworld. The trio called in a few more cronies and decided to teach a lesson to the 'foes of the community'. They began hunting for the long-haired drummer who played the dhol during Hindu festivals and was rumoured to have stabbed many people to death in the December riots. Armed with knives and swords, the group scanned the entire Dongri region throughout the night but failed to locate the drummer. It was at this point that they saw a Mathadi porter walking out of the godown of a transport company, and the trio decided to vent their anger on him. Other porters rushed out to rescue their colleague, but they, too, were attacked. Two of them, Laxman Kadam and Rajaram Kadam, died that night.

A year later, the police caught these youngsters, Jaseem included, but they were acquitted owing to a lack of evidence. Firoze Konkani escaped from police custody after getting a cop killed, but was later eliminated by another gang member, Chhota Shakeel.

By the next afternoon, the communal dominoes had fallen all across the city once again. The Shiv Sainiks attacked a Muslim colony in the Mahim area, and soon, a violent clash ensued between the two communities.[2] Bombay hadn't yet completely recovered from the December riots and was once again being painted with blood. Dongri, Pydhonie, Nagpada and V.P. Road were among the affected areas, with taxi drivers being some of the initial victims. Several cases of stabbing and mob lynchings were reported.

Years later, senior photojournalist and friend, Vijayanand Gupta, narrated to me how he lost his cousin Shashi, the father of a bubbly four-year-old, to one such event. A phone inspector in the Mandvi Telephone Exchange, Shashi was examining some equipment in the storeroom that day when a violent mob broke into the office. He was caught in the tsunami of violence, and Shashi's blood-soaked body was found about a 100-metres away a few hours later, with sixteen stab wounds. His family at Sahar received the news a day later. His body remained in Sir J.J. Hospital, which was in a Muslim area. On the special request of Vijayanand's journalist friends, Police Commissioner Shrikant Bapat arranged for Shashi's body to be escorted home by a police van.[3] That day, eleven people were stabbed to death and thirty-two injured.

The riots intensified on 7 January. Evening tabloids provided gory descriptions of the violence. Two passengers in Prateeksha Nagar were pulled out from a taxi and burnt alive. Places of worship were vandalized, and rioters of both communities clashed mercilessly, taking the day's toll to twenty-four deaths. We heard stories of the city burning in our as-yet-unharmed residence at Masjid Bunder.

Neither the curfew nor the desolate roads could prevent what followed on 8 January. That morning, a group of rioters locked a Marathi family in a room at Jogeshwari's Gandhi Chawl (which was misreported by various news outlets as Radhabai Chawl)[4] and set them on fire. Five men and a woman died a cruel death.

Like in the Bhiwandi riots of 1984, the Shiv Sainiks unleashed more violence as revenge, confirming their adherence to the radical Hindutva ideology. The party's prior agenda of fighting for justice for the 'sons of the soil' had offered no mileage beyond Bombay and Thane, while its Hindutva inclinations offered a fair chance of increasing its clout across Maharashtra and the rest of the nation.

During the 1987 Vidhan Sabha by-elections, party supremo Bal Thackeray had raised Hindutva as a political plank. He gave a venomous speech against Muslims at a public rally, after which the election commission stripped him of his voting rights.[5] Thackeray then began appearing in saffron clothes and was referred to as 'Hindu Hriday Samrat'—the 'King of Hindu Hearts'. The cadre-based party gathered Shiv Sainiks at different branch offices. Thackeray's inflammatory statements, *Saamana*'s editorials and the Shiv Sainiks' violence on the ground only served to aggravate the mayhem that Bombay was witnessing.

Commissioner Shrikant Bapat had recently assumed the chair and was touring the riot-affected areas round the clock. On 8 January, I saw his convoy heading towards Samuel Street, where my school was located. A few moments later, we heard a thunderous explosion and saw Bapat's associates rushing out of the street. They had been attacked by a crude bomb from a building next to my school and had escaped by a whisker. The blast left a crater on the ground and terror in our hearts as we wondered who was safe in this city.

To disperse the attacking mobs, the police had to open fire in thirty-one different locations, and twenty-eight people were killed as a result. Forty people were killed in incidents of stabbing and mob lynching. One place that saw much violence was the Imamwada area, where the residential quarters of fire-brigade workers are located. Some rioters attacked their homes with petrol bombs. It was ironic that the houses burning were the homes of firefighters, who were out to douse fires at others' homes.

My classmate Ahmed Sheikh recollects how a group of stone pelters hailing from the Hindu-populated area of Sandhurst Road attacked him and his friends at their Noorani Manzil building in Dongri. Irfan, Ahmed's older brother, joined a few others who retaliated with stones and empty bottles. Suddenly, a police van arrived and started firing at them. One bullet hit Irfan's friend in the eye, killing him instantly. Another casualty of the police firing was a potato seller who ran a stall outside the Dongri market. The third one was an unknown man who was shot in the abdomen. Soaked in blood, he crawled off the road but succumbed a few minutes later.[6]

How Fear and Hatred Fuelled Crime

Aslam Malkani, who lives about half a kilometre away from the Dongri market, recollects that streets leading to Muslim-dominated localities were barricaded using handcarts to block Hindu rioters and the police from entering. Rumour-mongering was rampant. People feared that the water and milk in Muslim areas had been poisoned and that a mob of Hindu rioters were planning to loot their houses. People collected knives, swords and empty bottles in their homes to confront the rumoured intruders. The criminal elements of the area stabbed any person from the other community they caught. The dead bodies were thrown into gutters or packed into drums and pushed on to the main road for the police to pick up. Many Muslims from Kerala also became victims of the violence, as they couldn't explain their identity because of linguistic constraints. Some youngsters moved around the streets shouting slogans such as, 'Nara e Takbeer', provoking others to join them. They then went on a rampage. Some Pathans fired on the police from terraces and escaped before the cops reached them.[7]

On the afternoon of 9 January, we heard gunshots for a long time coming from the direction of Minara Masjid, half a kilometre away from Wadi. Assuming that some terrorists with automatic weapons were firing from the terrace of Suleman Bakery, then joint commissioner of police, Ramdev Tyagi, reached the place and ordered his men to fire. Nine people were killed that day, but no terrorist or weapons was found. It appeared to be a false alarm. The deceased were poor bakery workers from Uttar Pradesh. Tyagi and his team members were later prosecuted for their excessive action.[8] That day, eighty-eight people died in the violence by rioters and police shooting across the city.

We had now started receiving disturbing news from near and dear ones. One of my uncle's friends had gone out to get his cooking gas cylinder refilled when he was murdered by rioters. Many like him, who went out for medical emergencies or to buy essentials, never returned home. Stalls and shops across the city were torched. Not even the ones near the police commissioner's office at Lohar Chawl were spared.

Amid the tumult, three or four men knocked on the Wadi's gate. Their faces were covered with handkerchiefs. My uncle and grandfather went down to meet them.

'We have heard that there is a gun shop inside the Wadi. We have to take few guns out of it. Those people have guns, and that's why our people are getting killed. We wish to reply to every bullet with a bullet,' one of them said.

It was clear that they intended to loot the arms shop. My uncle replied, 'There might be guns for sure in this shop, but they might be non-functional ones that have come here for repairs. Even if you break the lock of the workshop and take them, they will be of no use. And if you do get a gun in working condition, from where will you get the bullets? I don't think there are bullets in the workshop. No purpose will be served, and you guys will get entangled in a criminal case.'

Thankfully, they were convinced by my uncle's argument and left. Mama recognized them: they sold audio cassettes across the road. The atmosphere of hatred and insecurity was pushing them towards crime.

Homeless Again

The same day, someone threw a petrol-filled bottle and a fireball at the back of our Wadi. Someone spotted it at once, and, before the fire could advance, people doused it with buckets of water. The rioters who had thrown the fireball were threatening residents with a pistol. They were smiling—apparently deriving sadistic pleasure from our predicament. Although the fire was doused, the residents panicked. Many families fled and rushed towards Masjid Station with their belongings, defying the curfew outside. The Wadi was attacked for the first time that day, during the second phase of the riots.

My uncle Shashikant decided to shift us to a safer place. This time, taking refuge at Premshanker Sharma's home was not possible, as some of his relatives from the suburbs had already taken shelter there. The next option was a distant relative's place in Khetwadi. The three-kilometre-long route to Khetwadi passes through some Muslim-populated neighbourhoods, such as Mohammed Ali Road and Pydhonie. So, my uncle worked out another route that was seven kilometres longer, but safer—through Victoria Terminus, Kalbadevi and Bhuleshwar.

Two of my uncle's Shiv Sainik friends escorted us to the Masjid station, oblivious as we were to the government orders instructing all trains to not halt at Sandhurst Road and Masjid. We stood perplexed on the platform, watching trains pass us, one after another. Eventually, one train stopped about a hundred metres ahead of the platform because of a red signal. We ran on the tracks, hoping to catch the train. The signal turned green by then, but an accommodating guard helped us board the last bogie. The train was filled with families like ours, who had left their homes for safety. While a few women cried at their fate, the children sat looking puzzled at the turn of events.

We witnessed a mass exodus at Victoria Terminus. Affected by the riots, thousands of people were swarming in from all directions. People crowded into the outstation trains like cattle, blurring any distinction between the reserved and unreserved compartments. As per one estimate, around two lakh people left Bombay at this time. We pushed our way out of the station through the crowd.

We proceeded towards Kalbadevi Road via Mahapalika Marg. At the Metro Cinema junction, rioters had pounced like vultures on sports shops and had broken into them. They walked away with whatever they could lay their hands on—somebody with a cricket bat, someone else with footballs and badminton rackets. A man was seen running away with hockey sticks. All this was happening in broad daylight at a prominent junction. A police van passed by, but it did nothing to stop the loot, and the looters ignored them as well. Just next to the place where all this was happening is a monument related to Mahatma Gandhi's life. Close to Metro Cinema is the Small Causes Court, where Gandhi debuted as a professional lawyer in India. The story goes that he got nervous while arguing the case and refunded the fees to his client.

After walking for over half an hour, we reached Khetwadi. This area was completely populated by Hindus. About 500 metres ahead was a Shiva Temple named Gol Deval, and Muslim settlements such as Bhendi Bazaar and Null Bazaar beyond that. On 6 January, the riots in this area began after the end of a maha-arti, when the crowd leaving the event attacked the Muslim buildings in the area, leading to a carnage.

Such maha-artis were organized not only by the Shiv Sena, but also by the RSS and the VHP, which was banned after 6 December 1992. The time and venue of these maha-artis were announced on local notice boards of these organizations. The RSS and its affiliates used different names on these notice boards, such as 'Rama Sewak Sangh' and so on, to conceal their identities.

The city was officially under curfew, but in the streets of Khetwadi, people moved about fearlessly. Whenever a police van toured the area, everyone hid in the nearby buildings and came out as soon as the police left. It is rightly said that the death of a bird is child's play, and Khetwadi had turned into a playground. Young boys started playing pranks on passers-by on the street. They would cover their faces with handkerchiefs, interrogate anyone with a thin beard and threaten them with a toy pistol. If the person claimed to be Hindu, they would warn him to remove the beard.

The Congress takes pride in its secular credentials, but during the riots, the Congress workers and the Shiv Sainiks came together. In Andheri, a prominent north Indian Congress leader was seen moving around with the rioters. 'Hindu' and 'Muslim' were the only two identities that prevailed in the city, irrespective of political affiliation.

An Excess of Violence

On 10 January, I saw army columns passing down the main road next to our street in Khetwadi. The soldiers held their weapons, ready to fire. A jeep flying a red flag was escorting the convoy—it was the army's flag march. The government had now allowed the army to fire at troublemakers, when earlier they were only supposed to scare them.

The next day, on 11 January, the soldiers fired a few shots in Dadar to disperse some arsonists, but nobody was killed. On 12 January, a few people fleeing from their homes were caught by a mob of rioters in Antop Hill. The army jawans fired to rescue them. A similar situation erupted in a north-eastern suburb on the same day, and one person was killed while another was injured. The army, which is entrusted with the responsibility of protecting the country from external threats, had been compelled by circumstances to fire at citizens.

But 12 January saw an excess of savagery when two women were publicly stripped in Devipada. While one of them escaped, the other was burnt alive, along with an elderly man who tried to protect her. A family in Karupatil Chawl of Currey Road area was brutally attacked, and an old woman's fingers were chopped off. Two passengers near Kherwadi police station were pulled out from a taxi and burnt alive. At another location, a bus was attacked and a passenger set ablaze. In Jogeshwari, a truckload of rioters torched the slums; two children were burnt to death.

Atique-ur-Rehman, my political science teacher and an Islamic studies scholar at Bombay University, recollects how the maha-artis by the Shiv Sena had led to apprehensions in his area. Once, he had gone to the Minara Masjid for prayers when he heard a mob chanting 'Har Har Mahadev' approaching the mosque. This caused panic in the mosque. While some people began planning how to deal with the situation, others prepared to tackle the intrusion with violent resistance. People asked Rehman to join them to fight the advancing crowd, but his father stopped him. The situation grew tense as the slogans grew louder. Suddenly, all the masjids in the area blared the azan at the same time and, almost miraculously, the situation cooled down within minutes.

Rehman further recalls that Noor Hospital, close to his home, was inundated with dead bodies during the riots. Patients preferred private hospitals over the government ones out of fear of being booked as rioters. No funeral was arranged for many deads as they were buried secretly.[9]

The following days saw a decline in the number of rioting cases. By 15 January, peace had been established once again in most of the city, except Nirmal Nagar in Bandra.

The Political Repercussions

No other Indian city simmered like Bombay after the December 1992 riots. Prime Minister P.V. Narasimha Rao reached the city to tour the affected areas. He was greeted with black banners and taunts. Nowhere during his tour did Rao step out of his car, and neither did his convoy stop at any riot-affected area.

By 20 January, the second phase of riots ceased too. The curfew was withdrawn from several jurisdictions. The maha-artis were gradually discontinued. According to the Srikrishna Commission's Report, both phases of riots collectively killed over 900 people, and left 2,000 injured.[10] About 356 people from both communities died of bullet injuries. However, I am certain that the number of casualties was much higher. Former chief minister of Maharashtra Sharad Pawar has mentioned in his autobiography *On My Terms* that 2,000 people were killed.[11] Although life in Bombay inched back to normal, cynicism and hatred had taken root in every Bombayite's heart.

The system failed to prevent the bloodshed, and the incumbent politicians absolved themselves by blaming everything on the officers in charge. Five deputy commissioners of police (DCPs) were transferred to different cities, and Police Commissioner Shrikant Bapat was shunted out unceremoniously before the completion of his tenure. The city's former police commissioner, Rakesh Maria, has written in his autobiography, *Let Me Say It Now*, that Bapat was the chief of a force that was under-remunerated, outnumbered, overburdened, ill-equipped and manned by men who could not get adequate sleep for many days as they were busy controlling the conflict in the city.[12]

The riots led to political upheaval as well. The Congress leaders in Maharashtra were split into two factions led by Sharad Pawar and Shankarrao Chavan. The then chief minister, Sudhakarrao

Naik, was perceived as belonging to the Chavan camp. His failure to contain the violence led to murmurs growing for his ouster. Prime Minister Narasimha Rao invited Sharad Pawar, who was holding the defence portfolio then, to his home. After discussions lasting for over eight hours, it was decided that Pawar would go to Bombay and assume the chair of chief minister. It was Pawar's fourth time in office.

In the last week of January, the Maharashtra government announced a commission under Justice B.N. Srikrishna to investigate the riots. But before the work of the commission could gain momentum, the state government changed, and the new Shiv Sena–BJP government disbanded the commission. However, Prime Minister Atal Bihari Vajpayee urged the commission to be reconstituted with alterations in the scope of the investigation. In 1998, the commission completed its probe and submitted its report to the government.

The Damning Report

The commission concluded that the 1992 riots were an immediate reaction of Muslims after the demolition of the Babri mosque, but it also said that the Shiv Sena had engineered the January 1993 pogrom. The commission observed that no individual Muslim leader or organization had played a role in inciting the violence, but criminals from the Muslim community were involved in arson, killings and loot.

The commission made serious observations about the conduct of the Bombay Police in its report. Although the khaki uniform had no religion, those who wore it had been swayed according to their religious identity. They, too, seemed intoxicated with the same venom of hatred that had engulfed the entire city. The commission candidly stated that the Bombay Police had been biased. Not only did the police target Muslims, but they were lax in providing relief and registering their complaints. The curfew was harsher in Muslim-populated areas, and most of the victims of police bullets were Muslims. The commission specifically reported thirty-one policemen for dereliction of duty and conspiring with the rioters.

Retired Joint Commissioner of Mumbai Police Y.C. Pawar was posted with the SRP force during the riots and was asked to control the arson in Deonar. Referring to the police biases, he recollects, 'In the beginning, the police were not affected by the communal bias, but Muslim rioters attacked the police, and this led to a backlash. I remember recovering the bodies of two police constables cut into pieces and thrown into a garbage heap. I believe such incidents had affected the lower rung of the police force, but the senior officers were neutral.'[13]

Retired Assistant Commissioner of Police Surendrakumar Jayaswal was an inspector during the riots and was posted at the riot-affected Byculla. He concurs with JCP Pawar and adds, 'One cannot make a sweeping statement that the police were biased against Muslims. Most times, where Muslims lost their life and property, policemen themselves became complainants and filed the cases.'[14]

I spoke to a few constables who were deployed in the riot-affected areas. Hawaldar Baban Jadhav was posted at the Muslim-dominated Bhendi Bazaar. 'It was a very scary situation. We feared for our life. We were not against Muslims, but they were attacking us with bottles, stones and tube lights. The government had restricted us from firing at them. Fortunately, one day CM Sudhakarrao Naik passed through Bhendi Bazaar, and I got a chance to speak to him. I narrated the plight of the policemen on ground and asked, "Sir, for how long are we going to get beaten up like this?" After that he allowed the police to shoot at the rioters.'[15]

The hostility between the police and the Muslims could also be attributed to the anti-Rushdie riot that happened three years earlier. Muslims felt discriminated against when they were not allowed to protest at the British Consulate, and their leaders were arrested a day before the protests. The rioters and the police clashed on Mohammed Ali Road, and eleven Muslims were killed that day. Following the riots, some controversial statements made by senior police officers against Muslims only added to the acrimony.

There was only a minuscule number of Muslims in the police force. Many police families stayed in slums or chawls, which were affected by the riots. Their personal biases were reflected in their professional conduct.

The Shiv Sena–BJP government rejected the recommendations of the Srikrishna Commission report, but when the Congress returned to power in alliance with Sharad Pawar's newly formed Nationalist Congress Party, they created a Special Task Force (STF) and decided to implement the commission's recommendations. The STF was made up of policemen to act against the policemen named in the report. Its chief was K.P. Raghuvanshi, who had the reputation of being an upright and sincere officer. On the evening of 14 August 2001, a source called to inform me that former police commissioner Ramdev Tyagi had been arrested by the STF in the Suleman Bakery firing case.

'Yes, Jitendra. We have arrested Tyagi sir.' I remember the sadness in Raghuvanshi's tone when I called him to confirm the news. However, Tyagi was never jailed. Minutes before his arrest, he complained about being unwell and was admitted to Bombay Hospital. Shortly afterwards, he got bail as well. Tyagi later joined the Shiv Sena and unsuccessfully contested a Legislative Council election on the party's ticket. While many officers such as Tyagi were let off easily, one cop was dismissed and others lost their increments or promotions.

How Did Bal Thackeray Get Away?

When I met K.P. Raghuvanshi in 2016 after his retirement, I asked him why the STF hadn't arrested Bal Thackeray when the Srikrishna Commission categorically reported that he gave orders like a veteran general to his Shiv Sainiks to attack Muslims.

Raghuvanshi blamed the commission: 'How would I have arrested Bal Thackeray when the commission had not even recommended it? In the reports, they have given details of how Thackeray had instigated the riots, but our lawyers advised that the evidence on hand was not enough to prosecute him.'

Raghuvanshi explained that the STF had been established eight years after the riots, and it was difficult to produce evidence after so many years. The witnesses could not recollect the details of the incidents, and many didn't want to get into the hassle of court hearings.

While speaking to me and other journalists at his bungalow in Matoshri in 2000, Thackeray confessed, 'It is quite possible that I might have used that kind of language. It depends on the circumstances prevailing. Possibly, I may not use such language now, but the condition was that everyone was biased.'[16]

Action Elsewhere, Reaction in Bombay

The riots led to a mass exodus. While many people left for their home towns, others resettled in adjoining areas such as Mira Bhayandar, Navi Mumbai and Dombivli. Till 2008, I stayed in the Wadi along with twenty-five other Hindu-Gujarati families. Thirty years down the line from 1992, there remain none. The Ganesh Utsav celebrated at neighbouring Dabda Galli has been discontinued too. Like many others, Premshanker Sharma shut his business, sold his house and moved to Dombivli. Muslim families living in Hindu-populated areas shifted to locations such as Mumbra, Bhiwandi and Naya Nagar on Mira Road.

Over the years, Mumbai has witnessed some of the most outrageous reactions to national and international communal affairs, be it bloodshed over Rushdie's *The Satanic Verses*, the carnage following the Babri Masjid demolition or the reaction against atrocities meted out to Muslims in Assam and Myanmar in 2012.

6

12 March 1993: A Blood-Soaked Bombay

'GET OUT OF HERE FAST!'

I was engrossed in a history textbook at Dongri's study centre when I heard this hysterical shout from a middle-aged woman. 'Bombs are exploding everywhere in the city. It is not safe to stay out of home,' she continued, grabbing her son, who was sitting next to me. I had heard some explosions a few minutes ago, but I thought they were fireworks for some neighbourhood celebration.

On that Friday afternoon, 12 March 1993, I had walked to the study centre post lunch, to prepare for my Class VIII annual exams. For many students from middle-class families like ours living in congested homes, this public study centre was a boon because it gave us some much-needed quiet. The centre was like a big gazebo in the centre of a garden maintained by the Municipal Corporation. As news of the bomb blasts spread, the centre was vacated within minutes.

I quickly packed my belongings and headed home, which was about a kilometre away. On the way, I noticed a crowd gathered at the entrance of Katha Bazaar Street. I had stopped here to buy stationery on the way to the study centre. Police vehicles and the fire brigade were hacking their way through the crowd now. This was a commercial area next to the Masjid railway station, lined with shipping company offices, and this was where traders from across the city gathered to pick up various wholesale products. I learnt that one of the bombs had exploded here. It had been planted in a scooter parked opposite the Mandvi branch of Corporation Bank, and the explosion had killed five people. Burnt body parts were scattered on the street. This was the first time I saw human bodies in such a state, not knowing that later, my career as a journalist would make me see more such disasters.

Many shopkeepers pulled down their shutters in fear, while some kept them half-open. About half an hour after I reached home, both my uncles, Shashikant and Ramakant, returned home too. Ramakant Mama's hair shone with tiny fragments of glass. He told us that around 3 p.m., one of his clients had got a wristwatch repaired, and he had just taken a few steps away from the shop after getting his watch fixed, when there was a loud explosion, followed by flames and black smoke. As the smoke faded, Mama saw burnt human body parts all around. Because of the intensity of the explosion, the glass doors and windows of jewellery showrooms had shattered, and some of the fragments got stuck in his hair. My uncle had just survived a blast. It seemed like a miracle. His last client had bargained with him, and Mama had charged him less. 'He saved some money, but little did he know that in the next second, he wouldn't be able to save his life,' Mama said, sounding depressed.

Shashikant Mama, too, had escaped the blast by a whisker. He ran a stall selling imported goods and cutlery items just across the road from where the bomb was planted in Zaveri Bazaar—an enormous, crowded market for gold, silver and textiles. He had left the place for a few minutes for some work when the bomb exploded. He remembered how, just a few minutes before the explosion, a man had had an altercation with a hawker over the parking of a scooter. Later on, the investigations revealed that the explosives were planted in that scooter. The Mumbadevi temple was at one end of the road and devotees, after offering their prayers, often shopped at the stalls run by people from Uttar Pradesh and Bihar. In the Zaveri Bazaar blast, seventeen people were killed and over fifty lost their limbs.

A Blood-Soaked Day

Sharad Pawar had assumed the chair of chief minister just a week earlier on 6 March, replacing Sudhakarrao Naik. That afternoon, while he perused some files at his office in south Bombay's Mantralaya, he heard a loud explosion. As Pawar looked out of his window, he saw black smoke billowing from the Air India building in the southwest direction. By this time, he was also informed about the bomb blast at the Bombay Stock Exchange. Pawar decided to tour the city, but the then police commissioner, A.S. Samra, dissuaded him, as the blasts were still happening.

Pawar, in his autobiography, has written that his biggest concern was that the blasts would trigger another round of communal riots in the city. He straightaway rushed to the Doordarshan office to address people. In his televised speech, Pawar lied that the blasts had happened at thirteen locations instead of twelve, adding Masjid Bunder to the list. His intent was to prevent people from concluding that the attacks targeted a particular community. He believes it was this lie that thwarted the recurrence of communal violence.[1]

That evening, the Gujarati newspaper *Janmabhoomi* published a special edition carrying just the preliminary information available about the serial blasts. But it was enough to show the devastation that Bombay had witnessed. The serial blasts began around 1.30 p.m. and continued till 3.40 p.m. Twelve bombs went off in these two hours. The conspirators targeted almost every iconic location in the city, as well as the most crowded ones: a cinema hall, the airport, five-star hotels, public transport, the stock market. The bombs were mostly planted in cars and scooters, but hand grenades were also used at two locations. It was an attack on the pride of India, on its commercial capital and its gateway to the globe. The exact figures of the dead and injured were not available immediately, but in the days that followed, it became clear that the serial blasts had claimed at least 257 lives and left over 700 people injured.

The next morning, on 13 March, more details emerged in newspapers. The Shiv Sena's mouthpiece, *Saamana*, printed reports on the first page and devoted all the inner pages to graphic pictures of mangled human bodies. Four of the places bombed were known as bastions of the political outfit. One bomb exploded right outside the party head office at Dadar, another went off half a kilometre ahead at Plaza Cinema, the third at Century Bazaar in Worli and the fourth at Fishermens' Colony in Mahim. The deadliest of the four was at Century Bazaar, where a double-decker public bus was shattered, killing over ninety people. The highest number of casualties was at this location.

'Hundred Pieces of Glass Are Still Stuck in My Body!'

This is what Kirti Ajmera told me when I met him twenty-nine years after the blast. Working as a property consultant, Ajmera was about to step inside the Bombay Stock Exchange on that fateful afternoon when the bomb planted in the building's basement exploded. He was thrown a distance away, amid a heap of injured bodies, his right hand barely held in place by a thin strip of tissue from his body. His right cheek was torn apart, and he lay half-dead in a pool of blood. All he could think of in that moment was how badly he didn't want to die like that, lying on the road, as his body would be sent to the mortuary with other unidentified corpses, making it difficult for his family to locate him.

Ajmera awaited his death in that smoke-filled street when a taxi driver emerged as his guardian angel. He picked Ajmera up, taking him to the nearby St. George Hospital, which was overflowing with blast victims. He then took him to G.T. Hospital, but the situation there was no different. The driver then laid Ajmera under another patient's bed. After some time, the person lying on the bed died, and Ajmera was immediately moved up. He underwent surgery for his face and arm, and it took him several months to heal.

His life was upended after the blast. Over the last thirty years, he has had forty surgeries. 'Even today, glass pieces come out of my body. Some parts on the right-hand side of my body don't work, and I can't lie down on my right. So far, I have spent over 50 lakh rupees on my treatment,' Ajmera said.[2] He has decided to dedicate the rest of his life to fighting for financial relief for the other victims of the tragedy.

Like Ajmera, the lives of many other Bombayites were overturned in a matter of a few seconds. Somebody lost a dear one, while someone else was maimed for life. Bombay was recovering from the wounds of communal violence when, once again, it was soaked in blood. The devil was preying upon the City of Dreams. The perpetrators of the December 1992 and January 1993 riots were, by and large, known to everyone, but the brain behind these serial blasts was still a mystery. The blasts raised questions over the security of Bombay and the competence of Indian intelligence agencies to pre-empt such strikes.[3]

The Breakthrough

The Bombay Police began a rapid investigation and got its first clue within forty-eight hours of the blasts. Deputy Commissioner of Police (DCP) Rakesh Maria was informed about an explosive-laden scooter recovered at Dadar. The scooter led him to a flat at the Al Hussaini building near the Mahim police station. It was locked up. The neighbours informed him that the flat was registered in the name of Mushtaque Memon, who was better known as Tiger, the smuggler. Tiger stayed in the flat with his extended family, which included his parents, brothers Yakub, Yusuf, Essa, Ayub and Suleiman, and their wives. Everyone believed Tiger had links with Dawood Ibrahim.

Maria broke into the flat and found a key that fit the scooter recovered from Dadar. More links were found. Neighbours told Maria that Tiger had not been seen since 11 March. He had fled the country with his family hours before the blasts, but many people associated with the conspiracy were still in India. A manhunt began. Maria formed a team of 162 officers of varied ranks to investigate the case. The team spread across seventy-nine towns and cities in India, and arrested 189 suspects, most of whom were poor people associated with Tiger or his henchmen for different reasons.[4]

As the investigation progressed, a shocking truth was uncovered: the Pakistani intelligence agency, Inter Service Intelligence (ISI), was behind the blasts. To execute the conspiracy, the ISI used the resources and manpower of Dawood Ibrahim, who had escaped from India six years earlier and was now operating from Dubai. Although there was no extradition treaty between India and the United Arab Emirates (UAE), the strengthening of diplomatic relations between the two countries worried Dawood.

Meanwhile, the Bombay riots made the ISI's job easier. It was reported that Dawood received messages from Muslims in Bombay to avenge the riots. He was informed about the Shiv Sena's role and the police's biased approach. The ISI offered Dawood a quid pro quo deal to 'avenge' the Bombay riots for his help in executing their plan. The ISI promised to provide a safe harbour for him, his family and cronies in Pakistan, from where he could run his gang fearlessly.[5]

The ISI wanted Dawood to use his network of corrupt police and customs officials, who helped him smuggle gold and silver into India, to traffic explosives and weapons into Bombay. A series of meetings was organized in Dubai, which were attended by ISI agents; Dawood's brother, Anees Ibrahim; and Tiger Memon.[6] The Shiv Sainiks had burnt down Tiger Memon's office in Mahim during the riots, and the blasts offered him an opportunity to avenge his personal loss. But what confused investigators was the fact that the bomb blast at Zaveri Bazaar took place just outside Tiger Memon's beautiful glass building, which was shattered.

Three days after the serial blasts, it became clear to the Bombay Police that Tiger Memon had executed the conspiracy. Although Tiger had escaped, the police apprehended the bomb-planters, who further revealed how the RDX and the weapons dispatched by the ISI landed at the Raigadh coast near Bombay with the help of customs and police officials. Further investigation showed that the plan to rock Bombay had begun right after the January riots. While select people were sent to Pakistan, others were trained in nearby rural areas. Most were semi-literate and poor twenty- and thirty-year-olds with a criminal record. Some were the sole breadwinners of their families.

While covering the trial at the special court set up under the Terrorist and Disruptive Activities (Prevention) Act (TADA) in the late '90s and the early years of the twenty-first century, I interacted with a few of them. They were full of bitterness towards Tiger. One of the accused confessed, 'People like us could be easily misled under the circumstances. The Bombay riots infuriated us and Tiger capitalized on our anger. At present, while he relaxes in Pakistan, our families have been destroyed. I don't know if I will ever be able to lead a free life.'[7]

How Sanjay Dutt Became 'Khalnayak'

A cache of arms and explosives recovered from different parts of the city confirmed that there was more violence planned for 12 March and beyond, including multiple shoot-outs at the Municipal Corporation's headquarters and the Secretariat. The blasts were expected to trigger communal riots, for which the weapons could then be used. The investigators recovered 2,313 kilograms of RDX, 1,132 kilograms of gelatine and sixty-three AK-56 rifles. M.N. Singh, who was the joint commissioner of Bombay Police, supervised the investigation. He foresaw that the inquiry could get affected by revelations of high-profile names in the conspiracy. 'I warned my men that this is a case pertaining to national security and there would be allurements. If you fall prey to them, I will not spare you,' Singh told me.[8]

Some rifles from this cache were sent to Bollywood actor Sanjay Dutt by Anees Ibrahim through Abu Salem, who worked with Dawood at that time. Dutt's name in the blast conspiracy provided a fresh twist to the case. The Congress was in power in Maharashtra and the Centre at the time. Sanjay's father, Sunil Dutt, was a veteran film actor and a Congress Member of Parliament. He had led several relief campaigns in Muslim-dominated slum areas of his constituency and received threats as a result.

Around the same time, Sanjay was introduced to Anees Ibrahim during a film shoot in Dubai. It is believed that Sanjay expressed concerns about his father's safety to Anees, and the latter sent a cache of arms to Sanjay. The actor kept three AK-56 rifles, one 9-mm pistol and twenty-five hand grenades with him. After a few days, he returned all the arms except one AK-56 rifle. In an interview to me, former Delhi Police Commissioner Neeraj Kumar, who was part of the investigation during his stint with the CBI, revealed that Dawood had allegedly beaten Anees black and blue for supplying the weapons to Dutt. Dawood was furious that Anees had sent the weapons without his knowledge and approval.[9]

The weapons were transported to and from Sanjay's home by Samir Hingora and Hanif Kadawala, who were partners at Magnum Video Company. The duo revealed Sanjay's name during Maria's investigation.

Sanjay was not only booked under the Arms Act but also under the stringent TADA, which was generally applied to terrorists. What a startling coincidence that Sanjay got arrested at the time when his film *Khalnayak* was to be released! Many years later, I asked the former police commissioner A.S. Samra the reason for Sanjay being booked under TADA when he was not necessarily a participant in the blast conspiracy. Samra promptly asked, 'Are AK-56 rifles sold by greengrocers?'[10] He explained that the terrorists were using such Kalashnikovs, and the one procured by Dutt belonged to the cache of arms that were sent as a part of the serial blasts. Hence, Dutt had to be charged under TADA.

Before his arrest, Sanjay was often spotted at the Bhendi Bazaar junction, where he hung around with his friends. At times, he had dinner at Noor Mohammadi Restaurant there, and the restaurant owner, Khalid Hakim, composed a special dish, 'Chicken Sanju Baba', based on a recipe suggested by Dutt. Sanjay's close friend Yusuf Nalwalla, who lived in the same locality, was arrested too. The actor had earlier faced some notoriety when he got addicted to narcotics. An officer associated with the arms handling case remarked, 'Both times, Sanjay Dutt became a victim of undesirable company.'

Dutt was arrested and was initially reluctant to accept the rules of the jail. Swati Sathe, former superintendent of Arthur Road Jail, told me that Dutt was warned that physical force would be used if he didn't relent. The warning worked. Meanwhile, Sunil Dutt made concerted efforts to get his son out of jail. He wept during his meeting with Chief Minister Sharad Pawar, but the latter flatly refused to intervene. Almost every stalwart of the Congress distanced themselves from Sunil Dutt.

Many reporters recollect seeing Sunil Dutt waiting with his daughter, Priya, outside the gate of the special TADA court to meet Sanjay. People sympathized with Sunil Dutt, saying that the beloved veteran film star had to suffer because of the misdeeds of his son. M.N. Singh, under whose supervision the blast case was investigated, recollects that once Sunil Dutt met him and requested him with teary eyes to help in Sanjay's release. 'Mr Dutt, I sympathize with you, but I can't help you. Your son has confessed everything,' Singh bluntly told Dutt.[11]

The Dutt family got some relief when the Opposition parties, the Shiv Sena and the BJP, gained power in Maharashtra in 1995 and Manohar Joshi became the chief minister. Sunil Dutt met his political foe Bal Thackeray and requested his intervention for bailing out Sanjay. M.N. Singh acknowledges that there was pressure from Thackeray to give Sanjay bail. Everyone was flabbergasted that the Hindu Hriday Samrat wanted to help his political opponent's son, who was accused of being hand-in-glove with the killers of Hindus. On the one hand, *Saamana* vilified Sanjay Dutt, and on the other, Thackeray declared him to be entirely innocent.

With Thackeray's intervention, Sanjay did come out of jail. But before that, a review committee of TADA detainees was formed, which recommended his release. Sanjay's bail application was based on the committee's recommendation. When he came out of jail, Sunil Dutt took him to Bal Thackeray, where he touched

Thackeray's feet and thanked him. As per M.N. Singh, Thackeray had made a deal with Sunil Dutt over Sanjay's release. Dutt didn't contest the next Lok Sabha elections and Shiv Sena's candidate, Madhukar Sarpotdar, won from his seat.

A Historic Trial

After a seven-month-long rigorous investigation, the Bombay Police filed its charge sheet in the special TADA court. But this was no ordinary charge sheet. It comprised 9,392 pages and weighed 45 kilograms, and had to be packed in gunny bags and transported to the court in a truck. It contained the statements of 3,741 witnesses. Apart from sections of the TADA and the Indian Penal Code (IPC), the accused were also charged with sedition. This is believed to be the first case since Independence where such a charge was applied by the city police.[12]

Considering the large number of accused persons and the sensitivity of the case, the government didn't find it prudent to transport the accused every day from the jail to the court; it set up a separate court within the premises of Arthur Road Jail. Judge J.N. Patel presided over the court at the beginning of the trial, but three years later, on 11 March 1996, he was promoted to the High Court and Judge Pramod Kode succeeded him till the end of the first leg of the trial in February 2007. After that, the second leg of the trial began for the seven accused who were arrested later.

As a crime journalist, I got an opportunity to cover the historic trial and delivery of the verdict. Growing up in a locality that had witnessed tremendous bloodshed due to gang wars, communal riots and terror acts evoked my interest in crime reporting. In 1996, I got my first job as a journalist with the Hindi edition of the Shiv Sena's mouthpiece *Saamana*. After working at *Saamana* for three years, I landed a job with a newly launched national Hindi news channel in 1999. One of my initial assignments was to cover the trial of the 1993 serial blasts. When I visited the TADA court for the first time and looked at the faces of the accused, a feeling of disbelief hit me. The images of Katha Bazaar Street flashed in my mind, where I saw those burnt body parts of blast victims while returning from Dongri's study centre. The accused appeared to be simple men like the ones residing in my neighbourhood. It was difficult to believe that they could have perpetrated such a barbaric act.

Judge Kode had the reputation of not taking any leave. Even when his father died, Kode attended court after the cremation and conducted the proceedings of the day. He took his first leave in 2007, because of an injury in his arm. Kode was an approachable person and tried to keep the atmosphere light in the courtroom. During lunch breaks, he frequently invited reporters to his chamber and chatted with them. He often rebuked some of them mildly if he didn't approve of a court proceeding being reported in a certain way. Considering the sensitive nature of the case, Kode and Special Public Prosecutor Ujjwal Nikam were provided Z-category security.

During the trial in 2002, actress Parveen Babi sent a scandalous thirty-five-page letter to the TADA court that was widely covered in the media. Babi accused many people of being involved in the serial blasts, including Bollywood actors Sanjay Dutt and Amitabh Bachchan, Prince Charles, Bal Thackeray, several Hollywood celebrities and agencies such as the CIA, ISI, British Intelligence Agency and the Roman Catholic church. Everybody found these allegations to be ridiculous, but it was not widely known then that she was suffering from a mental illness. The court asked Babi to depose, but she claimed that there was a threat to her life. She was offered police security, but she still refused to go to the court.[13] Three years later, in 2005, she was found dead in her apartment. It was reported that she died due to complications arising out of diabetes and multi-organ failure.[14]

The inmates sat in a wooden box at the back of the courtroom, like school students, and were chatting away. They became acquainted with the regular court reporters as well, and often discussed with them their motivations for being involved in the blast conspiracy and how brutally they were being tortured by the police. Within that box sat Sanjay Dutt, attentively listening to the court proceedings. Dutt always made sure to put a *teeka* on his forehead before coming to court.

In that courtroom, I often noticed how most of the accused felt intimidated by Special Public Prosecutor Ujjwal Nikam. Every day after the court proceedings, Nikam used to brief the media about the happenings of the day. Once, when Sanjay Dutt came out of the court, all the cameras turned to capture him, and Nikam had to wait outside the court gate for mediapersons to return. After the next hearing, Nikam publicly warned Dutt, 'Sanju, you must not come out of the court before I leave.'

'Yes, sir,' Dutt replied. He knew that his conviction depended on how effectively Nikam argued against him in court. It was prudent to avoid his hostility.

Since then, Dutt never came out of the court before Nikam left.

How Yakub Memon Reached the Gallows

Once, under the leadership of Tiger Memon's brother Yakub, some of the accused created a big greeting card wishing Kode a happy Diwali. The card was displayed on the court's notice board on Kode's instructions. Given the judge's amiable nature, many believed him to be a gullible empath who would be lenient while delivering the judgement. But Kode was punctilious about his responsibilities and unbiased to the facts presented before him during the trial. This trial was conducted against 137 accused persons, out of whom fourteen died during the trial. Most of them were the ones who planted the bombs at various locations.

Kode convicted 100 accused out of the remaining 123. Yakub Memon, along with twelve others, received the death penalty. Memon was so furious when Kode announced his sentence that the security in the courtroom had a tough time controlling him. While being taken away, Yakub shouted he had been a fool to return to India and that he was paying the price for ignoring his brother Tiger's advice, who had told him not to surrender. That was the last time I saw him alive. After the judgement, he was shifted to the Nagpur jail, which housed the gallows.

The underworld grapevine has a story that explains why Yakub returned to India. He was the most educated person in the Memon family and worked as a chartered accountant before fleeing the country. 'It was because of the tussle between *deorani–jethani* that Yakub returned,' a former member of Dawood gang told me.[15] Wrangles between the deorani (the wife of the younger brother) and jethani (the wife of the elder brother) are a regular feature of Indian joint families. It is said that Yakub was fed up with the frequent quarrels between his wife, Raheen, and Tiger Memon's wife, Shabana.

After escaping from Bombay, Yakub's family became dependent on Tiger, and taking advantage of the situation, Shabana often tormented Raheen. Unable to bear his wife's nagging, Yakub decided to return. He believed that since his role in the conspiracy had been minimal, he would be out of jail in a few days. Yakub contacted his cousin based in Mumbai and informed him about his desire to return. On 5 August, he was arrested by the STF of the CBI at the New Delhi railway station. After the verdict was delivered, Yakub's wife, Raheen, told journalists that Yakub was paying for the sins of his brother and that he was innocent.

All the death penalties from the TADA court were commuted by the Supreme Court, except for Yakub Memon's. Eight years later, after all of Yakub's appeals and mercy petitions were rejected, the date of his hanging was fixed as 30 July 2015, which coincidentally was his birthday. His hanging was preceded by a dramatic controversy. In an article published on rediff.com, India's external intelligence agency, the Research and Analysis Wing (R&AW), officer B. Raman revealed that Yakub had been unofficially picked up in July 1994 in Kathmandu and the CBI staged his arrest at the Old Delhi railway station.[16] Raman remarked that based on Yakub's cooperation with the Indian agencies and his continuous pleas for his family, he didn't deserve the death sentence.

A week before Yakub's hanging, I interviewed Justice P.D. Kode to understand the rationale behind Yakub's death penalty. Kode told me he wasn't influenced by his good behaviour in the court during the trial, but found it fitting to award the death penalty based on evidence. 'Society makes laws, and if some accused is sentenced to death, it is in the interest of society and the country. The punishment is not given to the person, but the criminality within him,' he told me.[17]

I reached Nagpur a day before Yakub was to be hanged. The gallows in the jail were ready, and all the arrangements had been made, but there was much apprehension in the air. Out of nowhere, a massive group of civilians approached the Supreme Court with a last-minute mercy petition signed by several renowned lawyers, former judges, authors, politicians, journalists, actors and film-makers. This was an extraordinary circumstance, and unexpectedly, the court agreed to hear the petition at a very late hour that night.

I was witnessing an event of a lifetime. The petition pleaded for the commutation of the death penalty on the grounds of human rights violation, the twenty years that Yakub had spent in jail, international conventions and B. Raman's article. Some argued that since the killers of former Prime Minister Rajiv Gandhi, accomplices of sandalwood smuggler Veerappan and Khalistani militants were all pardoned, Yakub too deserved it. The lawyers of the petitioners and the government argued for about two hours. At around 4 a.m., the three-judge bench dismissed the mercy petition.

The Nagpur Police imposed a curfew in the area surrounding the jail and even the journalists were kept a kilometre away. At 6.35 a.m., a jail guard, who was appointed as the hangman, pulled the lever and Yakub's eyes shut forever. His post-mortem was performed within the jail premises, and the body was transported to Mumbai via an Indigo Airlines flight. I boarded the same flight. Yakub's brother, Suleiman, and another relative wept constantly throughout the journey.

Lakhs of people assembled at Mahim's Al Hussaini building, where Yakub's corpse was being taken. Police Commissioner Rakesh Maria was present to control the crowd. The crowd was intensely emotional, and there was a high risk of violence. For Maria, the bomb blast case had come a full circle. Twenty-two years ago, he began his investigation at this building as a DCP and now he was in front of the dead body of one of the accused at the same place.

The Bombay serial blasts, the trial and the execution of the accused were unprecedented. It ruptured Mumbai's soul. The city dreaded history repeating itself. But this was just the beginning.

7

Reign of the Underworld

'SALIM BADGUJAR SHOT DEAD!'

The headline left me numb. Just a few days before the 1998 Lok Sabha elections, Badgujar and I had been strolling down the narrow streets of south Mumbai's Nagpada, discussing local politics. This murder was the latest in a series of political killings that began in 1993.

Badgujar was allegedly killed by Dawood Ibrahim's second in command, Shakeel Ahmed Shaikh, aka Chhota Shakeel, who took offence at his association with the Shiv Sena and his facilitation of its inroads into Muslim-dominated Nagpada. Badgujar was a devout Muslim, who offered namaaz punctiliously every Friday. He had joined the Shiv Sena as Nagpada's branch chief, called the *shakha pramukh* in party parlance, a few days ago. I had met him as *Saamana's* reporter along with the Shiv Sena MP Mohan Rawale, whose electoral campaign in the locality he had launched.

I asked him why he would join a party accused of targeting Muslims during the Mumbai riots, to which he smiled and said, 'Violence was perpetrated from both sides. We must forget the past and move on. I like Balasaheb because he is a fearless man and talks about the interests of our nation.'

Nagpada was a bastion of Dawood Ibrahim's dreaded D-Company. Before fleeing India in 1989, Chhota Shakeel used to live on Nagpada's Temkar Street, along with his family. Dawood's widowed sister, Haseena Parker, lived in the Gordon Hall Apartments in the same locality. Just opposite her residence was Ahmed Sailor High School, from where Dawood dropped out in Class IX. Supporting the Muslims' adversaries at such a location was equivalent to betraying the community.

Many other Shiv Sena and BJP leaders were on Shakeel's hit list after the riots. A prominent name was BJP legislator Prem Kumar Sharma's, who had protested against the illegal constructions in the area, which resulted in the demolition of several properties—some of them owned by members of D-Company. In June 1993, when Sharma was heading to a restaurant to celebrate his daughter's exam results, two of Shakeel's men waylaid his car near Khetwadi and shot him dead.

The following year in 1994, they shot Ramdas Nayak, Bombay's BJP president, in Bandra, as he was heading to work. An AK-47 rifle was used for the first time by the underworld to assassinate a politician. Generally, the gangsters avoided attacking the police, but, in this case, Nayak's police bodyguard was shot dead too.

Nayak's assassination terrified the Shiv Sena and BJP leaders. The BJP announced a shutdown in the city. Nayak's funeral was attended by BJP bigwigs, including Atal Bihari Vajpayee and Lal Krishna Advani.

Though the killings may have had other motives, they were perceived as communally motivated. The prime reason for this was a split in Dawood's gang. Dawood's most trusted man had become his nemesis.

The Underworld's Communal Divide

When Dawood broke the backbone of the Pathan gang and established his supremacy in the Bombay underworld, he was aided by Rajan Nikalje, aka Chhota Rajan. Rajan was introduced to the crime world as a ticket black marketeer outside Sahakar Cinema in east Bombay's Chembur. With his mentor Bada Rajan's support, his notoriety soon grew in the city's netherworld. He came into contact with Dawood, and their proximity strengthened with time, leading him to become Dawood's most trusted man. In 1986, he moved to Dubai with Dawood. Dawood had given him wide authority within the gang, and this earned Rajan a few enemies. The in-group hostility spread like poison, and many gang members began maligning him in Dawood's presence. Chhota Shakeel and Dawood's younger brother Anees hated him.

In 1992, Dawood's brother-in-law Ibrahim Parker was shot dead by Arun Gawli's gang. A few days after the incident, the shooters were caught and beaten by the crowd when they fled after another shoot-out. The police arrested them and admitted them to Sir J.J. Hospital. Dawood wanted to avenge Parker's murder and asked Chhota Rajan to kill the shooters, but Rajan refused because of the heavy security around the hospital.

A few days later, Dawood assigned the task to another team led by Subhash Singh Thakur, who launched a daredevil attack on the hospital, killing one shooter, Shailesh Haldankar, and two policemen. Shakeel used this opportunity to question Dawood about Rajan's loyalty. Gradually, Dawood's consideration shifted towards another gang member, Sharad Shetty, aka Bada Idli, who now began receiving the privileges that Rajan once enjoyed.

While Rajan's future in the D-Company hung in the balance, Dawood's name emerged as one of the prime conspirators in the 12 March 1993 Bombay blasts. Rajan had no idea about the company's involvement in the blasts, and his exclusion from such an event shocked him. He realized he had no future with Dawood and quit the gang, relocating to Thailand in the following year. He even announced this in interviews.[1] He alleged that by conspiring the bomb blasts in Bombay, Dawood had betrayed India, and now Dawood's destruction had become his life's mission.

This narrative earned Rajan the reputation of being a 'patriot' and a 'nationalist don'. However, the former chief of Maharashtra Police, D. Sivanandhan, who is credited with a violent campaign against the underworld that crushed a large part of it, has a different story to tell. In a conversation with me, he pointed out that religion has no place in the dark world of the mafia. Everything is based on expediency, and Chhota Rajan's claim of being a Hindu sympathizer was just eyewash.

Another source from the underworld informed me that the prime cause of friction between Dawood and Rajan was extortion. Often, when Rajan threatened to extort somebody, they would approach Dawood and Anees directly, and Rajan would be instructed not to trouble them. However, this was not reciprocated when Anees or Shakeel threatened somebody and the victim contacted Rajan for relief. This disparity bothered Rajan. In Dubai, gang members often spent their evenings playing cards, and this issue led to altercations between them.

In an interview with *Frontline* magazine, Chhota Shakeel proclaimed that the split was due to Rajan's selfishness. 'Chhota Rajan says that he split with us because of the serial blasts. But why did he stay with us for a year after they took place? Why did he not leave two or three days after the blasts? After all, the names of all the accused, including ours, were in the newspapers by then. Why did he not give statements dissociating himself from us then? The truth is that he became selfish. He was making holes in the plate he was eating from. He wanted to portray himself as a white-collar person, but he cannot wipe off the stains from his white collar,' said Shakeel.[2]

To strengthen his image as a 'Patriot don', Rajan began ordering hits on the accused who were arrested for participating in the Bombay serial blasts. His shooters allegedly killed eight undertrials who had been flagged by Rajan. Hanif Kadawala, a partner in Magnum Video Company, was gunned down at his Bandra office one afternoon. Since Kadawala was a suspect in the blasts case, the Mumbai Police considered Rajan responsible for his murder. The CBI took over the case in 2015. However, Kadawala's son filed a plea in the trial court that a relative who wanted to usurp his property was behind his father's murder. His plea was rejected by the court on the grounds that there was no such claim made in the last sixteen years, and it was difficult to understand why such a claim was being made after such a delay.[3] Chhota Rajan was eventually acquitted due to a lack of evidence in the case.[4]

While Rajan claimed accountability for killing the blast suspects in media interviews, Chhota Shakeel retaliated by killing Shiv Sena office-bearers. Most of the targets were people indicted for rioting by the Srikrishna Commission. A prominent name among them was Milind Vaidya, Mumbai's former mayor, who survived two deadly attacks by Shakeel's gang.

Interestingly, although the gang wars between Chhota Rajan and Dawood had communal shades, both gangs had both Hindu and Muslim members. Dawood had Hindu loyalists such as Sharad Shetty; Sunil Sawant, aka Sawtya; and Anil Parab, whereas Muslims like Ijaz Lakdawala and Fareed Tanasha worked for Chhota Rajan.

Five Gangs That Ruled Bombay

There were many players in the 1990s gang wars other than Dawood's and Rajan's. A gang headed by a former mill worker,

Arun Gawli, aka Daddy, operated from south Bombay's Dagdi Chawl in Byculla. A short distance from Dagdi Chawl is Chinchpokli, from where another don Amar Naik, aka Ravan, ran his gang. These gangs had divided up the city, and every gang extorted money from different builders, hoteliers, mill owners, jewellers and eminent personalities.

Dawood dominated south Mumbai areas such as Nagpada, Mumbai Central, Masjid Bunder, Pydhonie, Zaveri Bazaar, Colaba, Mazgaon, Dongri and Crawford Market. Chhota Rajan had influence in north-eastern suburbs such as Chembur, Kurla, Govandi, Ghatkopar, Tilak Nagar and Parel of central Mumbai. Arun Gawli and Amar Naik fought for dominance over areas of south and central Mumbai such as Girgaon, Byculla, Lower Parel, Worli, Dadar, Matunga, Wadala, and suburbs such as Mulund, Bhandup, Vikhroli and Kanjurmarg. Members of these gangs often killed each other or tipped off the cops to eliminate rivals.

In 1997, a fifth gang led by Abdul Qayoom Ansari, aka Abu Salem, entered the scene. Salem earlier worked for Anees, but he could no longer ally with the D-Company after he eliminated music baron Gulshan Kumar without Dawood's approval. To escape Dawood's wrath, Salem left Dubai and moved to different cities in Europe. He established an independent gang, employing members from his hometown in Uttar Pradesh. The monitoring of the gang's activities by sleuths of the Mumbai crime branch revealed that Salem's main source of revenue was Bollywood, but he also extorted money from many real estate businessmen.

In 2018, I saw someone at the Mumbai office of a national political party. I was stunned. This man would have been killed or put behind bars, but he was now a political worker instead. Let's call him Brijesh Yadav for now. While reporting Shiv Sena Shakha Pramukh Kishore Pashte's murder in 1998, I had stumbled across his name as an accused. Over a cup of tea with him in 2018, when I revealed I knew about his past associations with the Amar Naik gang, he shared the rest of his story.

Brijesh forayed into the underworld when he was a first-year student at south Mumbai's K.C. College. He once got into a scuffle with a pedestrian outside his college premises, who turned out to be a member of Amar Naik's gang. Brijesh's friends told him that there could be a violent retribution and that he must meet Naik's henchman, Shashikant Sagvekar, aka Chikna Babu, to apologize. At the meeting, Chikna Babu noticed Brijesh's potential and made him an offer. In that moment, Brijesh knew his tea-seller father could never afford the power and glory possible in the underworld. He accepted the invitation and soon began extorting money from different sources, along with the gang.

Though Kishore Pashte hung around with the gang, Naik suspected him of being a police informer. This feeling only grew more acute when a gang member was killed in a police encounter. One day, in 1997, Brijesh and company shot Pashte in a crowded area in Bhuleshwar and fled to Hotel Oberoi. They confirmed Pashte's death at G.T. Hospital and celebrated the news with a bottle of champagne.

Although these killings had become regular news in Mumbai and newspapers had discontinued giving prominent space to daily shoot-outs, the coverage of Pashte's murder was important for *Saamana*, as Pashte worked for the Shiv Sena. My career as a journalist had commenced by working as a south Mumbai stringer for *Saamana*'s Hindi edition, and it came upon me to follow the murder investigations in detail. Based on inputs from the police, I had published a report the next morning in *Saamana* identifying all the suspects. Brijesh escaped to Nepal, but Chikna Babu and another accomplice were killed in an encounter. Three months later, Brijesh surrendered before the court, but, like most cases of the underworld, he was acquitted for lack of evidence. At present, Brijesh continues to hang around the party office.

Charan Sharma's (name changed) introduction to the underworld was similar to Brijesh's. In 1997, I attended a press conference held by Arun Gawli's wife, Asha Gawli, at the Mumbai Marathi Patrakar Sangh Hall. Surrounded by about twenty youngsters positioned as her bodyguards, she tried convincing the media of her husband's innocence. To my astonishment, one of these 'bodyguards' was Charan, my classmate from Wilson College. I had a quick chat with him.

Charan lived in a chawl in Worli with his father, a teacher in a Hindi-medium school. Once, Charan's girlfriend was molested in the college canteen. When Charan learnt about the incident, he thrashed the molester severely. The culprit was a member of Arun Gawli's gang. Charan's friends advised him to visit the Dagdi Chawl and settle the matter before the situation worsened. When he went to the chawl to meet Gawli's henchman, Raju Philip, he came across one of his acquaintances from his native village in Uttar Pradesh, who advised him to join the Gawli gang as well.

Charan couldn't resist the offer and soon became a shooter for the gang. He took part in many incidents thereafter, proud to be a 'company's man'. In the Mumbai underworld's parlance, a gang is referred as 'Company'. Dawood's gang is known as D-Company, Chhota Rajan's gang is known as Nana Company, and Arun Gawli's gang is known as Byculla Company or Daddy Company. In the perilous crime world, anybody stamped as a company's man held a distinct stature and felt powerful. By now, Charan had escaped two encounters. By the dawn of the new century, Arun Gawli's gang disbanded and Charan quit the underworld. He is now a political worker in a neighbouring city and acts in Bhojpuri movies. I wasn't surprised to know that he usually plays villains.

Although Brijesh and Charan's stories show how the underworld attracts youngsters, I can't guarantee their veracity, as it is quite possible that they lied or exaggerated the facts while talking to me. Neither of the two was ever found guilty by any court of law. Both of them are now political workers, but there were many like them who entered the dark alleys of the underworld and never returned. Either they were shot dead by the police or are still languishing in prisons.

Vasant Saraf, former police commissioner of Bombay, has researched extensively on the organized crime syndicates of the city. As per his findings, 66.5 per cent of the gangsters were between nineteen and twenty-eight years of age, whereas 26 per cent of them belonged to the age group between twenty-nine and thirty-eight.[5] As per a source from the underworld, prisons are the biggest recruiting grounds for gangs—prisoners charged with theft, pickpocketing, cheating and other petty offences are helped with lawyers and money for bail if they have the potential to work for a gang. Once the person is out of jail, he is provided weapons and details of the target, getting paid up to Rs 25,000 per shooting. Once the task is accomplished, the weapon has to be returned. Some gangs hire shooters on flexible salaries, but the consistency and time of the payment are not fixed.

Chhota Shakeel and Abu Salem appointed unemployed youths from Uttar Pradesh as shooters. After the target was eliminated, they were provided flight tickets to return. According to Saraf's report, 30 per cent of Mumbai's gangsters came from states other than Maharashtra. A glorified portrayal of the underworld in movies is another reason that continues to attract youngsters to this city of crimes.

The gangs operated in a fairly organized fashion. Each member had specific duties—some were assigned to keep watch on targets, some to kill them; some were assigned vehicle thefts; others had expertise in extortion; and some were deft in handling the gang's accounts. A few arranged lawyers for arrested gang members, bribed the cops and threatened witnesses as required. Every gang even had a 'jail unit', which looked after the arrested gang members and extorted money from white-collar prisoners by torturing them. Some gangs even arranged for the training of recruited shooters, usually at abandoned buildings, construction sites or deserted streets. Since most of the targets were shot point-blank, there was no need for target practice, but shooters were trained in weapon handling.

Most of the shooters from Arun Gawli and Amar Naik's gangs came from the families of mill workers. A prolonged strike called by the workers' union in the 1980s led to the permanent closure of over fifty textile mills in Bombay. Many mill owners packed up and moved their businesses to Gujarat. Apart from the textile mills, many other industries also shifted base to different locations because of aggressive unionism in the city. Bombay transformed from an industrial city to a commercial city. Unemployed workers lived miserable lives. The underworld capitalized on the situation and recruited the children of mill workers. Arun Gawli himself was a former mill worker.

Mafia dons such as Dawood Ibrahim, Chhota Rajan and Abu Salem ran their gangs from foreign countries. They made extortion calls to their targets in India. Gang members then picked up the money and dispatched it to their bosses through *hawala* channels. Whoever refused to pay was killed. Gangsters who got caught were shot dead by the police or put behind bars. The dons, safe in their foreign havens, easily got new boys for the job to replace those jailed or killed. But Amar Naik and Arun Gawli ran their gangs from Bombay. With the corrupt jail administration, they even operated their gangs from prison. Members of the Gawli gang proudly claimed, 'Our Daddy is not a fugitive. Despite being in jail he dominates everyone.'

The recession in the early 1990s led to a surge in underworld activities. During that phase, everyone who spent lavishly on events such as weddings received extortion calls from the underworld. Many people stopped printing their residential addresses on the invitation cards out of fear. By 1994, the underworld ruled the city. No area of Bombay remained untouched. Gang wars and high-profile murders made national headlines every other day. Nobody seemed more powerful than the mafia in Bombay. The police machinery seemed ineffective against them, and the underworld made the most of this terror that enveloped the city. The greater the fear, the greater the gang's income. Those who paid up had to pay the rival gang as well. In 1995, bullets of the underworld killed twenty-nine people. The number rose to ninety-nine in 1998.

Crime reporters such as me became chroniclers of these daily killings. Rushing from one murder spot to another became routine. The scenes were the same everywhere—blood spilt on the road, empty pellets, cops tracing outlines of corpses on the ground with chalk and officers registering statements from the witnesses. From the shoot-out spots, we hastened to the hospitals where wailing relatives of the victims gathered outside the mortuary.

The Mafia's Big Message

The case of Roopam, a famous clothing brand, evokes some of the most poignant memories of what may be called the most dominant phase of the mafias in Mumbai during the 1990s. The slate-grey multistorey showroom stands right opposite the Mumbai police commissioner's office as a reminder of the days when the police felt helpless before gangsters.

The forty-year-old owner of Roopam, Bharat Shah, was shot dead by Chhota Shakeel's men right outside the police commissioner's office. The gunshots would certainly have echoed in the chambers of the police chief. On 8 October 1998, Bharat had gone to a nearby public telephone booth, barely a hundred metres away, to make an overseas call. Two men appeared from the crowd, shot at him through the booth and fled, leaving a bleeding Bharat dead on the spot. This was no deserted road, but the centre of the city, swarming with Diwali crowds. And yet the shooters' swift escape seemed no big deal.

As informed by a friend, who is a member of Bharat's family, the businessman had received extortion calls for three years but decided not to yield to threats. Instead he lodged a police complaint each time, and the police provided him with temporary security. Bharat encouraged other businessmen to stand up to the underworld as well and even arranged security for some of them. However, as the number of extortion calls declined, he discontinued the security measures about eight months before his death. Little did he know that he was being observed all the while. The murder was Shakeel's revenge for Bharat's stand against the underworld.

Bharat Shah's death made national headlines and was the underworld's big message: They could kill anyone, anywhere, anytime, even if the target had police security. The mafia emerged supreme, and everyone had to bow before them. The ones who had earlier refused to pay extortion money immediately cleared all their 'dues' at once. Within a week of the assassination, the underworld earned crores. Mumbai Police was helpless.

According to Bharat's relative, the police began defaming the deceased and fuelled speculations in the media regarding Bharat's links with the underworld, just to protect themselves. They also spread the rumour that before getting killed, he talked to a gangster in Dubai. However, as Bharat lay dying in the booth, his younger brother Viren's good sense prevailed, and he redialled the number. It turned out to be a relative of theirs living in Dubai, and Viren made sure that this fact was recorded by the police. Since Chhota Shakeel came after Viren next with his threat calls, he eventually took security cover.

While Bharat Shah's murder was still under investigation, another shooting was reported within a week at Bhandup. Two youngsters rode their bikes to the crowded Madras Café and fired eight rounds, killing the Kurup brothers, Krishnadas and Haridas, who were the owners of the café, on the spot.

Another high-profile killing in the 1990s was that of fifty-one-year-old Sunit Khatau's. On 7 May 1994, Khatau's Mercedes stopped at a traffic signal near the Mahalaxmi Station, when shooters on a motorcycle, who had followed him from his Malabar Hill bungalow, smashed his windshield with a hammer and rained bullets on him. Khatau's murder was a repercussion of the gang war between Arun Gawli and Amar Naik. Khatau was about to sell his 50,000-square-feet mill in Byculla. Since Gawli had aided this deal by coercing the mill workers, he was to be given a share of the money. This deal implied more money, weapons, shooters and power for Gawli, which troubled Naik, and he commissioned Khatau's death.

Builder Pradip Jain was another big name killed by the underworld. Abu Salem had demanded a part of Pradip's property. His refusal cost him his life on 7 March 1995 at his Andheri office. Pradip's murder created a wave of fear among real estate businesspersons, and many of them paid extortion money almost immediately. On the thirteenth day after Jain's murder, Salem called his widow and, allegedly laughing demonically, threatened her that if Pradip's younger brother Sunil didn't fulfil his demands, he too would meet the same fate.[6]

Thakiyuddin Wahid's murder also made the news that year. After the Indian government allowed private players in the aviation sector, he founded the country's first private airline company called East–West Airlines in February 1992. As the airline began procuring new aircraft in its expansion drive, Thakiyuddin was attacked on his way home on 13 November 1995, at around 9.30 p.m., in a repeat of mill owner Khatau's murder over a year ago. Motorcycle-borne shooters waylaid his Mercedes, broke the windshield with a hammer and pumped fourteen bullets into him. In an interview with a weekly magazine, Chhota Rajan claimed responsibility for the incident. He believed Wahid had links with his adversary Dawood, who had invested in his airline company, so this attack was directed at Dawood.[7]

Investigative journalist Josy Joseph who, in his book *Feast of Vultures,* has written extensively about Thakiyuddin Wahid's murder, told me that he was murdered due to business rivalry and that his murder was orchestrated by the owner of a rival airline associated with Dawood.[8] Faisal Wahid, Thakiyuddin's younger brother, concurred with Joseph's findings when I spoke to him in 2021, twenty-six years after the incident. Faisal said his competitors had capitalized on the communal polarization in the country that followed the Babri mosque demolition. He said, 'East–West Airlines, being the first private airline in the country and the only big business conglomerate completely owned by a Muslim family, was most unfairly targeted by competitors through an organized smear campaign, which called it a Muslim-owned company. My beloved brother and managing director of the company was assassinated by the people who didn't believe in fair competition in the aviation business. We have never recovered from the great tragedy of losing the nucleus of our family. He was indeed one of the architects of private aviation in India.'[9]

Thakiyuddin's murder aggravated the fearful atmosphere in Bombay as the mafia continued with its 'kill-one-scare-all' policy. An Anti-Extortion Cell officer of Mumbai Police kept a collection of voice samples of several gangsters. I have heard some of them. What was common in almost all the conversations was how thoroughly informed the gangster was regarding the target's business performance and their families—where their children studied, at what time they travelled and so on. This would scare their targets and make the extortionists' tasks easier.

In the calls, such personal details were usually followed by the gangster detailing the consequences of approaching the police for help. Unlike most extortion callers, Chhota Shakeel usually began the conversations politely in chaste Urdu, and his tone changed if the target refused to pay.

Film Industry in Fear

The underworld had its eye on every business where big money changed hands. Till the early 1990s, the smuggling of gold and electronic items was an enormous source of income for underworld gangs. This practice ceased post liberalization as the customs duty on these goods reduced considerably. Extortion seemed like a promising alternate source of income, and the film industry was a gold mine. By the mid-1990s, the entire industry was in the grip of the underworld, and like those in other businesses, those who refused to pay were killed mercilessly.

Producer and director Mukesh Duggal, who had produced commercially successful movies such as *Gopi Kishan* and *Saathi,* became one of the first persons in Bollywood to be killed by the mafia's bullets on 7 March 1997. The police said that Duggal became a victim of inter-gang rivalry when he took financial support from one gang to produce a movie. When the rival gang learnt of this, Duggal was eliminated.

On 4 July 1997, a movie named *Gupt* starring actors Bobby Deol, Manisha Koirala and Kajol was released, which did well at the box office. The director and producer of the film was Rajiv Rai, who had delivered hits such as *Tridev, Vishwatma* and *Mohra* in the 1980s and 1990s. Rai's delight at his latest success was replaced by fear when the underworld demanded a share of the earnings. Rai decided he would not succumb to their threats and complained to the police, and he was assigned an armed constable for protection. On 31 July, at around 5 p.m., when he was leaving his office in the Tardeo area of south Mumbai, five people started firing at him. It rarely happened that a person with police security was targeted by the underworld. Generally, the gangs waited for the target to become careless and for his security to be withdrawn after an assessment that the threat had passed—as it had happened with Bharat Shah. While Rai looked for cover, his police bodyguard fired in retaliation. One gangster was injured by his bullets and was caught. Rai escaped the attempt on his life, but he got so scared after the incident that he settled down abroad and didn't return to Mumbai for a few years.

T-Series owner Gulshan Kumar, who had become a household name through his religious musical videos and bhajans, and was known as the 'Cassette King', wasn't as fortunate as Rai. On 12 August 1997, the most disturbing visuals of his bullet-ridden dead body were broadcast on TV. As always, Gulshan had gone to Andheri's Shiva temple for his morning prayers. As he was about to get into his car after the prayers, somebody shouted, '*Bahut ho gayi teri pooja* (Enough of your prayers).' Bullets rained down on him.

An injured Kumar tried to escape but was surrounded by three shooters and slaughtered. The post-mortem report revealed that sixteen bullets were pumped into his body.

Gulshan Kumar turned out to be one of the biggest preys of the underworld. After tasting success with his audio cassette business in Delhi, Kumar headed to Bombay. Apart from producing films, he made music videos that added to his prosperity. Kumar's rapid success disturbed his rivals and established players in the entertainment industry.

The police believed that Abu Salem accepted a contract to kill Kumar, and there were two reasons behind this. Musician Nadeem Saifi of the celebrated Nadeem–Shravan duo had produced a music album titled '*Hi Ajnabi*' and wanted Kumar to buy its rights. Kumar didn't like the album, but, under pressure, he bought it. As Kumar had assessed, the album flopped. Nadeem alleged that Kumar didn't promote the album adequately and asked Salem to kill him.

On the other hand, Mumbai Police also arrested Ramesh Taurani, owner of Tips, which was a rival company of T-Series. The police claimed that Taurani got Kumar killed owing to professional rivalry. Meanwhile, Nadeem Saifi moved to London. To extradite him back to India, Mumbai Police fought a legal battle in a London court but lost. Nadeem's lawyer, Majeed Memon, facilitated my phone call with him. When I spoke to him, Nadeem said that he was falsely implicated in the case. 'I am just an artiste. I can't even think of killing anyone,' he told me.[10] While Nadeem was out of bounds for the police, his partner, Shravan Rathod, was summoned by the Crime Branch several times and grilled for hours.

Two years later, another celebrity from Bollywood was targeted. Rakesh Roshan, who was undergoing a financial crisis, produced a film titled *Kaho Na … Pyaar Hai* (*KNPH*), starring his son, Hrithik Roshan, in the lead. The movie, released on

14 January 2000, became an instant hit. Roshan hoped that with the success of the film, his financial worries would be over. However, those were the days when the figures at the box office were monitored not only by film-makers but also by the underworld. When the underworld didn't get its share of the earnings, a death warrant was issued against Roshan. On 21 January, a week after *KNPH* was released, Roshan was shot at when he came out of his Santa Cruz office. The gangsters fired six shots at him, and two pierced his left arm. His driver had the presence of mind to take Roshan straight to Nanavati Hospital, and he survived the attack. This attack added to the atmosphere of terror in Bollywood.

Such shootings continued through 2001. One victim was Ajit Dewani, actress Manisha Koirala's secretary. On refusing to pay the desired amount to the Salem gang, Dewani was shot dead at his office on 30 June. Abu Salem soon emerged as the most dreaded mafia don in Bollywood. By this time, Ijaz Lakdawala, who had fallen out with Chhota Rajan, had formed a gang of his own. He attempted to extort money from Lawrence D'Souza, who had produced successful movies such as *Saajan, Dil Ka Kya Kasoor* and *Nyay Anyay* in the early 1990s. D'Souza refused to pay up, resulting in a deadly attack on him on 4 July 2002. He escaped by a whisker. Producer Manmohan Shetty and distributor Anil Thadani also just about got away in such attacks. Mumbai Police claimed there was a conspiracy involving the abduction of actor Aamir Khan, film-maker Ashutosh Gowariker and actress Manisha Koirala, but the timely intelligence inputs saved them.

While Bollywood movies celebrated the victory of good over evil, the industry itself survived at the mercy of the underworld. The protagonists who broke the bones of dreaded gangsters on-screen lived in fear of Mumbai's various 'companies'. The actors danced to the mafia's tune.

Don, Police and Forbidden Love

'My weapon has been snatched away, but that is for some higher good. When I am murdered, I will meet her in heaven. She is waiting for me there. We can't be separated for long.'[11]

These dreamy lines come from a real-life policeman's romantic saga. He confessed to me on camera about having an affair with a don's wife, who was allegedly murdered by her husband. The policeman now felt that he would be next.

Neeta Naik's murder stands apart from all the 1990s shootings that I covered. She donned two identities in Mumbai—first, of being a firebrand Shiv Sena corporator, and second, of being the wife of dreaded underworld don Ashwin Naik. She hailed from a wealthy Gujarati family, fell in love with and married Ashwin, who was the chief of one of the five ruling gangs of Bombay. He had taken over the gang after his elder brother, Amar Naik aka Ravan, was killed by the police in an alleged encounter.

Ashwin studied civil engineering at a foreign university and was known as the most educated gangster in the Bombay underworld, where only 29 per cent of mobsters had received primary education, while 42 per cent had gone to secondary school, as per research conducted by former Police Commissioner Vasant Saraf.[12] In April 1994, shooters of a rival gang attacked Ashwin Naik outside Bombay's Sessions Court. A bullet hit his head and permanently paralysed him below the waist, and he was restricted to a wheelchair for the rest of his life. The police arrested him for various crimes, but neither the prison's walls nor his physical handicap could prevent him from running his gang and orchestrating bloodshed.

It is believed that Naik learnt about Neeta's extramarital affair with a policeman, Laxman Ziman, during his imprisonment at Delhi's Tihar Jail. Laxman was a bodyguard of Narayan Rane, a Shiv

Sena leader and former chief minister of Maharashtra. An enraged Naik allegedly ordered his wife's murder. On 13 November 2000, the shooters fired at Neeta outside her residence.

A little-known fact about the underworld is that they follow the unwritten rule of not attacking women. When I reached the spot to cover the incident, police sources revealed Neeta had been a victim of her husband's suspicion. The next day, the picture became even clearer.

I got a tip-off that Laxman Ziman had been called to the Unit 2 office of the Mumbai Crime Branch at Jacob Circle. When I arrived there with my cameraman, we found the distraught Ziman sitting outside Unit In-Charge Dilip Patil's office. Patil had gone for an encounter with Chhota Shakeel's gang at Marine Drive, and Ziman was asked to wait till he returned. When I requested him for an interview, he refused and began mumbling. In his monologue recorded on my camera, he revealed that his official weapon had been confiscated and he could be murdered by Ashwin Naik soon. He said that he would meet Neeta in heaven. I kept the camera rolling and continued shooting questions, but he fled from the unit office.

Ashwin was acquitted of any charges in January 2009. In an interview with a newspaper, Ashwin said that he missed Neeta.[13] He published a remembrance on her death anniversary.

Journalists on Target

'Can you stay out of Mumbai for a few days? This is a question of your security,' Hemant Karkare, chief of the Maharashtra Anti-Terrorism Squad, asked me in an anxious tone one afternoon in April 2008.

Karkare had called me up two hours earlier, asking to meet me for something important. Instead of his office, we met at the headquarters of Mumbai Police in the joint commissioner's chamber. As I reached the chamber, the joint commissioner, who was Karkare's junior, left us to talk in private.

We shook hands, and he asked, 'Which of your stories has pinched Dawood's gang?'

Though it seems naïve now, but, at that moment, I took Karkare's question as a compliment. What more could a crime reporter ask for than his stories disquieting India's most-wanted mafia don? I replied that it was difficult to pick one, since I had covered so many stories that could have possibly irked Dawood. As a crime reporter for Star News, I had produced several reports related to the wrongdoings of the underworld.

'Please try to recall. It is important for me to know,' Karkare told me.

'Sir, I have recently filed many stories against Dawood. I have shown his ancestral bungalow in Ratnagiri. I have reported from his house at Pakmodia Street in Mumbai. Like all the Hindi news channels, I've referred to him as a traitor and an anti-national on camera. Is Dawood angry with me for this? I have only repeated what is already being said.'

Karkare then told me that his officers had intercepted a conversation between Chhota Shakeel and his men in Mumbai. Shakeel was seeking information about me. Karkare was concerned about a potential threat to my life and had called to warn me. He advised me to leave Mumbai for a few days, but I told him that was not possible. I was about to get married in the last week of April, and a week before that I had to attend my cousin's wedding. The preparations were on in full swing, and I was expected to remain in the city. Karkare then spoke to Milind Khandekar, my editor at Star News, who was his friend. Khandekar offered to transfer me to Delhi for a few days, which I refused again.

Seeing that I was adamant, Karkare offered to speak to Rakesh Maria, the then chief of the Crime Branch, to arrange security for me. I used to commute on my motorcycle at the time, and the idea of having an armed commando sitting pillion seemed bizarre. I declined this too. Ultimately, he said that his men would keep a watch on me in their special ways and then gave me some instructions for the coming days. That was my last meeting with Karkare. I followed his instructions for few days and then thought of asking Karkare for an update. However, my workload kept me occupied, and I was never able to meet him. Seven months later, he would be martyred in the 26/11 terror attacks in Mumbai. Many years later, a friend working for an intelligence agency told me that the threat to my life had been quite grave, but it had been pre-empted by timely action.

Like mill owners, builders, hoteliers and businessmen, the underworld targeted journalists as well. However, newspersons were attacked for reasons other than extortion.

On 12 June 1997, Baljit Parmar, the editor of *Bombay Eye* newspaper, came out of his home in front of the Antop Hill police station to drop his wife and children at Mumbai Central railway station as they were going to Punjab. Suddenly, a motorcycle stopped outside the gate. The man seated on the pillion seat fired five shots at Parmar. One bullet hit his right rib, another injured his underarm, the third pierced his palm and the other two injured his wrists. Fortunately, he reached the hospital in time and survived.

The investigation revealed that Parmar was attacked by the Chhota Rajan gang. The CBI had recently seized fifty-two containers belonging to Chhota Rajan from the Mumbai port, in which smuggled goods worth crores of rupees were being transported. Rajan suspected that the CBI acted on a tip-off from Parmar. Customs duty was relaxed for household products under Transfer of Residence (TR) for those who moved to India from abroad. The mafia misused this scheme in connivance with corrupt customs officers and smuggled in a substantial number of consumer appliances to be sold in Bombay's black markets.[14]

In 1997, Anandita Ramaswamy, a reporter at the *Asian Age,* was attacked outside Arun Gawli's residence in Dagdi Chawl. That morning, the newspaper had published a report claiming that Gawli had gone bankrupt after joining politics and couldn't pay his shooters. When she reached Dagdi Chawl for another story on the gang, stones rained down on her from all directions. Arun Gawli and two of his accomplices were arrested for this. Seven years later, in October 2004, Gawli was again accused of thrashing a reporter named Hafeez Mateen from the same newspaper because some questions irked him during an interview. He was arrested once again.

In July 2000, Mumbai Police arrested four members of Chhota Shakeel's gang who were wandering around Hindi *Saamana*'s chief reporter Prem Shukla's house in Saki Naka to kill him. Shukla told me that an attack on him was planned by a prominent north Indian politician with connections to Chhota Shakeel. Shukla was given an armed security guard for the next few years. He later became a spokesperson for the BJP.

The mafia was very sensitive about their public image. To run their businesses, they had to present themselves as dangerous, audacious and well-informed, and as never vulnerable or insignificant. Hence, if some journalists attempted to present a weak or lowly image of them, they didn't hesitate to kill them.

On 11 June 2011, Chhota Rajan's shooters killed my friend and veteran journalist Jyotirmoy Dey in the Powai suburb of Mumbai. He was the crime editor of *Mid-Day* and had authored two books on the underworld. As per the CBI, Rajan was told that Dey was writing a third book that could damage his image.

While sentencing Rajan with life imprisonment in the case, the special CBI court observed that Dey's writing would have hurt Rajan's ego and would have shown him as being weaker than his rival Dawood Ibrahim, which is why he ordered Dey's killing.[15] Another journalist, Jigna Vora, was also arrested in the case, but she was acquitted after the trial.

In September 2014, the Mumbai Crime Branch arrested three shooters from Ravi Pujari's gang who were about to kill a journalist from an English daily who had referred to him as '*chindi*'. or small fry in one of his reports.

How Corruption Irrigated the Underworld

In 1986, it was a tip-off from a corrupt cop that alerted Dawood, allowing him to escape to Dubai before a police team could raid his office. The 12 March 1993 serial blasts would never have happened had customs officials and the Raigarh police personnel not been so corrupt. It was due to a crooked jail administration that Arun Gawli and others could run their gangs and get people killed despite being behind bars. Corruption, right from the police stations to the incumbent politicians, was one of the many factors that helped the Mumbai underworld flourish. For gangsters, a bribe to a cop was like an investment.

On 25 December 2009, a video from a club party at Chembur went viral.[16] It showed an assistant police commissioner dancing with Chhota Rajan's gang to Bollywood music. Farid Tanasha and D.K. Rao, the two men spotted in the video, were dreaded gangsters and loyalists of Chhota Rajan. They had been released from jail just a few days ago. Five cops were reported to have been present at that party. This bonhomie between the police and the gangsters led to much public outrage. After the furore, Police Commissioner D. Sivanandhan recommended the suspension of those five cops and ordered an immediate inquiry into the matter. Unofficial investigations were also made to find out how the video got leaked.

Dawood allegedly had moles in the police department. In 2005 and 2008, two inspector-rank officers were dismissed from the service over their alleged links with the underworld. An assistant police commissioner was seen as close to Dawood's sister, Haseena Parker, who stayed in south Mumbai's Nagpada. He was also accused of extorting money from a builder on behalf of Parker. A constable named Rajesh Igwe worked in the armoury of Mumbai Police, but was also a member of the Dawood gang and trained the mafia boss's hitmen in Sanjay Gandhi National Park. On 17 November 1995, Igwe was killed in an encounter with the police. Coincidentally, the inspector who eliminated Igwe was Kader Khan, a classmate of Dawood's from Ahmed Sailor Urdu School at Nagpada. Khan told me that Dawood's men had given Igwe a list of high-profile people to be eliminated. In Igwe's hitlist was BJP leader L.K. Advani, Shiv Sena supremo Bal Thackeray, and IPS officers M.N. Singh and Rakesh Maria, who were investigating the Bombay blasts case. But he was killed before he could assassinate any of them.

Chandan Chowky, a police post in the Juhu area, was once infamously known as 'Extortion Chowky' because of some police officers posted there who were accused of extorting money from businessmen. Ironically, the *chowky* was officially titled 'Anti-Extortion Cell'. After receiving several complaints, senior police officers closed it down. Later on, the chowky was handed over to the Anti-Terrorism Squad.

It was reported that the underworld had its moles in the judicial system as well. In March 2000, a Sessions Court judge was arrested after the police came across purported telephonic conversations between him and Chhota Shakeel. In the call, the judge asked for

Shakeel's help in recovering his money from a chit fund, and in return, he assured the gangster action against the police officers who had killed Shakeel's men in fake encounters. This conversation was arranged by one of Shakeel's lawyers, who was later killed. Three years later, the judge was acquitted owing to a lack of evidence.[17]

Bombay Exports its Gang Wars

The bloodshed of gang wars in the city soon spread all over the world, as many gangsters operated from different countries. Their host countries were either hostile to India or had difficult extradition laws. They also befriended the local mafia and influential people.

For example, knowing that the rich sheikhs loved hobnobbing with film stars, Dawood Ibrahim frequently organized parties at his residence, called White House, and at various multi-star hotels. Bollywood stars were invited to mingle with sheikhs. He arranged events for sheikhs where prominent singers and actors performed. Some songs hailing Dawood were composed especially for such occasions.

But as glamorous as it may sound, the lives of gangsters abroad were not always easy. They carried the risk of death everywhere they went.

The first repercussion of Bombay's gang wars was felt on foreign soil in 1994 after Chhota Rajan defected from Dawood. Rajan's gang killed Bakhtiyar Khan, aka Feelu, by luring him to a hotel room in Bangkok. Dawood's gang found out that it was Feelu's bodyguard, Mangesh Pawar, who had tipped off Rajan. A manhunt followed, and Pawar was soon killed in South Africa.

In 1995, another hit by Chhota Rajan in Dubai convinced Dawood that he was no longer safe in the UAE, and so he shifted base. Chhota Rajan's shooters killed Dawood's henchman, Sunil Sawant, aka Sawtya,[18] outside Hotel Hyatt Regency in Dubai.

Rajan had been informed that Chhota Shakeel was also going to be accompanying Sawtya, but he didn't that day and, thus, escaped. After this attack, Dawood settled down permanently in Karachi. He had been contemplating leaving Dubai anyway, as pressure for his extradition mounted on the UAE government after he was declared responsible for the 1993 Bombay blasts.

The Mumbai underworld made its presence felt in Nepal as well. On 29 June 1998, Mirza Dilshad Beg, a Nepali parliamentarian, was gunned down by Chhota Rajan's men when he alighted from his car to enter his second wife's home. His driver was also killed in the incident. Rajan alleged that Beg was an agent of Pakistan's Inter-Service Intelligence and was helping Dawood.

D-Company was seeking an opportunity for retaliation after losing Beg. Their wait ended two years later, when Sharad Shetty met Dawood with information on the whereabouts of Chhota Rajan. Vinod Shetty, a hotelier from Chembur, leaked Chhota Rajan's Bangkok address to Sharad. Dawood asked Shakeel to immediately dispatch a hit squad to Bangkok. On 15 September 2000, a team of shooters, led by Munna Jhingada, attacked Rajan's apartment in Bangkok. Rajan received bullet injuries, but escaped. However, his confidant, Rohit Verma, was killed in the firing and Verma's wife was injured. The Bangkok Police arrested Jhingada. Shortly after the shoot-out, one of my colleagues went to Bangkok and interviewed Jhingada. He confessed on camera that 'Shakeel Boss' had sent him and that the gang would strike at Rajan again within six months.

An injured Rajan was being treated in a Bangkok hospital, but he escaped when he learnt that a team from Mumbai Police was coming to Thailand to pursue his extradition. While in hiding, Rajan found out that it was his friend Vinod who had betrayed him. On 2 November 2000, Vinod Shetty was killed on Uran-Panvel Road near Mumbai along with two others. This was the first shooting after the attack on Rajan, and it sent out the message that Rajan was still very much active and capable of getting his enemies killed. However, for Rajan, killing Vinod Shetty wasn't enough. To avenge the attack, he sent a squad of shooters to Dubai. On the evening of 20 January 2003, when Sharad Shetty entered India Club to attend a dinner hosted by his friend, a youngster shot him and escaped.

Sharad Shetty's murder was an enormous loss to D-Company, as he not only ran many hotels for them but also handled their cricket betting and match-fixing rackets. Although Shakeel's men could never reach Rajan again, they found Balu Dokre, a shooter from Rajan's gang in Kuala Lumpur, and promptly slaughtered him. Dokre had killed Dawood's alleged agent, Mirza Dilshad Beg, in Nepal. His head was almost severed, and there were multiple stab wounds on his body.

8

Bitter Pill: The End of the Underworld?

'Businessman Shot Dead Right Under the Nose of Police Commissioner'
'Music Baron Gunned Down in Broad Daylight'
'Shooters Walk Away After Killing a Builder in his Office'
'Mill Owner Shot Dead at Busy Traffic Signal'
'India's First Private Airline Owner Killed by Mafia'
'Innocent Citizens Killed by Gangsters because of Mistaken Identity'

SUCH DAILY HEADLINES CAPTURED THE SORDIDNESS of Mumbai while the city's prime law enforcement agency, Mumbai Police, struggled to restore its former prestige. The menace of the underworld was loosely equated with insurgencies in Kashmir and Punjab. Mumbai had turned into a national liability, and the union home secretary had to step in to assess the situation. Highlighting the failure of the law and order machinery, the saffron parties seized power in the state. Both the BJP and the Shiv Sena targeted the then chief minister, Sharad Pawar, and alleged that the underworld flourished under his regime.

Pawar was ousted from power in 1995, but even the new government failed to tackle this menace. Bal Thackeray announced Manohar Joshi as the new chief minister of Maharashtra, and the BJP's Gopinath Munde was appointed as the deputy chief minister while also heading the home ministry. Munde rose as the political boss of the police, which meant he was responsible for the city's safety and had to restore confidence in its business community.

Just a week before he was sworn in on 14 March 1995, the prominent builder Pradip Jain was killed by Abu Salem's gang. Munde called a meeting with some senior Mumbai Police officials to understand the gravity of the situation, and realized that two of the prime reasons for the spike in underworld activities were the absence of stringent laws and the loopholes in the legal system.

The TADA, which gave the police extensive powers—that were very often misused—had lapsed that year. Familiar with the conventional ways of the police, the underworld had devised new techniques to render them ineffective. The officers bluntly requested Munde to employ a different approach to deal with the menace. This prompted him to unofficially sanction a new policy, i.e. 'to protect the law, break the law'.[1,2] He gave the police a free hand to respond to gangsters in kind.[3] This illegal slant was a bitter pill to improve the situation in Mumbai.

A New Vocabulary

'I don't see them as human beings. I consider them to be mad dogs who deserve to be killed,' stated Vijay Salaskar when I questioned him about the moral grounds of killing someone. Salaskar was a police officer renowned as an 'encounter specialist', even though there is no such official designation in the police force.[4] The term grew popular in media reports to refer to cops who frequently killed gangsters in incidents that the police then declared as an 'encounter'. For Mumbai Police, the word meant a violent confrontation between the police and gangsters that always ended in the deaths of the latter. After every 'encounter', the police narrated a similar story to the public.

'After receiving specific inputs from our informants that a gangster named XYZ was coming to a particular place, we laid a trap. After spotting the gangster, we asked him to surrender. But he fired on the police team. In our retaliatory fire, he was killed. We have recovered a weapon from him.'

With the tacit support of Home Minister Munde, Mumbai Police went on a killing spree.[5] Various squads under deputy commissioners of police were formed to deal with organized criminal gangs. Lists of the top ten gangsters from each 'company' were prepared, and they were hunted down one by one. Also, anybody who had at least one murder case to his name was deemed '*fit* for an encounter'. Apart from surveilling mobile phones, the encounter specialists had developed an effective network of informers, known as '*zero numbers*', who helped them track down and kill gangsters. Informers are called so because they are considered policemen without actually being recruited to the force. Every policeman has a badge number as official identification, but these informers don't. An informer could be anybody from a petty criminal to a gangster, a call girl, a bar dancer or a taxi driver.

Seven encounters took place before Munde took charge of the home ministry in 1995. This number soared once he extended his support to the police. In 1996, fifty-nine alleged gangsters were gunned down by the police, and in 1997, the number rose to seventy.

With these encounters in daily headlines, the encounter specialists became heroes. Vijay Salaskar, Pradeep Sharma,

Daya Nayak, Praful Bhosle, Ravindranath Angre, Datta Ghule and Sachin Waze were among the prominent names being hailed by one and all. Pradeep Sharma and Daya Nayak, who operated as a pair, were even featured in *Time* magazine. Senior journalist Shekhar Gupta also interviewed them for his show 'Walk the Talk' on NDTV.

The officers soon specialized in killing gangsters of specific gangs. Salaskar mostly targeted Amar Naik and Arun Gawli's gangs, while Pradeep Sharma targeted Chhota Shakeel and Chhota Rajan. Ravindranath Angre focused on Suresh Manchekar's gang, which operated in Thane.

M.N. Singh, the former police commissioner of Mumbai, recollected when I interviewed him, 'The day I took charge in 2000 as the police chief, I announced that my priority was to finish the underworld. The government supported me, and I led a massive onslaught against the mafia.' This led to seventy-three alleged gangsters being killed in 2000 and ninety-four in 2001, during Singh's tenure.

Although these encounters saw murder rates by gangs fall in the city, the policy became controversial. Human rights activists accused the police of extra-judicial killings and of punishing the suspects before they were tried in court. They criticized the police for playing the role of investigator, prosecutor, judge as well as executioner, all at once.

In August 1997, Mumbai Police killed a person named Jawed Fawda at south Mumbai's Ballard Estate, citing his association with Abu Salem. The accused's family filed a petition in the Bombay High Court claiming the victim was a poor peanut seller named Abu Sayema. The family alleged that Sayema was apprehended outside a mosque and killed in cold blood. This petition was followed by two more in the same year. Vijay Salaskar had shot Sada Pawle, aka Mama, and Vijay Tandel in Ghatkopar. The petitioners alleged that the encounters were staged. The Bombay High Court ordered Principal Sessions Judge A.S. Aguiar to conduct an inquiry into the petitions and submit a detailed report. Judge Aguiar's March 1998 report was damning. He noted that the encounters were fake and the victims unarmed at the time of their killing.[6] The petitioners demanded murder charges against these officers.

After the Aguiar report, not a single encounter took place in the first five months of 1998. The officers feared prosecution. D. Sivanandhan, the then chief of the Crime Branch, told me that the morale of the police during those days hit an all-time low, despite his constant encouragement to continue the anti-mafia campaign. Underworld activities surged once again, with ninety-nine killings that year. In May, the encounter specialists took their guns out once again, and forty-eight alleged gangsters were shot dead. Despite Judge Aguiar's report and the judicial activism that followed, Mumbai Police resumed its policy of encounters, this time calling them 'operations' instead of 'encounters' to avoid any negative undertones. In the later years, encounters were used as a tit-for-tat measure—if a gangster killed somebody in the city, a gangster was killed by the police within twenty-four hours.

Guilty Until Proven Innocent

While encounters showed results, they remained controversial, and the police were on the lookout for an alternative. After TADA lapsed in 1995, a need was felt for another equally stringent law. Hence, Manohar Joshi issued an ordinance that matured as the Maharashtra Control of Organized Crime Act (MCOCA) in February 1999. It was the first legislation in India to be passed by a state to deal with organized crime. It overrode all other laws and armed the police with wide powers. An accused booked under the MCOCA could not get anticipatory bail, and their confessional statement given before a police officer could be used as evidence. The property of the accused could be attached if it was found that it had been gained from organized crime. The law increased the period for the police to file a charge sheet from ninety to 180 days. If a person was booked under the MCOCA, it was difficult to get bail. Generally, in the judicial system, a person is assumed to be innocent until proven guilty, but the MCOCA allowed the judicial process to assume a person to be guilty until they could prove their innocence in a trial. The burden of proof fell on the accused.

I vividly remember a hearing held at a special MCOCA court on 5 September 2000, where Mohammed Zuber Shaikh, Fazal Sheikh and Azizuddin Shaikh sat in the box, with copies of religious books in their hands, trembling with fear. They were allegedly members of Chhota Shakeel's gang and were booked for firing on Milind Vaidya, former mayor of Mumbai. Although Vaidya survived the attack, three of his associates succumbed to bullet injuries. During the trial, none of the witnesses turned hostile, and the three accused knew that the death penalty was imminent, and indeed Judge A.P. Bhangale ordered that the trio be hanged.

The accused could not control their tears that day, but the cops were jubilant. It was the first case booked under the MCOCA, and it had been successful. Pradip Sawant, deputy commissioner of police from the Crime Branch, was given the Best Detection Officer Award and was recommended for a President's Medal for meritorious service. The convictions added to Sawant's heroic image. The character of ACP Rathore in the film *Sarfarosh* is said to have been inspired by Sawant. However, when the MCOCA court's order was challenged in the Bombay High Court, two of the accused were set free, and the third's death penalty was commuted to life imprisonment.

Like the TADA, the MCOCA was labelled as a draconian law, and was met with vehement opposition from human rights and legal reform activists. It was slammed for having several provisions that could be misused by the police. The opponents argued that the law trampled upon fundamental rights and held people guilty even before they were tried in a court of law. But D. Sivanandhan confirmed to me that the law worked wonders for the city's crime scene.

'In contradiction to the popular erroneous perception that police encounters were behind neutralizing the underworld gangs, it was an efficacious law like MCOCA that acted as a deterrent. The MCOCA was tailor-made to deal with criminal gangs, and the cases were settled in a time-bound manner. It not only closed the legal loopholes that gangsters took advantage of, but also aimed at destroying their support system. Yes, the law is stringent, but don't we consume some bitter pills to remedy certain ailments? Just a handful of criminals have been booked under this law since 1999,' Sivanandhan told me in an interview.

These 'handful of criminals' amount to 209 alleged members of Dawood Ibrahim's gang and 167 alleged members of Chhota Rajan's gang, who were arrested under the MCOCA by 2009. The conviction rate of gangsters booked under this law was also encouraging for the police. In 58 per cent of the cases under MCOCA, conviction was secured, whereas the conviction rate under the Indian Penal Code was a meagre 25 per cent.[7]

D-Company: Why Did the Guns Fall Silent?

On 31 August 2017, Dawood's younger brother Iqbal Kaskar stood perplexed and terrified at south Mumbai's Pakmodia Street, where a dilapidated building neighbouring his had collapsed, leaving thirty-four residents dead. I came across him as I covered the rescue operations. He narrated the incident on my camera.

Iqbal seemed to be a simple and soft-spoken man, in sharp contrast to Dawood's flamboyant and intimidating image. His presence in Mumbai was one of the prime reasons no major shoot-outs or murders were attributed to the D-Company since 11 November 2002, when Ali Nanjiani, the owner of *Tehelka News,* was killed by Chhota Shakeel's shooters because of a property dispute with Dawood's younger brother, Noor.

In 2003, Iqbal was deported from Dubai and booked by Mumbai Police under the MCOCA. He was accused of grabbing land belonging to the Central Public Works Department in south Mumbai and illegally constructing a market named Sara-Sahara on it with his associates. It was no coincidence that after Iqbal's deportation to Mumbai, killings by the Dawood gang stopped. Haseena Parker, Dawood's sister, was booked in a criminal case too.

Dawood understood that if he continued to spill blood on the streets of Mumbai, his siblings would have to face the repercussions. Gang wars had already cost him his elder brother, Sabir, and brother-in-law, Ibrahim Parker, to the Pathan and Gawli gangs, respectively. Any violent act towards his enemies could jeopardize Iqbal's safety. Indeed, in 2011, Iqbal was attacked on Pakmodia Street, and his driver was killed. Despite this shoot-out, the D-Company abstained from retaliatory bloodshed in the city.

Dawood had been considering shrinking his gang's presence in Mumbai even before Iqbal was deported. In the mid-1990s, Dawood, in fact, offered to surrender through veteran lawyer Ram Jethmalani, with a pre-condition that he must be kept under house arrest. His offer was similar to the one made by Colombian drug lord Pablo Escobar to President César Gaviria in the early 1990s to prevent his deportation to the USA. Escobar had pleaded that he could be tried while under house arrest. It is not clear whether Dawood was inspired by Escobar.

After the 9/11 attacks, the new anti-terrorism policy adopted by the American government had repercussions for Dawood as well. In 2003, the USA declared him a 'Specially Designated Global Terrorist'. India always maintained that Pakistan was hosting Dawood and helping him run his terrorist activities. It would have been embarrassing for Pakistan if Dawood made his presence known on its soil. In the same year, the United Nations Security Council (UNSC) also listed Dawood as a terrorist, alleging he had links with the Al-Qaeda, Taliban and Lashkar-e-Taiba. He was accused of financing terrorist activities in India. This, coupled with at least three attempts on his life by Indian intelligence agencies, compelled him to lie low.

D-Company's key men in Mumbai were either killed or arrested under the MCOCA, and his recruiting agents were under the police scanner. The law enforcement agencies launched financial attacks on him as well. In December 2000, an auction of eleven properties allegedly owned by him was organized in Colaba's Hotel Diplomat by the Income Tax Department.

I covered the auction and reported on TV that nobody dared to bid out of fear. Soon after, I received a call from a Delhi-based lawyer Ajay Shrivastava, who was enraged by my report. He claimed to be a member of the Shiv Sena and was interested in bidding on one of the properties. The next year, the auction was organized again. Shrivastava turned out to be the lone bidder and won two shops at Jairajbhai Lane, Nagpada. However, Shrivastava could never get possession of the properties as they were under Haseena Parker's custody. He approached the Small Causes Court for possession, but to no avail. Meanwhile, Parker died due to a cardiac arrest while the matter was sub judice.

In an auction held in 2021, Shrivastava won Dawood's ancestral bungalow at his native village in Ratnagiri. He was successful in taking possession of this property and announced that the place would be converted into a Hindu religious school named '*Sanatan Dharma Pathshala*'. Shrivastava received a few threats over this project, but there was no actual attempt by the D-Company to harm him.

However, the gang still made its presence felt in Mumbai to some extent. Its members now entered the real estate business, and bought old buildings by fair and unfair means to reconstruct them as multistorey residential towers. Chhota Shakeel continued to give TV interviews. His last interview to be aired was in 2015, wherein he protested the hanging of Yakub Memon, claiming Memon's innocence. Ever since, Dawood's reign in Mumbai seems to have been on the decline. However, sleuths in the intelligence world believe that Dawood has to continue being 'useful' for the ISI in lieu of the safe haven provided to him in the country. It implies that if ISI assigns him some task, he is bound to deliver.

Disintegration of the Nana Company

As a journalist, I have filed many stories on Chhota Rajan, aka Nana, but it was only in September 2015 that I saw him in person. In the orange uniform of prisoners, Rajan looked like any ordinary criminal. His appearance differed from the image that I had in mind through our limited conversations and some footage of him, which was repeatedly telecast on news channels.[8] The sick, old and vulnerable Rajan was being escorted from the Crime Branch office to a lock-up in Bali.

Chhota Rajan was arrested at Bali's Denpasar airport on 25 October 2015, as soon as he alighted from a Garuda flight from Sydney, Australia. He was found carrying a passport issued under the fake name of Mohan Kumar. But the Bali Police had been passed on more information about Rajan by their Australian counterparts based on a Red Corner notice issued against him by Interpol.

Rajan's arrest was big news in India, and many Indian journalists like me were airdropped to Bali for the follow-up coverage. The news on the underworld grapevine was that Rajan had planned his own arrest. He operated from Newcastle, a picturesque harbour city in Australia, but the city no longer remained safe for him as Chhota Shakeel had apparently discovered his location from Rajan's cook in April 2015. Rajan got wind of the conspiracy and escaped. The D-Company vowed to kill Rajan, and he knew that the next attempt on his life could happen soon. He saw no point in fleeing from one country to another. His deteriorating health also added to his distress. It is conceivable that he found it prudent to surrender and return to India. However, while in the custody of the Bali Police, Rajan stated that he had not surrendered and that he was not scared of anyone.

On 1 November 2015, a six-member team of the CBI, Mumbai Police and Delhi Police landed in Bali for Rajan's deportation. A volcano eruption in the nearby Mount Rinjani led to a shutdown of flight operations, and the police had to wait to deport Rajan. On 6 November, a special flight of the Indian Air Force brought Chhota Rajan to Delhi. He returned to India twenty-seven years after fleeing to Dubai, following his then-boss Dawood. Chhota Rajan's arrest led to the shutdown of his gang's operations. The second major gang of the Mumbai underworld after Dawood's was now silenced.

Chhota Rajan's downfall had begun back in 2000, with an attack on him on 15 September in Bangkok by Chhota Shakeel. Although Rajan survived, his decline had begun. He frequently changed his location after that. His distrust towards his people grew, and he suspected they would reveal his whereabouts. This affected the operations of his gang, and some of his most trusted lieutenants deserted him. A few formed independent gangs, such as Ravi Pujari, Bunty Pande, Ejaz Lakdawala, Hemant Pujari, Santosh Shetty and Bharat Nepali.

Adding to this, Rajan's close associate Balu Dokre was stabbed to death on 22 May 2005 near Kuala Lumpur, Malaysia, by Chhota Shakeel's men. Dokre had forty-three serious charges filed against him and had taken part in many hits ordered by Rajan, including the murder of Nepalese politician Mirza Dilshad Beg. Mumbai Police turned the heat on against the gang, especially after 2002, by killing shooters of the company and arresting Rajan's key associates, including Ravi Mallesh Vora, aka D.K. Rao, Farid Tanasha and Vicky Malhotra.

The campaign by the city's police also led to the arrest of Rajan's wife, Sujata, in December 2005 under the stringent MCOCA on charges of extortion from builders. Rajan had married Sujata in 1987, and their wedding reception in Dubai had been attended by Dawood and his wife, Mehazbeen. The couple had three daughters. Sujata managed a construction firm, Khushi Developers Private Limited, named after their youngest daughter. Two years later, in 2007, Sujata was released by the court.

In the face of so many setbacks, Rajan could not afford to be seen as a weak and emasculated don. A perception was building that his gang had gradually become dormant after the Bangkok attack. In 2011, Rajan once again brought the Mumbai underworld into the prime-time news when his alleged shooters killed Arif, a bodyguard of Iqbal Kaskar, in Dawood's bastion Pakmodia Street.

On a rainy afternoon on 11 June 2011, Chhota Rajan's alleged shooters killed my friend, the veteran journalist Jyotirmoy Dey. He was attacked from the back while riding his motorcycle towards his mother's residence. Dey's death led to an uproar by journalist organizations and political parties across India, and compelled the police to launch an aggressive campaign against Rajan.

The remaining devoted members of his gang were also arrested, and the company collapsed.

After Dey's murder, Rajan supposedly called four journalists to accept responsibility for the murder. He said that he regretted killing Dey and that it was the result of some misinformation passed on to him. A few days before he was killed, Dey had asked Rajan to meet him in the Philippines. Rajan suspected that Dey had acted at the behest of the D-Company, and it was a ploy to trap him. However, the CBI in its investigation came up with another motive: Dey was writing a book titled *Chindi: Rags to Riches*. The synopsis of the book was leaked to Rajan, which led him to believe that Dey would present him in a poor light while glorifying his rival Dawood Ibrahim.

Dey's murder shocked me. During our conversations, he always sounded appreciative of Chhota Rajan and stressed that Rajan was a genuinely 'patriotic' don, who helped Indian intelligence agencies eliminate anti-national elements. He often had long telephonic conversations with the mafia boss. The tragedy of losing my friend reinforced my belief that the pen is indeed mightier than the gun. However, this incident also made me ponder over the perilous nature of crime reporting. It is like playing with fire. Dey's writing would have contradicted the powerful image that Rajan wished to project of himself. Hence, he was killed, and his book could never be completed. Dey had invited me home for tea on Sunday morning to share some exclusive pictures of the underworld. That Sunday, I attended his funeral instead. Rajan was convicted by the CBI in the J. Dey murder case and was sentenced to life imprisonment. He challenged the conviction in the Bombay High Court.

Before being deported to India, Rajan claimed that all cases against him were false and that some officers in the police force were hand-in-glove with Dawood and there was a risk to his life. Shortly after his deportation, the Maharashtra government announced that all seventy cases registered against him would be transferred to the CBI, and he was kept at Tihar Jail in Delhi. This was a massive blow for Mumbai Police, as it could not interrogate one of its most wanted criminals. In the recent past, a few other high-profile cases such as the J. Dey murder and the Sheena Bora murder case were also handed over to the CBI. A frustrated Mumbai Police officer told me, 'Now what remains for Mumbai Police is to catch the pick-pockets and chain snatchers.'[9]

Game Over for Gawli Gang

On the first day of the Maharashtra Legislative Assembly's winter session in 2004, Arun Gawli embarked in his minibus towards Vidhan Bhavan at Nariman Point in south Mumbai. Gawli had recently earned the new identity of a Member of the Legislative Assembly (MLA) by winning the election from the Chinchpokli constituency. He was the first and only MLA from his newly founded political party, Akhil Bhartiya Sena (ABS), and I was the only journalist present in that minibus as it moved out of Dagdi Chawl—Gawli's den. The mafia boss's personalized security could be compared to the official Z category security provided to VIPs. There were at least ten youngsters on the bus, and a few of them were armed. The mini bus was escorted by five to six motorcycles and followed by a few cars. Dawood was still a looming threat, as Gawli's gang had killed Dawood's brother-in-law.

Gawli was neither a good orator nor did he have any political experience. His personality was not charismatic either. How he became an MLA was a wonder to many. Some political observers attributed it to money. Most of the voters in his constituency were poor or belonged to the lower–middle class and lived in slums or old chawls, ignored by civic authorities. Gawli tried to solve their issues, such as repairing public toilets, fixing broken taps and so on. He funded Ganpati *mandals* and offered monetary help to those suffering from major maladies. People queued up outside his party office for help. Gawli became a local Robin Hood of sorts.

En route to Vidhan Bhavan, I interviewed Gawli. He avoided speaking against his political opponents and expressed his happiness that people had given him an opportunity to serve them. His priority would be to address the issues of unemployment and housing of slum dwellers. 'They [the police] can't kill me now. I am an MLA,' he smiled.[10] Just a hundred metres away from the Vidhan Bhavan, Gawli's minibus stopped. A black Mercedes waited for him there. Gawli's arrival at the Vidhan Sabha in a sedan was a statement to his political rivals—that he too was one of them now.

Gawli's foray into politics, however, came with a cost to his gang. He had attracted hostility from existing political players, especially the Shiv Sena. In fact, Gawli's party was set up 'to teach Shiv Sena a lesson'. Indeed, in the late '90s, Gawli's ABS became a challenger to the Shiv Sena and made that party's leadership uneasy.

Things were different till the 1995 Vidhan Sabha elections. During his political campaigns, Bal Thackeray openly admitted to Arun Gawli's associations with him and Dawood Ibrahim's with the Congress. The bonhomie between the two diminished as soon as the Shiv Sena–BJP coalition assumed power in Maharashtra, and, within a year, the friends became foes. Assuming that the new government was favourable to it, the Gawli gang audaciously intensified its operations. However, Munde ordered a blanket offensive against all underworld gangs, and Gawli's was no exception. Munde's confidante, Keshav Upadhyay, told me, 'Munde ji instructed the cops to reply to bullets with bullets. Those who kill others don't have any human rights.'[11] In 1995, when Munde took over as the home minister, only one member of the Gawli gang was killed on 7 August at Mulund by the cops. As the police intensified its crackdown, the number of Gawli gangsters killed rose to seven in 1996.

Apart from killing his gang members, the government also strategized to demolish the infrastructure through which the gang leaders operated from jails. Gawli expected the Shiv Sena to come to his rescue, but the party failed him. Gawli was suddenly shifted from the Aurangabad jail to the Amravati jail, which shattered his arrangements with the Aurangabad jail administration and cut off his communications with his gang. He gradually gained favours from the Amravati jail authorities as well, and soon learnt that he had been transferred at the behest of Jayant Jadhav, known as Bal Thackeray's *manas putra* (godson). An enraged Gawli ordered Jadhav's murder on 30 April 1996 at Prabhadevi, near his residence, and this became the turning point in his relationship with the Shiv Sena.

Gawli announced his own political outfit, Akhil Bhartiya Sena (ABS), in January 1997 with the aim of making it a national party. Gawli structured the ABS exactly on the lines of the Shiv Sena. The branch head of a local unit was called '*shakha adhyaksh*', like Shiv Sena's '*shakha pramukh*'. Gawli was guided by Jitendra Dabholkar—an ex-Shiv Sena leader who had been affiliated with the party's labour union, Bhartiya Kamgar Sena. He brought not only competent organizational experience with him, but also a mass following. The first elections to be contested by the ABS were of the Mumbai Municipal Corporation. Out of 227 seats, the ABS fielded candidates on forty. The party could not win a single seat, but its candidates stood second in ten seats. However, Dabholkar attributed the loss to Gawli being in jail during the election campaign.

After coming out of jail, Gawli decided to exhibit his political strength. On 11 July 1997, ten people were killed in a police firing during a protest following the desecration of a statue of

Dr B.R. Ambedkar at Ramabai Nagar. Gawli, just out of jail, picked up the issue and announced a protest rally at Azad Maidan on 17 July. It was attended by over 75,000 people from Mumbai, Nasik, Kolhapur, Solapur, Ahmednagar and other districts. Unexpectedly, Gawli himself did not attend the rally, citing security concerns. His wife, Asha, aka Mummy, and Jitendra Dabholkar led the demonstration. Ironically, they targeted the coalition government in their speeches by alleging that law and order had failed the state.

Within a year, the party grew rapidly. About 3,50,000 people enrolled as members and 221 shakhas were set up. It is said that many Shiv Sena members were pulled into the ABS by hook or crook. Some were offered money, while others were coerced into switching loyalties. Shiv Sena *shakha*s were physically captured like forts won in a war and their signboards replaced with ABS ones. The labour wing of the ABS also earned major victories. At Oberoi Hotels, Tata Memorial Cancer Hospital and government organizations such as SICOM (State Industrial and Investment Corporation of Maharashtra) and IRCON (Indian Railway Construction Limited), which were prime sources of revenue for the party, the Bhartiya Kamgar Sena was replaced by the ABS.

The ABS's growth endangered the Shiv Sena's existence. Gawli announced that his party would contest the next BMC elections as well. The Shiv Sena had been in power at the BMC for over a decade by then. Being the largest civic body of India and having a budget bigger than that of many small states', it was a prime source of funding for the Shiv Sena. It was opined in party meetings that Gawli's wings needed to be clipped urgently.

In 1997, twelve of Gawli's henchmen were eliminated in encounters. Police action intensified against his company and many prominent gang members were shot dead. One of them was Gawli's manager, Sada Pawle, aka Mama, who had been booked for several offences. On 26 September, a month after Gawli's maiden political rally, Pawle was killed by Vijay Salaskar's team in Ghatkopar. Pawle's associate Vijay Tandel was also shot. This was a major blow to Gawli, for Pawle managed the gang's finances and supervised the operations in the leader's absence.

Along with the police killings, Gawli's party functionaries were being eliminated by rival gangs. Party secretary Jitendra Dabholkar's murder on 4 October 1997 was a massive blow for the ABS and temporarily paralysed the party's activities. Gawli's political career had begun to crash. Many members who had joined the ABS from the Shiv Sena returned to the old party, as they feared being targeted by Gawli's rivals.

Despite these setbacks, Gawli was reluctant to quit politics. In fact, he got involved even more vigorously. In 1999, the Shiv Sena–BJP government was replaced by the Congress–NCP alliance. Gawli was at loggerheads with the new dispensation as well. The menace of the underworld was not yet over, and the crackdown by Mumbai Police continued. Gawli believed that the only way to remain powerful and safe was to become a legislator.

In 2004, he contested the Lok Sabha polls from the south-central constituency of Mumbai. Mohan Rawale, Gawli's prime opponent and Shiv Sena's candidate, had already won this seat four times in the past. Another contender in the fray was Gawli's nephew, Sachin Ahir, from the NCP. On the polling day, I went to the Dagdi Chawl to follow Gawli till the polling booth and capture visuals of him. That was when I witnessed him as never seen before. Gawli saw the encounter specialist Vijay Salaskar roaming around Dagdi Chawl's gate and began mumbling in fear, 'He is a murderer. He has killed many of my men and he will kill me as well. I am scared.' He refused to step out of his home.

Even though Gawli could not vote, the results delighted him: he had ranked third with 92,000 votes. Shiv Sena's Mohan Rawale emerged victorious once again, followed by Sachin Ahir.

T.K. Chowdhary, a retired IPS officer, also contested from the same seat and was behind Gawli with a mere 10,000 votes. The gangster outshone the cop! Gawli had never expected to win. His candidature was just to test the waters for the upcoming State Assembly elections. This defeat maximized his chances of getting elected as an MLA later.

The polling day of the Maharashtra Vidhan Sabha elections fell on 13 October 2004. Gawli had filed his candidature from the Chinchpokli seat. This time, he reached the polling booth as soon as voting began in the morning. Gawli was irked by the slow movement of the queue and sensed a conspiracy in the air. He was confident of winning this time, but the slow voting process meant fewer votes. Gawli asked a petrified polling officer in an intimidating tone about why the queue was moving at snail's pace. He then turned towards a gang member and, pointing a finger towards the polling officer, instructed, 'Find out his name and address. We will see him.' The situation would have perhaps turned violent, but Gawli soon noticed my camera rolling. He was always apprehensive about displaying his gangster avatar on TV, and preferred assuming a soft-spoken, well-mannered character whenever I interviewed him. He gave the officer a fierce look and entered the voting compartment. Remarkably, the queue started moving faster after Gawli left the polling centre.

He emerged victorious with 31,964 votes, while the Congress candidate, Madhu Chawan, secured 20,146 votes. It was the culmination of Gawli's political career, which had begun in 1997. The person who was often sent behind bars for breaking laws was now officially a lawmaker. However, Gawli's criminal past travelled with him even when he was a legislator, and many cases of extortion still piled up against him. The cops continued prowling around Dagdi Chawl, where he lived on the third floor of the Gitai building and had offices on the second and fourth floors. There was one room called the 'Bhajanachi Kholi (room for chanting prayers)', where various businessmen were called and threatened for extortion.

Once, in 2005, I tagged along with a Crime Branch team when it went to fetch Gawli from his residence in a case of extortion. The cops searched every room of the multistorey building; broke down locked doors; and checked the cavities of the sofas, beds and cupboards. But Gawli was not found. It is believed that he had constructed secret tunnels to help him escape whenever the police raided the chawl. He later got admitted to a hospital and was technically arrested.

Gawli once again became the focus of national news when a model named Preeti Jain was arrested by Mumbai Police. Jain was accused of contracting Naresh Pardeshi, a member of the Gawli gang, for killing the film-maker Madhur Bhandarkar. She had also filed a criminal case against him previously. The prosecution's case was that Jain paid Rs 75,000 to Pardeshi for the job. When Gawli learnt of this, he tipped off the police, and Jain and Pardeshi were arrested. Jain told me she was framed in the case and the police wanted to implicate Gawli through her.

Gawli's criminal career ended when he was convicted and sentenced to life imprisonment for the murder of Kamlakar Jamsandekar, a Shiv Sena corporator. On 2 March 2007, four men on two motorcycles arrived outside the chawl at Saki Naka, where Jamsandekar lived. One of them entered his room and shot him right in the head, killing him on the spot. A year-long investigation by the Crime Branch found that Jamsandekar's political rivals had given Gawli a contract of Rs 30 lakh to kill him. Gawli was arrested. His term as an MLA ended while he was still in jail. In 2012, the Bombay Sessions Court sentenced him to lifetime imprisonment. However, his political outfit, ABS, survived. His daughter, Geeta Gawli, contested and won the BMC elections in

2007, and repeated her success in 2012 and 2017. Ironically, in one election, the Shiv Sena supported Geeta by not fielding any candidate against her, and she was appointed as the chairperson of the civic body's health committee.

Abu Salem: The End of His Gang and Love Story

I landed in Oslo, the capital of the Scandinavian country of Norway, on the chilly night of 24 November 2005. A thirty-minute train ride from the airport took me and my cameraman to Drammen, 45 kilometres away. The temperature dropped to -5 degrees Celsius. I was 6,660 kilometres away from Mumbai in this sunlight-deficient part of the world for one reason only—Mumbai's underworld.

Mafia don Abu Salem and his film actress wife, Monica Bedi, had been deported from Portugal's capital, Lisbon, to Mumbai and had become a big story for the media. Bedi's involvement added the 'filmi touch' that the Hindi media used to thrive on in those days. She had worked in a few movies such as *Surakshaa* and *Jodi No. 1* with high-profile co-actors.

My editor-in-chief, Udayshanker, had a brainwave that Star News could have an exclusive scoop if we could trace Monica Bedi's family in Europe and explore how she became a moll. This was my first foreign assignment, and I had got in touch with Monica's brother, Bobby Bedi, in Drammen after pestering an officer friend from the Crime Intelligence Unit through several phone calls. Before leaving Mumbai, I had called Bobby requesting an interview, to which he responded sharply with a strict warning against me coming to Norway. I had still landed in this freezing country to try my luck.

Before leaving for Oslo, I acquainted myself with Abu Salem's criminal career through a few informers and officers of the Crime

Branch. Salem's real name was Abdul Qayoom Ansari. At fourteen, he ran away from his native village, Sarai Mir, in the Azamgarh district of Uttar Pradesh and worked for a few years as a taxi driver in Delhi. He moved to Mumbai in the late 1980s and worked as a telephone booth operator for some time at Andheri's Arasa market, where he came in contact with a politician who was allegedly associated with the D-Company. This man introduced Salem to Anees Ibrahim, Dawood's younger brother. Salem joined as Anees's driver, but rose swiftly through the ranks and looked after the extortion business from Bollywood. Salem arranged for unemployed youngsters from Azamgarh to execute shoot-outs at the gang's behest.

After the 1993 Bombay blasts, Salem escaped to the UAE and then to Pakistan. However, after he orchestrated the murder of music baron Gulshan Kumar, differences between him and other members of the D-Company, especially Chhota Shakeel, cropped up. Salem decided to run his own gang and began operations from Dubai. The gang grew rapidly, as did his terror. His expansion troubled the D-Company, as they did not want more rivals.

Once, Anees led a group to barge into Salem's house in Dubai, but he was able to escape. An angry Anees then ransacked his house and showered expletives on Salem's first wife, Samira. Later, Dawood called Samira and apologized on Anees's behalf, as women were always to be left untouched.

Shakeel kept track of Salem's movements and tipped off authorities when he travelled to Sharjah. Based on a Red Corner notice issued against him by Interpol, Salem was detained in October 2001. He claimed to be a Pakistani national, identifying himself as Mohammed Ali. Indian authorities swung into action to get him deported, but failed to produce his fingerprints before the UAE government to establish that he was actually an Indian fugitive. Before the Mumbai Police team could reach Sharjah, he was released from custody.

Salem then thought it prudent to leave the UAE. He moved from country to country—from the UK, the USA, Singapore, Nepal and Germany. However, his globe-trotting came to a halt on 18 September 2002, when he was arrested in Lisbon along with Monica Bedi, who he claimed was his wife. At the time of their arrest, Salem and Monica carried a Pakistani and an Indian passport, respectively, under the names Arsalan Mohammed Ali and Sana Malik Kamal.

After learning about his arrest in Lisbon, my thoughts went directly to Mumbai's relationship with Portugal. It was the Portuguese who began the urbanization of the seven islands that were later unified by the British as the city of Bombay. Salem, a conspirator of bombing the city, was caught in the very country that urbanized Bombay. However, India and Portugal had had a turbulent past since the early 1960s, when the Indian government launched a police action called the 'Liberation of Goa'. The question now was whether the Portuguese government would cooperate with India or not.

While Abu Salem and Monica Bedi were charged for travelling with fake documents in Portugal, Indian authorities attempted to extradite them—though there was no extradition treaty between the two countries. After a three-year-long legal battle, the Indian government secured the couple's extradition to India, but with certain conditions. Portugal is a signatory of a convention of European countries, which rules that no criminal can be deported to a country where they could be punished with death. Hence, one term of the extradition was that Salem would not be given capital punishment. Other conditions included that he would not be sentenced to jail for over twenty-five years and would not be tried for cases other than the eight presented before the Portuguese government for his deportation.

We reached Drammen around 11 p.m. and checked into Hotel Rita Park in the city centre. The Bedi family lived in the Engene area, which was about a five-minute drive from our hotel. En route, I attached a hidden camera to my shirt. This was a standby arrangement in case the Bedi family refused the interview. Since my channel had invested so much on this assignment, I could not afford to return empty-handed.

An elderly man in his late fifties answered the door. He was Premkumar Bedi, Monica's father. After I introduced myself, he allowed me inside. After a brief conversation, he offered me tea, but refused to give an interview. I tried to convince him that this could help swing public sympathy towards Monica. Since all the news coverage thus far presented her as a criminal, and her perspective needed to be shared. There was nobody to defend her. Her concerned father gave it some thought and eventually relented.

Premkumar Bedi hailed from Chhabewal village of Hoshiarpur district in Punjab. In 1975, when Monica was just a year old, he shifted to Drammen, where he ran a garment store named 'Euroteksil' and a video library of Hindi movies. Premkumar told me that Monica, whose nickname was Nicky, completed her primary education in Drammen and then went to the UK for higher studies. She then went to India to pursue her childhood dream of becoming an actress.

'Monica used to tell us about a friend named Sanjay in Mumbai who was helping her get movie assignments. It was only after he was arrested that I got to know that his real name was Abu Salem. I met him when he was in the custody of the Lisbon police. He was a small, soft-spoken man. Looking at him, you could not imagine that this man was accused of so many serious crimes. He addressed me as "Papa" and said that he was innocent,' Premkumar told me.[12]

Shakuntala Bedi, Monica's wheelchair-bound mother, was also in the house that day and agreed to an interview. 'When she went to work in Mumbai, I also joined her there. I accompanied her wherever she went for her shoots—Hyderabad, Chennai and many other places. She didn't even go to the markets without me. When I was in Mumbai, I never heard Abu Salem's name. She loved me a lot and told me everything. Once, I came back to Norway and suffered a paralytic attack; I got stuck to this wheelchair since. She is an innocent girl who has been trapped,' Shakuntala told me, crying.[13]

Shakuntala's sobs awakened Bobby, who was asleep in an adjacent room. Bobby, a tall, bearded man in his late twenties, was enraged to see me and asked me to leave immediately. An altercation ensued. His father pacified him, after which he returned to his room. At my request, Premkumar then drove me to the school where Monica had studied. After I took a few shots of the building, Bedi took me to his garment store, where he gathered a few Indians who knew Monica, and I interviewed them as well.

What Monica's parents didn't know was that she had come in contact with Abu Salem as early as 1997. My former colleague and veteran crime journalist Sheela Raval met Salem's first wife, Samira Jumani, who shared details of the Monica–Salem relationship with her. Salem used to organize stage shows of Bollywood stars in Dubai for the D-Company. In one such show, film producer Mukesh Duggal introduced Monica to him. Later, when Duggal visited Salem's home in Dubai, he introduced Monica as his girlfriend to Samira. When Duggal was shot dead by Shakeel's men in Mumbai on 7 March 1997, Monica grew closer to Salem and began staying with him. Salem claims to have married Monica in Los Angeles in November 2000. Jumani alleged that after she moved to the USA, Monica coerced her to divorce Salem, but she refused.[14]

Abu Salem's arrest in 2002 put a stop to the activities of his gang, which had been shrinking since his shooters killed Gulshan Kumar in 1997. Mumbai Police went after them in full swing, and by 2002, twenty-seven of his alleged shooters were shot dead. Many of his affiliates were also arrested under the MCOCA.

Salem escaped two attacks on his life in jail. In 2010, Mustafa Dosa, another accused in the 1993 bombing case, slashed his face with a sharpened spoon in Mumbai's Arthur Road Jail. In 2013, after Salem was shifted to Navi Mumbai's Taloja Jail, a murder accused, named Devendra Jagtap, shot at him, but Salem escaped with injuries to his hand. He was convicted in most of the cases presented against him in Portugal and was sentenced to life imprisonment in 2017 for participating in the Mumbai blast conspiracy. The next year, he was convicted for killing builder Pradeep Jain and, in this case as well, he was awarded life imprisonment.

A few years after Monica was released from jail, I tracked her down at Hotel Samraj in Andheri. She was finding it difficult to rent a home in Mumbai due to her history and had to live in the hotel. I asked her for an interview, but she refused and checked out of the hotel as well.

Ashwin Naik: From Engineer to Gangster to Builder

Had Ashwin Naik not been a gangster, he would have been an inspiration to many. An inspiration to achieve one's goals despite adversities, physical disability and confinement. The wheelchair-bound gangster did everything he set out to do, except many of his activities were criminal.

In July 1996, when Amar Naik was killed in an alleged encounter with Inspector Vijay Salaskar, it was assumed that one gang had been eliminated from the fabric of Mumbai's underworld. However, despite being imprisoned and paralysed waist down, Amar's brother, Ashwin, successfully ran the gang for at least eight more years. Naik's gang had diminished by 2003. Most of his shooters were killed either in police encounters with Inspector Vijay Salaskar and Inspector Ravindranath Angre, or had been eliminated by rival gangs. Many surrendered to escape death.

After being acquitted in one of the major cases filed against him from a Pune court, Ashwin Naik came out of jail in 2009. In an interaction with the media at his residence in Chinchpokli, he told me, 'I have lived the worst days of my life. I want to live peacefully now. Please don't call me a don.'[15]

A few days before that press interaction, Naik had met Bal Thackeray and Raj Thackeray at their residences, leading to speculation that he was planning to join politics, much like his rival Arun Gawli. But Naik clarified he had no political ambitions and planned to start a real estate business. He claimed to be a supporter of the Shiv Sena, and wanted Uddhav Thackeray and Raj Thackeray to end their animosity.

It is said that after his release, Naik partnered with some big builders and exited fully from the underworld. But the underworld is like quicksand, difficult to get rid of. In 2015, Naik was once again arrested by Mumbai Police on charges of kidnapping and extorting a builder. After a trial that stretched for about six years, he was finally acquitted in September 2021. In fact, Naik has been acquitted in almost all the cases in which he was prosecuted.

The End of the Ravi Pujari Gang

'This Ravi Pujari is the creation of a few policemen. Eventually, I am going to arrest them,' Inspector Vijay Salaskar told me just a few months before he was killed in the 2008 attacks in Mumbai. As per Salaskar, a few corrupt police officers used Pujari to extort money and settle personal scores.

Although most Mumbai gangs had fallen silent by the first decade of the twenty-first century, Pujari continued to be a menace and was a nuisance for law enforcement agencies across India. He was one of those breakaway members of Chhota Rajan's gang who formed his independent group after September 2000, when Rajan was injured in a shoot-out by Chhota Shakeel's hitmen.

Ravi Pujari was born in the coastal town of Malpe in the Udupi district of Karnataka, but grew up in the western suburbs of Mumbai. A short stint in petty crimes introduced him to Chhota Rajan's gang, and soon he became one of Rajan's top lieutenants. After breaking away from Rajan, he adopted the same strategy as his former boss—of presenting himself as a patriotic don by targeting lawyers who took the cases of terror accused and those who spoke of minority rights.

On 4 July 2005, two of his alleged shooters fired on veteran lawyer Majeed Memon near his Bandra residence. Memon had defended several suspects of the Bombay blasts cases in courts and also led a legal battle to get justice for Khwaja Yunus, a terror accused who was allegedly tortured to death in police custody. Memon escaped the bullets while his car was damaged. After the incident, Pujari called up an Indian news channel and announced that his boys had attempted to kill a traitor. In 2006, he allegedly planned to kill film-maker Mahesh Bhatt, and threatened him for his liberal views and for speaking up for minorities, but the plan was foiled. In 2016, he threatened the leader of the hard-line Hurriyat Conference, Syed Ali Shah Geelani, a pro-Pakistan politician from Jammu and Kashmir.

Apart from the image-building exercise of being a patriotic don, Ravi Pujari allegedly extorted money from many hoteliers and builders from Mumbai, Navi Mumbai and Thane. His operations extended to Kerala and Karnataka, where he also intimidated politicians and businessmen.

Pujari's game ended when he was arrested in Senegal in January 2019. He was living there under the fake name of Anthony Fernandes, on a Burkina Faso passport, and ran a restaurant named

'Namaste India'. In 2020, he was extradited to India for ten cases registered against him in Mumbai and Karnataka.

The Indian government's diplomatic efforts ensured that many other gangsters who operated from foreign countries were apprehended as well. In 2010, Prakash, aka Bunty Pandey, was arrested in Vietnam and brought to India. Pandey was once loyal to Chhota Rajan and claimed that he attempted to kill Dawood thrice at Rajan's behest. Pandey told investigators that some differences cropped up between him and Rajan over helping the families of gang members killed in police encounters, and he consequently quit the gang.[16]

In 2011, Mumbai Police got hold of Santosh Shetty, another former accomplice of Chhota Rajan. After Rajan was attacked by Chhota Shakeel's shooters, it was Santosh Shetty who helped him escape from Bangkok. He was with Rajan till 2002, but left him over a monetary dispute. In 2011, Shetty was arrested in Bangkok and deported to India. Like Rajan, Pujari and Pandey, he, too, claimed to be a patriot, that he had helped Indian agencies unearth a counterfeit currency racket run from Pakistan.[17]

By 2022, most of the gangsters who wreaked havoc in the city have been killed, arrested or silenced. The Mumbai underworld of the 1980s and 1990s does not exist any more, and shoot-outs, extortion calls and kidnappings have become rare. However, with time, narcotics abuse has expanded. In 2021, the Narcotics Control Bureau (NCB) unearthed a factory manufacturing mephedrone, also codenamed MD, or '*Mummy-Daddy*', in the Dongri area of south Mumbai. A man named Chinku Pathan was arrested. In actor Sushant Singh's suicide case of 2020 and the Cordelia Cruise Party case of 2021, the NCB came across a few WhatsApp chats stating that drugs were easily available in the city, and many famous personalities were discovered to be regular consumers. In one such chat, a famous actress is seen asking her manager, 'Do you have *maal*?'[18]

Drug abuse in Bollywood isn't new, but the issue appears before the public eye only when popular figures like Sanjay Dutt or Fardeen Khan are implicated. The actual concern is that the drug menace affects the youth from lower- and middle-class families. To support their addiction, they often resort to theft and other crimes. One of my Bombayphile friends rightly remarks, 'As long as Mumbai remains "Mumbai", it can never get rid of its underworld. It will always resurface in some form or the other. It will keep reincarnating.'

9

Tears of Khaki

AND THEN THE FIERCE DAYA SUCCUMBED TO A miserable prey.

Tall, well-built and moustachioed, Daya Nayak emerged as an encounter specialist in the late 1990s—his personality the antithesis of his name, which means 'mercy' in Hindi. The man who had become synonymous with fear after having killed over fifty gangsters was now a wreck. My camera recorded him weeping, but my mind could not accept the sight.

A daredevil cop, the blue-eyed boy of all his superiors and an ever-so-efficient officer, Daya Nayak never hesitated to pose for my camera at the encounter spots, flashing his Kalashnikov.

Men cry. Policemen cry. And anyone who believes they can't or shouldn't fails to see the human in them. The first police officer to cry in front of my camera was Dr P.S. Pasricha, who was appointed as the police commissioner of Mumbai in 2004 when his predecessor was embroiled in a scam pertaining to fake stamp paper, named the Telgi Scam after the kingpin, Abdul Karim Telgi. A Special Investigation Team (SIT) was set up by the Bombay

High Court to investigate the case, which led to Home Minister Chhagan Bhujbal's forced resignation and sent several cops to jail.

Bhujbal was succeeded by R.R. Patil, aka Aabaa. Patil was a modest man with an upright image, and his appointment as the home minister promised to improve the NCP's soiled image. Pasricha was announced as the police commissioner of Mumbai in November 2003. He pledged to restore Mumbai Police's splendour and crackdown on corruption. Although he had a background that was free of corruption and controversies, Patil seemed inclined to revamp the police force by allotting key postings to his favourites. Hence, just two-and-a-half months later, Pasricha was promoted and transferred.

This was sudden and insulting, and Pasricha was most definitely disappointed. His patience had been put to the test, and he did something that shocked everybody in the police and the media. On 3 February 2004, when his transfer was announced, Pasricha refused to vacate the chair or comply with the order. High drama ensued when his successor, Anami Roy, could not take office till Pasricha relieved his charge. Outdoor broadcasting (OB) vans lined up at the police commissioner's office, and crime reporters gathered outside Pasricha's cabin to get a sound byte, but he refused to meet anyone. This was when I sent him an SMS insisting on an interview. I reminded him of his initial ambitions as a commissioner and convinced him that this interview might actually become the medium for him to narrate his story of unfair treatment. Ten minutes later, he invited me in with my cameras.

The ever-so-jovial Pasricha sat anguished this day. A weighty silence enveloped the room as I prepared for the interview. Mics were set and camera angles adjusted. He struggled with an unusual heaviness in his throat before breaking into tears in front of the camera.

> *'Puttar, jab hatana hi tha, toh police commissioner banaya kyon? Ye theek nahi hua. Mujhe samajh nahi aata ki sarkaar ko main kahan galat lagaa. [Sharad] Pawar saab, Patil saab, CM saab—sab mere kaam se khush the. Lekin ab aisa kar diya!'*[1]
>
> (Son, why did they appoint me as the Police Commissioner in the first place when this is how the situations turned out, eventually? This is unfair. I am unaware of any distress that I caused the government. Sharad Pawar sir, R.R. Patil sir, CM sir—everyone seemed content with my work. But now this is where they've landed me!)

In a landmark event, the visuals of the weeping police commissioner immediately aired on my news channel. A police commissioner publicly expressing his emotions on being removed from office was highly unusual, to say the least.

I felt sorry for Pasricha, but my role was limited, so I couldn't help him. Most IPS officers from the Maharashtra cadre dream of being awarded the coveted post of Mumbai's police commissioner at the peak of their career. He who holds this position is deemed as one of the most powerful and prosperous police officers of the state, and carries more prestige in the public eye than the state's police chief, which is, in fact, a higher position. Pasricha's dream was realized briefly and then forever snatched, and the repeated telecast of his visuals on Star News was poignant.

Pasricha explained that the reason he had not handed over charge to his successor was a call from a lawyer, who had filed a PIL against his transfer in the High Court. The lawyer informed Pasricha that the court had ruled to maintain the status quo. If Pasricha relinquished his charge then it would be contempt of the court. Even after many hours when the court order was not produced before him, Pasricha signed off from the office.[2]

Daya Nayak's Distress

A year-and-a-half later, here I was, capturing yet another police officer's breakdown. Daya Nayak was charged in a case of possessing disproportionate assets. The honour that he had earned over the years seemed to fade in front of the fear of an impending arrest. Nayak hailed from a village in coastal Karnataka and had moved to Bombay with his relatives to pursue a college education. To make ends meet, he worked petty jobs, including that of a waiter at a tea stall. After clearing the Maharashtra Public Services Exam, he was recruited as a sub-inspector in Bombay Police in 1995. Posted in the Juhu police station, Nayak came across Inspector Pradeep Sharma, who was impressed with the potential he saw in the young man. Soon, Sharma inducted him into his squad, and the duo conducted several encounters together. Nayak's fame spread like wildfire, and the duo became the favourites of many senior officers. To his peers' envy, he was the only sub-inspector–rank officer with a separate cabin like his senior officers.

Nayak's troubles began in early 2006, when a Marathi newspaper reported about a high-tech school that Nayak had opened in his native village, Yennehole. Named after his mother, Radha Nayak, the school's inauguration ceremony was attended by celebrities such as Amitabh Bachchan, Suniel Shetty and Aftab Shivdasani. He had allegedly spent crores of rupees on this project, which seemed unaffordable for a sub-inspector. It was speculated that Nayak misused his position and extorted money from businessmen. Soon, a case of amassing assets disproportionate to the known source of income was registered against him by the Anti-Corruption Bureau. Nayak went into hiding and applied for anticipatory bail. As the bail application got rejected, and his imprisonment appeared imminent, Daya gave me an interview at an undisclosed location before finally surrendering.

Miserable and tormented, he alleged that his former colleagues had conspired against him out of jealousy: 'I am a victim of infighting in the force.'[3] His wife and two friends were also booked in the case. He was imprisoned for two months and was granted bail when the Anti-Corruption Bureau failed to file the charge sheet against him within the stipulated time period of sixty days. Later investigations couldn't gather any substantive evidence against him, and he was eventually discharged. He was later reinstated into the force.

The War Within

As gangsters bayed for each other's blood on the streets, a parallel war was ensuing among the people who were supposed to eliminate them. Since a few of my fellow crime reporters and I often interacted with the police, we had a clearer picture of this. Pradeep Sharma and Daya Nayak together had killed over eighty alleged gangsters and were portrayed as heroes. While the duo inspired many Bollywood films, at the start of the twenty-first century, like many Hindi movie scripts, their friendship was affected as more officers joined Sharma's squad, leading to disagreements and misunderstandings between them. Nayak's fame was said to be overshadowing his superior's, and there were whispers that his wings must be clipped.

Another rift that was talked about was between Pradeep Sharma, aka Bawa, and Vijay Salaskar, aka Maharaj. Both Sharma and Salaskar belonged to the 1983 batch of recruits. They were posted together in Bombay and became close friends. They also worked briefly in the Anti-Narcotics Cell of the Bombay Police. However, later in their careers, they became parts of the two warring factions of IPS officers attempting to outperform the other. This affected their relationship. There were some informers who were common for both. They were dissuaded by one faction from working for the other. They also began arresting each other's informers and tried to sabotage their operations. The acrimony between them divided journalists as well. Some grew closer to Sharma, while others to Salaskar. Neither received stories from the other. My friend, ACP Avinash Dharmadhikari, who had good offices with both Sharma and Salaskar, attempted to broker peace between them, but in vain.[4]

The unhealthy divide was clear even among senior IPS officers. In the late 1990s and at the dawn of this century, factionalism within the force was such that most officers identified with one or the other. Rakesh Maria, former commissioner of Mumbai Police, in fact, in his autobiography, *Let Me Say It Now*, has acknowledged these factions and claimed to be a victim of internal politics himself. He has written that inquiries were slammed against him on flimsy charges of generating false terror alerts and that attempts were made to stall his promotion. He says he was not considered for important posts and that his image was deliberately tarnished. However, during the last few years of his career, Maria was appointed to various significant positions, including joint commissioner of Crime Branch, chief of Anti-Terrorism Squad and finally police commissioner of Mumbai.

Lobbies based on the regions from where the IPS and IAS officers hailed, such as the 'Punjabi lobby', 'UP–Bihar lobby' and the 'Marathi lobby' have always existed. However, rarely have there been reports of conflicts between these groups. Instead, they operate covertly and try to get favourable appointments for their members by pulling strings with incumbent politicians in the state and the Centre.

Some police officers get identified with specific politicians and enjoy plum postings during their tenure. For example, Devendra Fadnavis' tenure as the CM of Maharashtra proved favourable for a handful of IPS officers, who were then sidelined when Uddhav Thackeray took over as CM in 2019. Some of them even faced criminal charges.

The Paradox of Encounter Cops

'I have a network of one-thousand informers across India. Doctors, engineers and judges aren't my informers. Somebody who is remotely "connected" and has some cases against them could be my informers. I have to keep in touch with them on a day-to-day basis. It is because of advanced information received from them that we have been able to save people's lives. I made such a network for the police work.'[5]

These are Pradeep Sharma's words as he defended himself on my camera. He had been dismissed from Mumbai Police on allegations of working for the organized crime syndicate in August 2008. In an interview at his residence, Sharma justified his communication with some of the accused by claiming they were his informers. Ten months later, he was successful in revoking his dismissal by challenging it in the Maharashtra Administrative Tribunal (MAT), which ruled in his favour. The tribunal made strong observations against the government and remarked that the charges against Sharma were baseless.

Two years later, however, Sharma was arrested for allegedly killing Ramnarayan Gupta, aka Lakhan Bhaiya, a purported member of Chhota Rajan's gang at Versova back in 2006. Lakhan Bhaiya's brother alleged that he was killed in cold blood, and the story of an encounter was invented to cover the crime. After spending four years behind bars, Sharma was acquitted of the murder charge in July 2013. However, thirteen other policemen who took part in the alleged fake encounter were convicted and sentenced for terms in jail.

Sharma was reinstated in the police force and posted in the Anti-Extortion Cell of the Thane Police. The arrest of Dawood Ibrahim's younger brother Iqbal was one of his major successes during his second stint in the police. However, he resigned from the force in July 2019 to fulfil his political ambitions. Initially, he sought a ticket from the BJP to contest the Vidhan Sabha elections in October that year. However, his desired seat was with the Shiv Sena as per the seat-sharing arrangement created with the BJP. Hence, Sharma joined the Shiv Sena and contested from the Nala Sopara seat against Kshitij Thakur, who was a candidate of the Bahujan Vikas Aaghadi and the son of local strongman, Hitendra Thakur. Sharma lost by a margin of around 43,000 votes. He was arrested for another murder in June 2021.

Other encounter cops such as Ravindranath Angre, Datta Ghule and Sachin Waze, too, have been entangled in different controversies. The breed of encounter-specialist cops that emerged as a quick-fix solution to the menace of the underworld turned out to be double-edged swords. They thrived initially, but they later claimed to have been 'used and thrown' by senior officers and politicians. Their remarkable feature, however, remains their ability to survive. They are probably the fittest of the lot and, despite an ample number of cases filed against them, suspensions and imprisonments, they bounce back with more audacity and rigour every time.

As a crime reporter, I have observed that fighting the underworld has its own perils. It is difficult to keep one's hands clean while cleaning dirt. To bring down one gang, an officer has to be in touch with its rivals and enrol a few members of the targeted gang as informers. Often, it becomes arduous for the police officers to work by the book, and this remains one of the grey areas of policing in Mumbai.

Telgi Scam

During one of my daily visits to the Mumbai Police headquarters in late 2002, I met my friend, the veteran crime journalist J. Dey, who worked for a morning paper in those days. Dey usually preferred to keep his emotions private, but that day, as we sat together over a cup of tea, his feelings got the better of him. When I asked him what the matter was, he took out a piece of paper from his pocket and said, 'This is a bomb! If this gets published in any newspaper, it is going to create a stir in the Maharashtra Police establishment and many heads will roll. But my editors cannot understand its significance and are planning to print it on some inner page like regular news. I have withheld it. I don't want to kill such a great story.'[6]

The paper had details of a letter addressed to the Maharashtra police chief by S.M. Mushrif, the additional commissioner of Pune Police, complaining about corruption in his organization. Mushrif wrote that in the multi-crore fake stamp paper scam, some names of accused had been added and others dropped mysteriously. He suspected it was done to extort money from Abdul Karim Telgi, the kingpin of the scam. He was displeased that, although the investigation into the case was technically conducted under his supervision, the investigating officers directly reported to the Pune police commissioner.

Abdul Karim Telgi was not an ordinary criminal. He hailed from Khanapur of Belgaum in Karnataka. While his father, Ladsaab, worked as a coolie, he sold eatables in trains at the town's railway station. Telgi shifted to Bombay, seeking better opportunities. He started a travel and placement agency, through which he defrauded people who aspired to work abroad and soon got arrested. In jail, he met a stockbroker who taught him how to make counterfeit documents. Upon his release, Telgi applied this newly gained skill to pursue his dream of becoming a millionaire.

He learnt that India Security Press was planning to sell used printing blocks as scrap. The blocks were used for printing legal stamp papers. According to the rules, the blocks had to be dismantled before they were scrapped, but Telgi connived with some officials and bought it from them intact. With those blocks, Telgi began running a parallel printing press. He hired young graduates who sold the counterfeit stamp papers to various firms at lower rates. His business flourished across eight Indian states, and he earned in crores. But his lavish lifestyle and blooming trade came to a halt in November 2001, when he got arrested by Karnataka Police. Cases were registered against him in other states as well. Pune Police were the next to get his custody, where a case was filed in the Bund Garden police station. Mushrif's letter alleged corruption in this particular case.

A frustrated Dey was willing to share the contents of the letter with me. He believed that a national television channel picking up this story would do it justice and make his editors regret their lukewarm response to his scoop. I could not understand why Dey wanted to give away the credit for such a major story. Even if the story got printed somewhere in the inner pages of a newspaper, he could later claim credit for it. Perhaps there was more to it than his editors' attitude. Maybe he wanted to avoid antagonizing senior police officers. But the story had merit, and not publishing it would have been unfair.

I noted down the details of the letter and checked the veracity of its contents from my end. The next morning, the first headline of *Aaj Tak*, where I worked in 2002, flashed, 'Scam of Pune Police! Suspiciously adds and drops a few names from the accused list of multi-crore Telgi scam.' From the first bulletin at 7 a.m., the news was repeated throughout the day. As Dey had expected, it created a furore not only within the police establishment but also in the political corridors. The story was picked up by all the national TV channels and newspapers. The Opposition parties took it up as well. An embarrassed state government transferred the investigation from Pune Police to an SIT headed by Deputy Inspector General (DIG) Subodh Jayaswal.

DIG Jayaswal's inquiry concluded that some of his colleagues in the Maharashtra police force had indeed extorted money from Telgi. In a confidential report submitted to the state police chief, Jayaswal further exposed dealings where Telgi had offered bribes for a comfortable police custody and protection of his relatives from arrest.

Sanjay Singh, a crime journalist working for NDTV, leaked this explosive report. This led to another round of tumult in the state, and the matter reached the Bombay High Court. The court ordered that it would monitor the investigation and formed another SIT, headed by the former director general of police S.S. Puri. Subodh Jayaswal was made a member of this SIT as well. The team was given police powers, which implied that it could make arrests in the case.

Puri and his staff were camped at Worli's Police Housing Department's building. The SIT investigations were accompanied by a series of arrests. Mumbai Crime Branch officers were accused of being hand-in-glove with Telgi, and of allowing him to stay and party at his apartment in Cuffe Parade while in police custody. The joint commissioner, the deputy commissioner of police, the assistant commissioner of police and inspectors of the Crime Branch were all implicated, and put behind bars.

The prestigious and most reliable wing of Mumbai Police was undergoing its darkest period in 2003-04, and its symbolic black stone building, aka *kaale patthar waali imaarat,* was cloaked in gloom.

It was heart-wrenching to shoot visuals of teary-eyed arrested policemen every other day—in stark contrast to how they'd been depicted thus far as heroes who protected the people from the underworld—while they were taken out of the SIT office to be produced in court. The media-friendly cops who rarely hesitated to parade the accused in front of our cameras were now captured sandwiched as the accused themselves between SIT officers in Tata Sumos.

The SIT had Home Minister Chhagan Bhujbal and his nephew Sameer Bhujbal on their target too. Rumour had it that the duo could be arrested any time. In November 2003, the probe got transferred to the CBI, and the Bhujbals were not arrested.

The Shiv Sena announced its support for the arrested policemen, and *Saamana* published articles sympathizing with them. Many supporters of the arrested cops speculated that the probe by the SIT was a ploy by the underworld to silence them. Some senior IPS officer friends told me that DIG Subodh Jayaswal faced castigation and boycott from the police fraternity, and he opted for a deputation with the Central government. In May 2021, he was appointed as the CBI chief.

The Telgi Scam is remembered as the case in which everyone from constables to commissioners got arrested. While many officers were later declared innocent by courts, the period remains the darkest chapter of the Mumbai Police's history.

The Disappearance of Khwaja Yunus

In the beginning of January 2003, I was undergoing a pre-launch training of Star News at the World Trade Centre when a source rang me up. 'Khwaja Yunus has escaped! Waze was taking him to Aurangabad for investigation, but their Gypsy overturned near Parner. Waze got injured, while Yunus ran away.' Sachin Waze was an assistant police inspector, and Khwaja Yunus was an accused in the Ghatkopar bomb blast case.

Waze was an audacious, intelligent, tech-savvy, cunning and erratic cop. He was one of the first police officers I got acquainted with in my career as a crime reporter. Waze defied the stereotypical image of a police officer with his benign nature, gentlemanly manner, and an attire of plain formal shirts and jeans. He seemed more of a banker or corporate executive than a policeman.

Waze was part of Inspector Pradeep Sharma's high-profile 'encounter squad'. Cops such as Waze catalysed crime reporting in Mumbai. They updated us about police encounters and other newsworthy information, which often totalled about a hundred encounters a year. How quickly you got news of an encounter was one parameter to gauge the worth of crime reporters back then.

Commissioned in the 1990 batch, one of Waze's initial postings was with Thane Police. He soon rose as the then Thane police chief Bhujangrao Mohite's favourite. Mohite was transferred to the post of Mumbai Crime Branch chief in 2001. He posted Waze at the Andheri office of the Crime Intelligence Unit (CIU), headed by Inspector Pradeep Sharma.

On the evening of 2 December 2002, a colossal explosion was triggered when a bomb went off in the BEST bus number 416 outside the Ghatkopar railway station. Two people were killed and many injured. Mumbai Police swung into action and swiftly arrested nine people who were allegedly affiliated with the Students' Islamic Movement of India (SIMI), a banned outfit. One of the accused was a twenty-seven-year-old software engineer from Parbhani named Khwaja Yunus. Being a CIU officer, Sachin Waze was also a part of the investigation.

In January 2003, Waze narrated how their Gypsy met with an accident on the way to Aurangabad, and Yunus took advantage of the situation to escape. This tale took on a different hue when another co-accused Mateen Basit alleged that Yunus, in fact, may have just died because of the extensive torture in custody, and a story had been spun to make it sound like he'd escaped. A tremendous uproar over Yunus' disappearance followed, and the matter reached the Bombay High Court.

The Maharashtra government transferred the case to the state's Crime Investigation Department (CID). In 2004, Waze and three other policemen got arrested and were suspended. The CID alleged that Yunus was tortured to death and, to cover up the custodial killing, a false narrative had been created. In fact, till date, Yunus has not been traced, dead or alive. The other eight persons arrested with Yunus were acquitted, which led people to infer that Yunus was possibly innocent as well.

After getting out on bail, Waze submitted his resignation from the police, but it was not accepted. Around 2008, he joined the Shiv Sena and took part in national debates on news channels. Briefly, he also served as a consultant for TV9. Waze had been a bibliophile, and soon got busy reading and writing books. He authored *Jinkun Harleli Ladhai*, a book based on the 26/11 Mumbai attacks. He also developed a mobile application named '*Laybhari*' modelled on WhatsApp but more secure—as he claimed at the app's launch event at the Mumbai Press Club. He took part in live chats and gave sound bites as an IT expert to TV channels. Waze always maintained that Khwaja Yunus was alive and under cover. Despite all their laurels, the disappearance of Khwaja Yunus was one case that severely tarnished the image of Mumbai Police and questioned the institution's credibility.

The Antilia Conspiracy

The Telgi Scam and the Khwaja Yunus disappearance case had rocked Mumbai Police in 2003-04, and seventeen years later, history repeated itself with the Antilia Conspiracy in 2021. This case shook the police and political establishment in Maharashtra.

Billionaire Mukesh Ambani lives in south Mumbai's Altamount Road. He named his twenty-seven-storey residential tower Antilia after a mythical island in the Atlantic Ocean. The building has been a source of awe since its construction in 2012. However, what drew public attention to Antilia in 2021 was a Mahindra Scorpio SUV loaded with twenty gelatin sticks parked near the building on 25 February.

Sachin Waze was one of the first officers to reach the spot. After his suspension in 2004 and reinstatement in May 2020, Waze was now posted in the Crime Intelligence Unit (CIU) of Mumbai Police as an assistant police inspector once again. His reinstatement led to raised eyebrows, but there were more shocks in store. Although a junior-ranking officer, he was made in-charge of the powerful CIU and reported directly to Police Commissioner Parambir Singh, bypassing all his superiors. All high-profile investigations were assigned to him, overlooking his controversial past and sixteen years of suspension.

There were no detonators found attached to the explosives in the Mahindra SUV. It had a letter inside threatening the Ambanis: '*Ye to sirf ek trailer hai, Neeta Bhabhi, Mukesh Bhaiya* (This is just a trailer, dear Neeta and Mukesh).' The police also came across another message on the Telegram app by an organization named Jaish-ul-Hind that repeated the threat. When the SUV owner, Mansukh Hiran, was traced in Thane, he stated that the vehicle had been stolen from the Eastern Express Highway near Airoli junction.

While the CIU investigated the case, a parallel probe was launched by the Anti-Terrorism Squad (ATS) and the National Investigation Agency (NIA), since the matter concerned explosives and the prime minister's industrialist friend Mukesh Ambani.

Devendra Fadnavis, the BJP leader of Opposition, had developed a circle of police officers when he was CM of the state. There was a perception that some of these officers were still loyal to him and kept him abreast of the happenings in the police department. Fadnavis also kept a tab on the developments in the Antilia case via such officers.

In the Vidhan Sabha session held on 5 March 2021, Fadnavis stunned everyone when he alleged that Mansukh Hiran, the owner of the SUV, was known to Sachin Waze. He also revealed that Waze had used the car before it was stolen. Fadnavis's suspicions against Waze were firm. As he concluded his speech, the news of Mansukh Hiran's death broke out. This was shocking. His body was found at Thane Creek with ten new handkerchiefs stuffed into his mouth. Hiran's wife suspected Sachin Waze of killing him. Following an uproar, Waze was transferred out of the Crime Branch a week later. Nevertheless, CM Uddhav Thackeray defended him on the floor of the House. 'Sachin Waze is not Osama bin Laden. It is not right to target a person, hang him and then investigate.'[7]

The tables were turned when the NIA officially took over the case. On the morning of 13 March, Waze said in his WhatsApp status that he had been falsely implicated in the Khwaja Yunus case in 2004 and that history was being repeated. His story read, 'Then probably I had 17 years of hope, patience, life and service too. Now I will neither have 17 years of further life, nor service, nor patience to live. I think the time to say goodbye to the world is coming closer.' The message implied Waze was contemplating suicide, but before he could actually attempt to do so, he was arrested by the NIA.

The NIA alleged the policeman had parked the explosive-laden SUV near Antilia and played a pivotal role in Hiran's murder. Four other serving and former cops were arrested, including Pradeep Sharma, who had accepted voluntary retirement from the police force to contest elections on a Shiv Sena ticket. The charge sheet filed by the NIA in the court read:

> 'As evident from the threat, [the] note placed along with the explosives in the vehicle planted by accused Sachin Waze himself was an act of terror. The intent was clearly to terrorise wealthy and prosperous individuals and also to extort money by instilling fear of dire consequences. The post on Telegram channel Jaish-ul- Hind appears to be a deliberate attempt to add credibility to the above said act of terror, and the murder of Mansukh Hiran was a direct outcome of the said act of terror.'[8] Waze has refuted all the charges against him.

An embarrassed government removed Police Commissioner Parambir Singh on 18 March and transferred him to the less reputable Home Guard department. Shortly after this, Maharashtra's home minister, Anil Deshmukh, gave an interview to Marathi channel ABP Majha and blamed Singh for the whole mess. Singh responded with a damning letter to CM Uddhav Thackeray and Governor Bhagat Singh Koshyari on 20 March, alleging that Deshmukh often summoned Waze to his bungalow and compelled him to extort money from bar and restaurant owners to the tune of Rs 100 crore per month.[9]

Parambir Singh's letter opened a can of worms. Never in the history of Maharashtra had a senior IPS officer made such a grave allegation of corruption against his political boss. The BJP seized the opportunity and pressured the government to sack Deshmukh. On 5 April, the minister was asked to resign, just as Chhagan Bhujbal resigned from the home ministry after the Telgi Scam.

After a few activists approached the Bombay High Court, the CBI conducted a preliminary inquiry into Singh's allegations against Deshmukh. A case on the charge of money laundering was registered by the Enforcement Directorate as well, and Deshmukh was arrested. A series of criminal cases, ranging from charges of extortion to some other atrocities, were filed against Parambir Singh in different police stations of the state. Singh even went missing for a while, only to reappear when the Maharashtra police force was about to seize his property by declaring him an absconder. He presented himself before all the police stations where he was booked, but none of them could arrest him since he came with a No Arrest order from the Supreme Court. Some junior-ranking officers named along with him in cases of extortion were arrested. Later, the Supreme Court transferred all the cases registered against Singh to the CBI.

10

A New Politics

IN MAHARASHTRA POLITICS, 1995 WAS A WATERSHED year. For the first time in thirty-five years, the Congress and its breakaway parties had lost to the Shiv Sena–BJP combine. The impact of the events of 1992-93 was now clear on the state's politics as the saffron alliance assumed power. The Assembly elections held in 1995 was the first one after the Ayodhya episode. The polarization caused by the communal riots evidently benefitted saffron parties.

Communal Polarization

The Vishwa Hindu Parishad (VHP) had announced 6 December 1992 as the day of 'karseva' at the disputed site in Ayodhya. The word 'karseva' means to voluntarily offer one's services for some religious cause. It was supposed to be a symbolic event for the construction of the Rama temple. Soon, members of the VHP and its affiliates began pouring into Ayodhya. Since the Shiv Sena had announced its support for the Rama temple agitation, the party sent its *sainiks* from Bombay and other regions.

When Nandu Satam, former mayor of Bombay, reached Ayodhya along with seventy-two Shiv Sena corporators on 6 December 1992, it was afternoon, and the Babri masjid was almost demolished. Satam told me the train that they had taken from Bombay to reach Ayodhya was attacked by trackside slum dwellers near Jhansi, and hence, they got delayed. Another set of Shiv Sena leaders, led by Manohar Joshi, could reach only by the next day. It was unclear if the Shiv Sainiks from Bombay had any role to play in the demolition of the mosque, but shortly after, Bal Thackeray announced, 'If my Shiv Sainiks have demolished the mosque, then I am proud of them.'[1]

Satam told me that Thackeray's statement came when Sundarlal Bhandari, a BJP leader, blamed Shiv Sena for the mosque's destruction. 'After the structure was demolished, all the top BJP leaders got scared and disowned their party from the demolition. Only Balasaheb had the guts to take the responsibility,' said Satam.[2] Bal Thackeray made the statement at the risk of a criminal case because Bhandari put in words exactly what the Shiv Sena wanted to be seen as: a militant Hindu outfit.

This admission strengthened the Shiv Sena's image as a champion of the Hindutva ideology. The party had gained the reputation of being a militant Hindu organization since it took part in the communal riots at Bhiwandi in 1984. In an Assembly by-poll in 1987, the Shiv Sena officially employed Hindutva as a political plank. Thackeray gave inflammatory speeches against Muslims and solicited votes for Shiv Sena candidates on communal grounds. The Shiv Sena adopted the slogan, '*Garv se kaho hum Hindu hain* (Admit with pride that we are Hindus).'

The events following 6 December clearly led to communal polarization across the country, not just Bombay. I could sense a political shift within personal spaces where families, friends and neighbours stood divided. Since two Shiv Sainiks had escorted my family to safety when my uncle abandoned our home during the second phase of the riots, my family felt indebted to the Shiv Sena. A general sentiment that engulfed the Hindus of the city areas was that to save Hindus from becoming a minority community, the Shiv Sena–BJP alliance must come to power.

Damage by Demolition Man

A magnificent building once stood in Pakmodia Street, right opposite Dawood Ibrahim's childhood home, incongruent with the surrounding dilapidated buildings and modest chawls.

It was known as the Qadri Building until May 1992, when Dawood's men purchased it and evicted the tenants by paying them paltry sums. At the time of the purchase, the building was in a decrepit state, and permission was sought from the Bombay Municipal Corporation for repairs. After receiving permission, however, the building was demolished, and a new five-storey structure was erected.

The facade of the fully air-conditioned building was fitted with glass imported from Belgium. Precious marble- and gold-plated taps were fitted in the bathrooms, and the first floor had a fancy swimming pool. The house reeked of luxury. Dawood was the Shah Jahan of this Taj Mahal and Mehazbeen, his Mumtaz. Qadri Building was now called the Mehazbeen Tower. Dawood had organized a luxurious life for his relatives in Bombay, similar to the one he was living in Dubai.

While the city was abuzz about the splendour of this architectural wonder, a middle-ranked municipal officer, Govind Raghav Khairnar, reached Pakmodia Street one fine day in 1993 with a humongous hammer, a few bulldozers and an army of over a hundred labourers. Anticipating a violent confrontation, the officer had come with an assembly of policemen, who cordoned off the area before the demolition began. Mehazbeen Tower was reduced to a heap of debris within a day's time.

The hammer hit Dawood's dreadful reputation severely. Nobody had ever dreamt that a mid-level BMC officer would dare to destroy the don's house. For Khairnar, Mehazbeen Tower was just another illegal site in Dawood's possession, and he was duty-bound to get rid of it. He was an honest, audacious and no-nonsense officer, known for his campaigns against illegal hawkers, and the destruction of liquor and gambling dens run by slumlords. Khairnar also demolished bomb blast–accused Tiger Memon's building at Zaveri Bazaar and Dawood's henchman Salim Talwar's building at Dongri.

Khairnar emerged as a national hero, and was given the sobriquet 'Demolition Man of Bombay'. In his autobiography, titled *Ekanki Jhuj* (A Lonely Struggle), Khairnar mentioned that after Sudhakarrao Naik was replaced by Sharad Pawar as the CM of Maharashtra in March 1993, he began facing obstacles in his anti-Dawood campaign. It became difficult to get a police escort to demolition sites, and cooperation from government officials gradually faded. His superiors in the BMC suggested he should watch his pace. Khairnar was accused of targeting illegal buildings only in Muslim-dominated areas, which could reignite communal tensions. When Khairnar didn't succumb to the pressure, a committee was set up with a mandate to approve or reject demolitions of illegal buildings.[3]

An enraged Khairnar openly claimed that his powers were being curtailed at the behest of CM Sharad Pawar. Accusing the people of Pakmodia Street for his plight, he went to the extent of saying that the expense of the stage on which politicians addressed election meetings in Dawood's area was met by the mafia boss's men.[4] Such outbursts painted Sharad Pawar as Dawood's empath. The Pawar government briefly contemplated filing defamation cases against Khairnar, but the idea never came to fruition. Khairnar was eventually suspended in 1994 on charges of violating service rules and acts of indiscipline.

After his suspension, Khairnar launched an anti-corruption crusade. He was invited by social organizations across the country to deliver speeches in which he narrated how he was punished for doing his duty and taking on Dawood Ibrahim. After the 1993 blasts, Dawood had emerged as Bombay's 'Enemy Number 1' and Khairnar as the hero on a mission to fight his supremacy in the city. Action against Khairnar was perceived as favouring Dawood. Many prominent citizens rallied in his support and demanded his reinstatement to the BMC.

The Shiv Sena–BJP alliance capitalized on Khairnar's anti-establishment tirade, but Sharad Pawar was never prosecuted. The truckload of evidence against Pawar that Khairnar once claimed to have possessed was never produced.[5] Khairnar was reinstated in the service in 2000. Ironically, the Congress played a role in his suspension and also supported his reinstatement later. The Shiv Sena, which won the elections partly due to his anti-corruption campaign, was against reinstating him.[6]

Allegations of Criminalizing Politics

Apart from protecting Dawood's interests, Sharad Pawar was also accused of facilitating the admission of various criminals into politics. In August 1994, a police officer named Ulhas Joshi filed an affidavit in the Bombay High Court, alleging that the CM was protecting the interests of some gang lords from Bombay's neighbouring areas such as Vasai, Virar and Ulhasnagar.[7]

On the night of 30 April 1991, a trawler loaded with silver ingots capsized near the coastal village of Vadrai, about a hundred kilometres from Bombay. When the tribal villagers got a whiff of the accident, they rushed to the spot in large numbers and took away the contraband from the damaged trawler. The silver ingots were smuggled by Dawood's gang and were to be transported into Bombay. When Dawood was informed about the incident, he called up his local agent, Jayendra, aka Bhai Thakur, to recover the silver. Thakur was a feared gangster in the Vasai–Virar region adjoining Bombay.

On Dawood's instructions, Bhai Thakur and an army of bikers raided Vadrai, and brutally tortured the villagers. All the silver ingots were recovered, but three villagers lost their lives to the torture. The matter came to light only eight months later, since nobody dared to file a complaint against Thakur, who fled to Dubai after the case was registered. He was arrested on 23 July 1993, when he came to Delhi via Kathmandu.

During Sharad Pawar's chief ministership earlier, in 1990, Bhai Thakur's brother, Hitendra, had been offered a candidature by the Congress in the Vidhan Sabha elections, a year before the Vadrai bloodbath. Later, Hitendra Thakur was arrested under TADA for conspiring to kill a builder and possessing illegal arms. 'I work for the people and that is why I am elected repeatedly. I had been falsely implicated in the criminal cases,' Thakur told me in an interview in 2004.[8]

Just as the Thakur brothers dominated the Vasai–Virar coastal belt, Suresh, aka Pappu Kalani, ruled using his muscle power in Ulhasnagar—a satellite town of Bombay, densely populated with Sindhi migrants from Pakistan. Kalani's gang was the most powerful of several warring gangs in Ulhasnagar that thrived on extortion and various other illegal businesses. Pappu Kalani had entered politics as early as 1986 by joining the Congress, but it was during Pawar's tenure in 1990 that he became an MLA.

Thakur and Kalani's entry into the Legislative Assembly became an electoral issue, and Pawar's detractors accused him of criminalizing politics. During the election campaign, Pawar toured their constituencies and addressed rallies in their support. In his autobiography, *On My Terms*, Pawar rejected the accusations and claimed that the names were proposed by local units of the party. He went to campaign for them as a part of his state-wide election tour, as instructed by the party.[9]

Pawar faced another storm of allegations when veteran lawyer Ram Jethmalani revealed having received a call from fugitive Dawood Ibrahim, wherein the latter expressed his willingness to surrender. Jethmalani alleged that he had informed Pawar about this offer, but the proposal was rejected. Questions were raised as to why Sharad Pawar did not want Dawood to return to India.

Pawar explained that the conditions set by Dawood could not have been met. Dawood demanded that he be kept only under house arrest and wanted relief from the trials of the Bombay serial blasts. The senior police officers and the Centre conveyed to Pawar that a criminal like Dawood couldn't dictate terms to the government, and so his proposal was rejected. Pawar dismissed Jethmalani's disclosure as a mere publicity stunt.[10]

The accusations against the Congress continued to rise. On 12 September 1992, Dawood's shooters attacked J.J. Hospital, in which Shailesh Haldankar, a shooter from Gawli's gang, had been admitted after being beaten up by a mob. He had killed Dawood's brother-in-law, Ibrahim Parker, on 26 July 1992, and Dawood had vowed to avenge the murder. This was one of the major shoot-outs involving the Bombay underworld, and Shailesh Haldankar and two policemen were killed.

The investigations revealed the accused used the official car of Jaywant Suryarao, president of Bhiwandi–Nizampur Municipal Corporation, to flee. That Suryarao was a member of the Congress gave the Shiv Sena–BJP combine another reason to attack the Congress. This shoot-out happened when Sudhakarrao Naik was the CM. Naik had started a crackdown against criminals, which didn't spare members of his own party. Both Hitendra Thakur and Pappu Kalani, despite being Congress MLAs, were booked under TADA during Naik's tenure.

There were also attempts to tarnish Pawar's image within the Congress itself. The state unit of the party was divided into two factions. Intimidated by Pawar's ambition, which some believed was to become the PM, the opposing faction gave air to the negative perception of Pawar,[11] which was a cocktail of truths, half-truths, rumours and lies.

'Shivshahi'

On 30 September 1993, Maharashtra experienced the deadliest earthquake in its history, with an intensity of 6.4 on the Richter scale. The epicentre was Killari village in the Latur district, 500 kilometres away from Bombay. Over 10,000 people died in the catastrophe and dozens of villages were devastated. The state also witnessed unseasonal rains, which damaged crops and ruined farmers' livelihoods. All of this acted as fodder for the Opposition. Bal Thackeray, in his election rallies, often exclaimed that Sharad Pawar, as CM, had proved incapable of mitigating the impact of such disasters.

On 23 November 1994, around 5,000 members of the Govari community marched to Vidhan Bhavan in Nagpur to demand Scheduled Tribe status for the community, which would make them eligible for reservation benefits in jobs and education. A lathi charge on the protesters caused a stampede, leading to 114 deaths and over 500 injuries. Most of the victims were women and children. The incident happened four months before the Vidhan Sabha polls and added to the anti-incumbency wave against the Pawar government, and was constantly referenced by leaders of the saffron combine.

Above all, it was the Shiv Sena supremo Bal Thackeray's personal charisma that contributed to the defeat of the Sharad Pawar–led Congress government. He campaigned vigorously across the state with speeches filled with mimicry and expletives, narrating the 'failures' and 'misdeeds' of the Pawar government.

On 11 March 1995, when the Shiv Sena–BJP were declared the winners, Thackeray announced that he would not hold an official post. Among the many vows that he had taken, this was one. Declaring Manohar Joshi as his choice for the CM seat, Thackeray said, 'The remote control of the government will be in my hands.'[12]

Out of the total 288 seats in the Maharashtra Vidhan Sabha, the saffron alliance won 138. Ten independent MLAs offered their support to the combine, which pushed them beyond the magic figure of 145 seats. Prior to their win, the Shiv Sena had promised to introduce 'Shivshahi' in Maharashtra—good governance resembling the administration of Chhatrapati Shivaji. However, the five years that the alliance was in power were marred by allegations of corruption, failure of developmental schemes, criminal cases, infighting within the Shiv Sena, tussles between the coalition partners and various other controversies.

Gandhian activist Anna Hazare accused ministers Shashikant Sutar, Mahadeo Shivankar and Babanrao Gholap of corruption. Although they were later cleared of the charges, Hazare's accusations embarrassed the government. Manohar Joshi came under fire over the alleged involvement of his son-in-law, Girish Vyas, in a land allotment scam in Pune. The allegation was that a 30,000-square-foot plot of land in Pune's prime area, reserved for a school, was de-reserved in favour of a company owned by Vyas to construct a housing project.[13]

Bal Thackeray's nephew, Raj Thackeray, got embroiled in Ramesh Kini's murder case. Kini was found dead in a cinema hall in Pune, and a confidant of Raj Thackeray was arrested in the case. Based on accusations levelled by Kini's wife, the Congress alleged that Raj Thackeray himself had played a role in the conspiracy. Kini's wife revealed that their landlord wanted them to vacate the flat by paying them a pittance. On Kini's refusal, the landlord used his proximity to Raj Thackeray to harass him. Thackeray was extensively interrogated by the CBI, but was eventually given a clean chit.

In July 1997, riots broke out in Ramabai Nagar—a slum in the eastern suburb of Ghatkopar—following the desecration of Dr Babasaheb Ambedkar's statue. Ten people were killed and twenty-six others were injured in the police firing. After the incident, the Opposition parties labelled the saffron government as anti-Dalit.

An anti-incumbency sentiment against the BJP–Shiv Sena government started gaining momentum, which was reflected in the 1998 Lok Sabha elections, where the Congress swept most of the seats. The chances of returning to power for the alliance in the next election seemed bleak. Several differences between the Shiv Sena and the BJP also came to the fore. The acrimony got so intense that Gopinath Munde even refused to attend the Cabinet meeting once.

Bal Thackeray's disappointment with Manohar Joshi also grew over time. Joshi's actions gave the impression of self-assertion and a desire to create a parallel power centre, which didn't go down well with Thackeray. When Rebecca Mark, an executive of the Enron power project, went to meet Bal Thackeray before meeting CM Joshi for negotiations, an enraged Joshi cancelled her appointment, riling Thackeray further. *Saamana* began publishing articles against the Joshi government. Some of Joshi's casual comments praising Sharad Pawar added insult to injury. Thackeray announced his *sanyas,* or renunciation, from politics. He was soon pacified by Shiv Sena leaders, ministers and Shiv Sainiks, who gathered at his residence, Matoshri, in Bandra and he reversed his decision.

Thackeray then asked Manohar Joshi to step down. Konkan's strongman Narayan Rane was announced as the new CM, which came as a surprise to many since there were few other senior leaders such as Sudhir Joshi, Pramod Navalkar and Subhash Desai who were seen as contenders for the coveted post.

Veteran journalist Vageesh Saraswat told me that Smita Thackeray, the wife of Bal Thackeray's estranged son, Jaideo, had pitched for Narayan Rane. She had become powerful in the Shiv Sena and ganged up with Raj to put pressure on Bal Thackeray. Rane returned the favour as CM by allotting a 17,000-square-metre plot of land at a prime location for Smitha's NGO, Mukti Foundation. Another merit was his ability to fill the party's coffers. Saraswat recollects Rane had gifted Land Cruiser cars to Uddhav and Raj.[14]

The saffron government was successful in renaming Bombay as Mumbai in 1996, but failed to deliver its other pre-poll promises—ranging from housing schemes for slum dwellers to providing employment to Marathi youths. The *Zunka Bhakar* centres allotted to private individuals to provide affordable food to the poor were converted to fast-food joints. Some of the combine's only accomplishments included the construction of fifty-five flyovers in Mumbai, the commencement of work on the Mumbai–Pune Expressway, and the silencing of the Mumbai underworld.

The next state Vidhan Sabha elections were held in 1999, six months before the completion of the government's tenure. Sharad Pawar had broken away from the Congress and established his own outfit, the Nationalist Congress Party (NCP). The Congress and the NCP fought the elections separately, and the Congress emerged as the single-largest party with seventy-five seats. The NCP won fifty-eight seats.

However, there was another pre-poll alliance between the Shiv Sena and the BJP, and they bagged 125 seats in all. This was a fractured mandate, but having a pre-poll alliance in place, they had a chance to stake the claim for government formation. Narayan Rane was confident of getting support from independent MLAs and smaller parties to cross the majority mark of 145 seats, but he alleged the BJP was dilly-dallying over issuing the required support letter. Rane suspected that Gopinath Munde was two-timing the Shiv Sena and was seeking support from the NCP to fulfil his ambitions of becoming the CM. Eventually, the NCP allied with the Congress and a government was formed under the chief ministership of Vilasrao Deshmukh of the Congress.

When the Protégé Took on the Mentor

One July afternoon in 2000, Bal Thackeray called Mumbai's then police commissioner, M.N. Singh.

'MN, will you arrest me?' he asked.

'Yes, Balasaheb. I have to.'

'Not only Mumbai, but the whole of India will burn. Do you know that?' Thackeray threatened.

'Balasaheb, India is yours and Mumbai is yours. If you want it to burn, then let it burn. Please tell me why you have called.'

'Is it necessary to arrest me? Can't you file the charge sheet directly?'

'No, saheb. We have to arrest you.'

'All right, so will you handcuff me and parade me on the streets?' Thackeray asked in a lighter vein.

'No, Balasaheb. You are a respected leader and an elder. We will treat you with due respect.'

'I trust you, MN, but not that Lakhoba.' Thackeray referred to Chhagan Bhujbal as 'Lakhoba', an antagonist from a Marathi drama.

'No. Bhujbal saheb has not given me any such order, and I will not comply if at all it is given.'

'So shall I come to you or will you come to me?' Thackeray asked.

'Why don't you come, Balasaheb? I will be happy to show you this grand British-era building of the police commissioner's office.' Singh smiled as the conversation ended.[15]

This telephonic conversation between Bal Thackeray and Commissioner Singh took place a few days before the former was arrested by Mumbai Police on 25 July 2000. It reflects Thackeray's anxiety and his distrust towards Chhagan Bhujbal, the man whom he had mentored in politics. Thackeray wasn't afraid of getting arrested, but he wanted to avoid it—for it would have been perceived as a symbolic victory of a man whom he derided.

In Maharashtra's political circles, Bal Thackeray's arrest is remembered as a case where a protégé took revenge on his mentor. Chhagan Bhujbal, a vegetable seller at Byculla market, was enthused by the fiery speeches of Bal Thackeray, the leader of the newly founded Shiv Sena in the late 1960s. Thackeray's campaign to fight for the pride of the local Marathi population appealed to Bhujbal, and he joined the Shiv Sena. Bhujbal emerged as a firebrand leader and worked hard for the party's advancement. He rapidly rose through the ranks and soon became one of Thackeray's top lieutenants.

In the 1985 Vidhan Sabha elections, Bhujbal was the only candidate from the Shiv Sena to win. In the 1990 elections, Bhujbal repeated his victory. This time, the Shiv Sena emerged as the largest Opposition party by winning fifty-two seats. He expected that the coveted post of the Leader of Opposition would be offered to him, but, to his disappointment, Thackeray instead chose Manohar Joshi. He was asked to become the mayor of Bombay, which he saw as a demotion from state politics to city politics. Bhujbal was offended. Another issue that irked him was Bal Thackeray's opposition to the Mandal Commission's recommendations. Bhujbal was seen as a leader of the OBCs (Other Backward Classes), and Thackeray's stance had put him in a dilemma.[16]

Congress leader Sharad Pawar noticed Bhujbal's resentment and strategized to capitalize on it. He persuaded Bhujbal to defect from the party along with eighteen other Shiv Sena MLAs. Most of them later joined the Congress. This was a major jolt for Thackeray, being the first major revolt witnessed since the Shiv Sena's formation. Owing to the defections, the number of the Shiv Sena MLAs in the Vidhan Sabha was now reduced, and Gopinath Munde from the BJP staked the claim for the post of Opposition leader.

Thackeray declared Bhujbal a traitor and decided to punish him. He seized one such opportunity in 1997 when the Shiv Sena–BJP combine was in power. Bhujbal's official security cover was withdrawn. On 13 July 1997, several Shiv Sainiks entered Bhujbal's official bungalow in south Mumbai and began searching for Bhujbal, who had locked himself up inside a room. Unable to find him, the disappointed Shiv Sainiks ransacked the interiors and burnt some documents. A police team arrived to rescue Bhujbal. Thackeray supported the attack by saying that his Shiv Sainiks were only reacting to provocative speeches made by Bhujbal. The attack satiated Thackeray's urge to teach Bhujbal a lesson, but also filled the latter with a desire to take revenge.

Bhujbal got his chance once the Shiv Sena–BJP government was replaced by the Congress–NCP alliance, and he became the home minister. He learnt of an old case against Bal Thackeray, wherein he was charged with writing inflammatory articles in *Saamana*. Bhujbal asked Mumbai Police to reopen the file and approved the arrest of Thackeray.

Initially, Thackeray contemplated presenting himself before the police, as advised by Commissioner Singh, but BJP's Pramod Mahajan cautioned him against doing so.[17] On the morning of 25 July 2000, a police team reached Thackeray's residence, Matoshri, and arrested him. He was produced before a Metropolitan Magistrate in Bhoiwada court, and after about a forty-five-minute-long hearing, the case was closed and Thackeray was let off. Although there was tremendous tension in the city and shops were shut in fear, the heavy police deployment ensured that there was no ensuing rampage by Shiv Sainiks. Thackeray's arrest was symbolic, but Bhujbal had avenged his attack. Many years later, Ajit Pawar, Bhujbal's colleague in the NCP, revealed that he had been against arresting Thackeray. 'It was because of [the] obstinacy of certain people that the arrest was carried out,' said Pawar, without directly naming Bhujbal.[18]

Kidnap Drama: Operation Topple Fails

Although Narayan Rane was CM for only nine months, he aimed to be back on the coveted chair by hook or crook. After the 1999 Vidhan Sabha election results were out, there was a chance for him to return to power, but that opportunity was not realized because of Gopinath Munde's non-cooperation.

In June 2002, Rane saw an opportunity to topple the Congress–NCP government led by Vilasrao Deshmukh. The 1999 election saw a fractured mandate where no party or alliance got a clear majority, so Deshmukh's government was a mix of many small parties and independent MLAs. Owing to certain disagreements, the Peasants and Workers Party (PWP) withdrew its five MLAs from the combine, and Deshmukh's government went into a minority. The CM was given ten days by the governor to pass a trust motion on the floor of the House. Rane seized the opportunity and strategized for a few more MLAs to vote against the motion.

As per the plan, on 5 June 2002, Rane took a few Congress–NCP MLAs to Matoshri Club at Jogeshwari. The club was secured by hundreds of Shiv Sainiks, especially Rane loyalists. The Congress and the NCP alleged that their MLAs were kidnapped by Rane, and were made to sign affidavits withdrawing their support from Deshmukh's government under duress.

Padmakar Valvi, one of the MLAs, attempted to escape the heavily guarded club but was caught and sent back by Rane's men. On the government's instructions, Mumbai Police launched a midnight operation to rescue the MLAs. About a hundred cops, encounter-specialist officers and two NCP MLAs reached the club. Rane came out in his undershirt, and showered expletives and threats on the police team. He embarrassed some officers by reminding them of the favours they had gained from him when he was CM. Seeing Rane's aggression, the officers concluded that any police action could lead to a law-and-order situation in the city and retreated.

The next day, Rane invited me and a few other journalists to interview the captive MLAs. In the presence of Rane's men, all the MLAs admitted on record that they were not kidnapped and that they were staying at the club willingly.

On 13 June 2002, the day earmarked for voting on the trust motion, Rane took all the MLAs to Vidhan Bhavan in a bus. Before the Vidhan Sabha could assemble, Padmakar Valvi escaped under the pretext of using the bathroom and met Speaker Arun Gujrathi. After Valvi complained that his life was under threat, Gujrathi ordered him to be protected by the marshals of the House. Gujrathi also declared seven MLAs of the NCP and the Janata Dal (Secular) JDS parties as ineligible to vote during the trust motion. Five PWP members abstained from the voting. This brought down the majority figure to 138 from 145. Vilasrao Deshmukh won with 143 votes in favour, while 133 MLAs voted against him. Rane's plan to topple the Deshmukh government was thus foiled.

After Deshmukh won the trust motion, jubilant NCP and Congress workers began celebrations outside Vidhan Bhavan. This enraged Rane further, and a violent clash between the celebrating workers and his men ensued. An angry CM Deshmukh called up Police Commissioner M.N. Singh and thundered, 'Singh, we are in the government, but our men are getting beaten up. What are you doing?'[19]

After being reprimanded by Deshmukh, Singh reached the road outside Mantralaya, which had, by then, turned into a battleground. He noticed that most of the rioters were hiding inside Narayan Rane's bungalow on the side of the road. An enraged Singh entered the bungalow and warned, 'Mr Rane, I am giving you five minutes to stop this. After that, my men will enter the bungalow.'

'Don't raise your voice, Singh. Don't you know I am the former CM of Maharashtra?' Rane retorted aggressively.

'I am not here on a courtesy call, Mr Rane. Ask your men to disperse. This is my order.' Singh was firm.[20]

His warning worked, and the riots ended.

Narayan Rane's 'Operation Topple' failed. In his autobiography, titled *No Holds Barred*, Rane blamed Uddhav Thackeray and Gopinath Munde for its failure. According to him, Thackeray didn't take much interest in the operation, while Munde, although part of the saffron alliance, acted as a mole for the opponents.[21]

More Revolts in the Shiv Sena

The defection of Chhagan Bhujbal to the Congress was the first rebellion in the Shiv Sena, and around fifteen years later, the party saw another major rebellion with Narayan Rane as its fore.

Rane began losing his grip on the party when Uddhav Thackeray started taking part in the party's affairs. The first spark of hostility between Uddhav and Rane can be traced back to 1999, when Uddhav replaced fifteen Vidhan Sabha election candidates recommended by Rane. In 2003, their relationship soured further when Uddhav was anointed the executive president of the Shiv Sena.

Rane felt sidelined from important party meetings and the decision-making processes. He didn't receive adequate support from Uddhav in his operation to topple the Vilasrao Deshmukh–led Congress–NCP government. Rane was disregarded during the party's ticket distribution strategy for the 2004 Vidhan Sabha elections, and his loyalists were denied candidature. He suspected Manohar Joshi and Subhash Desai of conspiring against him, leading to his animosity with Uddhav. He was also peeved about the attention that Milind Narvekar, Uddhav's personal assistant, was receiving in the party. Rane brought up the topic of his humiliation to Bal Thackeray, which, as reported by Rane, even led to a heated argument between Bal Thackeray and his son, Uddhav. In a fit of rage, Uddhav threatened to leave Matoshri with his wife.[22]

Rane could no longer contain his anguish. At a party meeting held in 2005, he minced no words while speaking against Uddhav and his loyalists. He alleged that the party tickets were sold under Narvekar's supervision. The Shiv Sena then expelled Rane. He joined the Congress and was appointed as a minister. According to Rane, he was also assured that the party would consider him for chief ministership.

Narayan Rane's rebellion was followed by Raj Thackeray's a few months later. Bal Thackeray's nephew, Raj, had actively engaged in politics since the late 1980s, as an in-charge of the party's student wing, Bhartiya Vidyarthi Sena. He displayed an aggression that resembled his uncle's and had similar fiery oratory skills. He was grooming himself to be Bal Thackeray's successor. However, Uddhav, the youngest of Thackeray's three sons, also began taking an active interest in the party affairs by the early 1990s. Contrary to Raj, Uddhav was soft-spoken and shy. Their ideas and style of functioning differed, and the Shiv Sena was soon divided into two camps.

The Ramesh Kini case of 1996 marked a turning point in Raj's career. Although he got a clean chit in the case, his clout diminished in the party. Some of his detractors criticized his lavish lifestyle and the company he kept. At the same time, Uddhav began volunteering more assertively in the party's decision-making. Like Narayan Rane, Raj, too, started feeling sidelined. His loyalists were denied tickets in various elections and were not given any important posts in party. Preference was given to Uddhav's men in appointing chiefs of state-run corporations when the saffron government was in power. In the 2002 BMC elections, Raj's loyalists were once again ignored and didn't get any party tickets.

The situation worsened for Raj when Uddhav was anointed as ageing Bal Thackeray's successor. Raj openly opposed Uddhav's policies and programmes. One such programme was

'Me Mumbaikar', wherein Uddhav sought to bring all citizens of Mumbai—irrespective of their regional and linguistic background—close to the Shiv Sena. Uddhav also launched the Hindi edition of *Saamana* to build bridges with the north Indian community. On the contrary, Raj's men attacked north Indian candidates for a railway exam at the Kalyan railway station, sabotaging Uddhav's idea of inclusiveness.

Feeling suffocated under Uddhav's shadow, Raj announced his resignation from the Shiv Sena in November 2005. Four months later, in March 2006, he founded his own political party, the Maharashtra Navnirman Sena (MNS). The party adopted 'sons of soil' as its agenda, and staged violent attacks on people from Uttar Pradesh and Bihar. In the 2009 Vidhan Sabha elections, though the MNS won only thirteen seats, it led to the defeat of many Shiv Sena candidates because of a division of traditional Marathi votes. Regional politics couldn't help the MNS in subsequent elections, and the party couldn't win over one seat in the 2014 and 2019 elections. Raj Thackeray reflected on the potential causes and adopted Hindutva as his party's ideology in 2020.

The Biggest Revolt

The Shiv Sena faced its biggest coup in June 2022 when its stalwart, Eknath Shinde, rebelled along with forty MLAs of the party. The drama ensued for eleven days, in which Shinde and the rebels travelled to Gujarat, Assam and Goa, the states ruled by the BJP. Governor Bhagat Singh Koshyari ordered CM Uddhav Thackeray to go for a floor test in Vidhan Sabha, which was challenged in the Supreme Court. However, after getting no reprieve from the court, Thackeray resigned. On 30 June, in a hastily arranged swearing-in ceremony, Shinde took oath as the CM of Maharashtra. BJP leader Devendra Fadnavis became the deputy CM. Differing from the previous coups, the revolt by Shinde was the biggest blow to the party, and it threatened to snatch away control of the Shiv Sena from the Thackeray family.

There were several factors that led to Shinde's rebellion. Most of the rebels were unhappy with the Maha Vikas Aghadi government formed in November 2019 following a drama that continued for over a month. The rebels complained that by aligning with parties like the Congress and the NCP, which conflicted with the Shiv Sena's Hindutva, Uddhav Thackeray made an unnatural alliance. They felt the NCP was dominating the government and was clandestinely working towards finishing the Shiv Sena and getting hold of important portfolios such as finance, home, housing and so on in the government. Shinde's ambition to become the CM, too, had a role to play. He was one of the most resourceful leaders in the party, with both muscle and money power, and had clout across Maharashtra. The rise of Uddhav's son Aditya's clout in the party and the government was also resented by Shinde. Aditya was a minister in Thackeray's cabinet. Uddhav Thackeray's inaccessibility was also cited as one of the major causes of the revolt. It was alleged that Thackeray lost connect with party leaders and was confined to a coterie of men who advised him. Uddhav's camp defended his limited interaction with people by attributing it to his health issues. The BJP, which felt betrayed by Uddhav Thackeray in 2019, was also waiting for a chance to seize power. After Shinde conveyed his decision to part ways with Uddhav to the BJP, the party's central leadership, guided by Home Minister Amit Shah, swung into action and engineered the coup.

It was not just a group of forty (out of fifty-five) Shiv Sena MLAs that announced allegiance to Shinde, but the coup spread to the Parliament as well. On 19 July 2022, twelve members of Parliament from the Shiv Sena in the Lok Sabha announced their support of Shinde. Many former corporators from various municipal corporations—like Thane, Navi Mumbai, Kalyan-Dombivali, Mira-Bhayandar and Aurangabad—and a few others from Mumbai, joined the Shinde camp. The Shiv Sena's many office-bearers of different ranks, too, left Uddhav and joined the rebels. Shinde announced that the 'real Shiv Sena', which adhered to Bal Thackeray's Hindutva ideology, was with him and notified the Election Commission of the same.

During the whole political fiasco, two things intrigued political pundits—the BJP's support of Eknath Shinde, who had a fewer number of MLAs than the BJP as the CM, and demoting a stalwart like Devendra Fadnavis to the deputy CM's post, who had had the experience of working as the CM twice. The party insiders explained to me that both the decisions were taken considering the long-term strategy of the BJP, especially the 2024 Lok Sabha elections. The BJP didn't have a strong Maratha face, which is a politically dominant community in Maharashtra. By installing Shinde as the CM, who is a Maratha, the BJP strategized to win over the community. Fadnavis was asked to swear in as deputy CM because the party wanted to keep its control over the government, and there appeared no better person than Fadnavis, who had good administrative expertise and knew how to control the bureaucracy.

11

Pramod Mahajan: The Man, His Murder and His Politics

IT WAS AROUND 9.15 A.M. ON 22 APRIL 2006 WHEN THE thud and jerk of the plane's touch down at the Mumbai airport awakened me. I had barely slept the previous night. The anchor shoot for my crime show, *Red Alert,* in Delhi had extended till 5 a.m., post which I immediately rushed to catch my flight back home to Mumbai. Amid a few crying babies on board, some snoring passengers and an irritating migraine, I struggled to steal a nap.

As soon as I switched on my phone upon landing, I received a panic-stricken call from a source in the BJP: 'Sir, Pramod Mahajan has been shot dead!'

My exhaustion vanished, and I immediately rang the local DCP to check the veracity of what I had just heard. His phone was constantly engaged that morning.

As I thought about whom I could contact next, Vinod Tawde's name instantly occurred to me. Tawde was a BJP leader and often consulted me on matters of organized crime to take them up in the legislature. He confirmed that Pramod Mahajan had indeed been shot and had been rushed to hospital. He was still alive. A source at the Worli police station, under whose jurisdiction Mahajan's residence fell, also confirmed the news and offered some more information. Pramod Mahajan had been shot by none other than his younger brother, Pravin. I headed directly to Poorna Building at Worli, where Pramod Mahajan lived on the fourteenth floor.

At around 10 a.m., my channel broke the shocking news to the nation. In a phono to my channel, I recounted whatever I had gathered so far about the incident. Soon, the lane outside Poorna Building saw a flood of mediapersons and OB vans queued up on the road.

That morning, at around 7.30 a.m., Pravin Mahajan had reached Pramod's living room when the latter was engrossed reading a newspaper. Pramod's wife, Rekha, and a helper, Harish, who were also present in the room till then, went to the kitchen to prepare tea. Pravin wanted to talk to Pramod, but while he spoke, Pramod didn't acknowledge his presence and continued reading the paper. An enraged Pravin impulsively took out his licensed F.N. Browning 0.32 bore pistol and fired three shots at Pramod's abdomen.

Pravin then straightaway went to the nearby Worli police station and surrendered. His confession left the officers numb, and they took a while to determine their response.

Meanwhile, Pramod Mahajan was rushed to P.N. Hinduja Hospital by Gopinath Munde, his brother-in-law and BJP colleague, who stayed in the same building.

On his way to the hospital, a conscious Mahajan asked Munde, 'What was my mistake that Pravin shot me?'[1]

Soon, he lost consciousness. The bullets had damaged his liver and pancreas. A police team reached the hospital to record Pramod's statement, but the doctors informed them of his precarious condition. Despite availing the best medical arrangements, and after battling for his life for several days, Pramod was finally declared dead at 4.10 p.m. on 3 May—the flag at the state BJP office was lowered. His last words to Munde were taken as his dying declaration. His death marked the end of an era in BJP history.

PM Who Aspired to Be 'The PM'

Referred to as PM in the political corridors, Pramod Mahajan was one of the most prominent faces of Indian politics during the 1990s and would have been a man of consequence now, had he been alive. He joined the RSS and became a worker of the BJP when he was still relatively young. With excellent oratory, organizational and interpersonal skills, he swiftly rose through the party ranks. He was the one who planned and coordinated Lal Krishna Advani's rath yatra in 1990. In the later years, he grew close to Atal Bihari Vajpayee as well. During Vajpayee's tenure as PM, Mahajan became his one-point contact. After Lal Krishna Advani, Atal Bihari Vajpayee and Murli Manohar Joshi, Mahajan belonged to the second generation of BJP leaders, along with Arun Jaitley, Sushma Swaraj, Rajnath Singh and others.

Abhimanyu Shitole, political editor of *Navbharat Times*, said, 'Mahajan spoke to Mamata Banerjee in West Bengal, Jayalalithaa in Tamil Nadu and Chandrababu Naidu in Andhra Pradesh. He brought all those parties to the fold of the NDA, who considered the BJP to be untouchable due to its Hindutva stance.'[2]

Mahajan networked with some of the top industrialists of the country and is credited for introducing the 'five-star culture' in the BJP—which displeased the RSS, for it opposed Mahajan's ostentatious lifestyle. In turn, Mahajan disapproved of many RSS ideologies. In a lighter vein, he often ridiculed RSS veterans by saying, 'These old and unmarried people have nothing else to do in life. Hence, they keep arranging meetings.'[3]

In 1998, when Vajpayee became PM for the second time, Mahajan was appointed as his advisor. During this time, Mahajan began nurturing his ambition of becoming the PM himself. Veteran journalist Vageesh Sarawat recollects an off-the-record interaction, wherein some journalists questioned him about who could be the next PM from the BJP, to which Mahajan smiled and countered, 'Who else is the option?' In his autobiography, *Majha Album*, Pravin Mahajan too elaborated on his older brother's ambition of becoming the PM.

Mahajan's aspirations received a setback in 2003, when he was removed as the minister of communications and information technology from Vajpayee's Cabinet and assigned to look after the BJP's organizational affairs. His name had cropped up in many controversies by then, like the murder of journalist Shivani Bhatnagar and disputed dealings with a major telecom company when he was telecommunications minister.[4] Apart from these controversies, Mahajan's ouster was also seen as an outcome of the intra-party rivalry between the Advani and Vajpayee camps. Narendra Modi, who was then chief minister of Gujarat, was close to Advani. During the 2002 Gujarat riots, PM Vajpayee publicly taunted Modi to follow the Rajdharma.[5] Modi's supporters believed it was Mahajan who instigated Vajpayee to make such a comment.

In 2004, Mahajan was made in charge of the BJP's Lok Sabha election campaign, 'India Shining', which failed to bring the BJP into power a third time. However, those who know Pramod Mahajan believe he had a resilient spirit and would have bounced back soon. Had he been alive, Indian politics would have appeared different today. 'I doubt if Mahajan would have accepted subordination to Modi, like Arun Jaitley, Sushma Swaraj, Rajnath Singh and others did,' remarks Shitole.[6]

Relationship with Shiv Sena

Mahajan had brought the Shiv Sena and the BJP together in Maharashtra, and was known as the architect of the saffron alliance. Whenever any issue arose between the two parties and Bal Thackeray expressed his displeasure, Mahajan knew the tactics to placate him. Based on Pramod Mahajan's suggestion, some senior BJP leader, such as Atal Bihari Vajpayee or L.K. Advani, would visit Thackeray's bungalow, Matoshri, after which his temper would inevitably cool down. However, the situation changed when Uddhav started becoming powerful in the Shiv Sena and realized that Mahajan was taking undue advantage of Thackeray's trust in him.[7]

During the Rama temple campaign, Bal Thackeray's popularity as a firebrand Hindu leader spread beyond Maharashtra as well. Nandu Satam, former mayor of Bombay, who went to Ayodhya on 6 December 1992 with a group of Shiv Sena corporators, recollects that north Indians were crazy about Thackeray. Whenever any helicopter passed over Ayodhya, people would shout, 'Balasaheb! Balasaheb!' assuming that Thackeray would visit Ayodhya to supervise the demolition.[8]

The leadership of the Shiv Sena wanted to expand the party beyond Maharashtra, and was even successful in winning its first-ever MLA seat outside the state—in Uttar Pradesh. But to establish a party, Thackeray needed to visit Uttar Pradesh, and participate in rallies and public meetings. During the NDA rule at the Centre, whenever Thackeray contemplated going outside Maharashtra, Mahajan dissuaded him by citing inputs from the

Intelligence Bureau, claiming that there was a threat to his life. The tour was cancelled immediately.[9]

Was dissuading Thackeray a ploy to limit the Shiv Sena's expansion? Was it a trick to prevent the party from becoming BJP's rival at the national level? Whatever the truth may be, Uddhav Thackeray had begun disliking Mahajan and Mahajan knew that. Prem Shukla, the executive editor of *Saamana's* Hindi edition who became a BJP spokesperson later, states, 'Once, when I sought an interview with Mahajan, he asked me where I would publish the interview. I replied obviously in *Saamana*. To that he said, "Your Uddhav will not allow you to publish my interview in his newspaper." Mahajan told me that Uddhav and he were not on speaking terms since the 2004 Lok Sabha elections, and Uddhav had stopped receiving his phone calls.'[10]

Sanjay Nirupam was the executive editor of Hindi *Saamana* before Shukla. He wrote a series of articles against Mahajan—over how he opposed the proposal of the Tata–Singapore Airlines joint venture in Parliament to save the interests of Jet Airways. One morning, Bal Thackeray rang the Hindi *Saamana's* office. The call was received by senior sub-editor Abhimanyu Shitole.

'Where is Nirupam?' Thackeray asked, sounding furious.

'Sir, he has not yet come in.'

'Why is he writing against Pramod Mahajan? Doesn't he know that his party is our alliance partner? Tell him not to write anything against Mahajan,' he thundered before disconnecting the call.

Ten minutes later, Thackeray called again. This time, too, Shitole received the call. Thackeray spoke gently: 'Ignore what I said in my previous call. That Mahajan came to my residence, and started crying and complaining. So, to stop him, I said those things in the last call. Tell Nirupam to write whatever he wants to write. I have no objection.'[11]

Nirupam once told me, 'Balasaheb never reprimanded me for anything I wrote against the BJP.'[12]

'Pramod Mahajan Would Have Been Alive if ...'

'Pramod Mahajan would have been alive today had he affectionately patted his brother's back that morning. It would have calmed Pravin's rage, and he would not have shot Pramod.'[13] This is the opinion of the man who investigated one of the most sensational murder cases in India. Inspector Anil Mecwan mysteriously resigned from Mumbai Police as soon as he finished preparing the charge sheet of the Pramod Mahajan murder case in 2006. Fifteen years later, I traced the elusive inspector. After his resignation, Mecwan joined Star India as its vice-president (internal affairs). He rarely entertained journalists, but, being his former colleague from the same group, he favoured me. He agreed to share his observations, and we met one afternoon in January 2022 at a coffee shop near St. Carmel Church, Bandra. Mecwan said he was a law graduate and resigned from the police force to become financially better off by working in the corporate sector as a legal consultant.

'Pravin Mahajan was interrogated for two hours every day while he was in police custody. My behaviour with him was not like a regular police officer's. I was never harsh with him, and, in fact, tried to make him comfortable by behaving in a friendly manner and getting him breakfast of his choice. I wanted to understand the case from his point of view,' said Mecwan.[14]

Pravin became friendly with Mecwan and spoke his heart to him, which offered the cop insights into the relationship between the brothers.

'After Pramod Mahajan's murder, there was so much speculation, and many strange theories floated around, but all that is rubbish.

Through my interactions with Pravin, I understand he murdered Pramod because he felt he was denied of his entitlement,' said Mecwan.[15]

Pravin informed the cop that after their father's death, the family had been through some tough times and had suffered immensely. Pramod had four siblings—two sisters and two brothers. As the eldest of the brothers, Pramod became the head of the family at a very young age. The family prospered as Pramod flourished in politics. Initially, Pravin handled Pramod's finances, but after his older brother's daughter, Poonam, married Anand Rao, Pravin felt sidelined, and many people who were close to Pramod, like his secretary Vivek Moitra, irked him.

'If we have suffered penury together, we must enjoy prosperity together,' Pravin told Mecwan.[16]

Pravin admitted to Mecwan that his family survived on the regular flow of income that Pramod had arranged for them. However, he also felt that Pramod humiliated him.

'Pramod neither gave him respect nor brotherly affection. Hence, one day, Pravin decided to teach Pramod a lesson,' said Mecwan. That's when the shooting happened.[17]

Mecwan recollects that Mahajan's family was very inquisitive about everything that Pravin said in police custody and kept a tab on the investigation. They had never guessed that Pravin could go to such an extent. In the trial, Pravin made many sensational disclosures, which prompted the court to record his statement in-camera. Since the trial court prevented the media from making them public, many facts regarding the case remain undisclosed.

Pravin was convicted for Pramod's murder in 2007 and was awarded life imprisonment. Two years later, he published his autobiography *Majha Album,* which reflects his hatred for Pramod and his hostile views towards other relatives, like Gopinath Munde.

Series of Bad News

Pramod Mahajan's murder was followed by a series of ill-fated events in the family. On 2 June 2006, just a month after his death, his secretary, Vivek Moitra, his son, Rahul, and three other people had gathered at Mahajan's bungalow at 7 Safdarjung Road. Delhi Police recovered a bottle of champagne and some white powder from the scene. Moitra had died, while Rahul Mahajan was found in an unconscious state and was admitted to a hospital.[18]

Four years later, on 3 March 2010, Pravin died in a Thane hospital from a brain haemorrhage. He had come out of jail on parole. Except his elder brother, Prakash, nobody from the Munde–Mahajan family attended his funeral.

On 3 June 2014, shortly after taking oath as the Union minister for rural welfare, Gopinath Munde's Maruti SX4 was hit by another car that had jumped a signal. Munde's liver got ruptured in the accident, and he suffered a massive heart attack because of the shock.

By the time he was brought to AIIMS by his driver and assistant, he was declared dead. The following day, his body was taken to Parli in the Beed district of Maharashtra for the funeral. A riot broke out at the cremation ground, and Munde's supporters burnt a few police vehicles, suspecting that he had been murdered. Eventually, the case went to the CBI, which ruled out any foul play in its charge sheet against the driver whose taxi had hit Munde's car.

Maharashtra Politics after Mahajan

Pramod Mahajan was remembered by the political circles in Maharashtra when there was turmoil in the state after the 2019 Vidhan Sabha elections. Although the Shiv Sena and the BJP fought the elections together and won enough seats to form the government, a dispute broke out between the two over who would get the CM's chair. Shiv Sena chief, Uddhav Thackeray, claimed that the BJP had promised him the coveted position for half of the tenure, but Devendra Fadnavis from the BJP denied this. The political drama in the state continued for thirty-five days after the election results were declared in October, and ended when the Shiv Sena joined hands with its political opponents, the NCP and the Congress, and formed a tri-party government. Uddhav Thackeray became the chief minister, and the alliance was named the 'Maha Vikas Aghadi'.

The dispute over the CM's chair was an immediate cause for the divorce between the two parties. Several other issues piled up over the years too. Pramod Mahajan's presence would have certainly taken Maharashtra politics down a different route. Many unfortunate circumstances may have been avoided. Perhaps the saffron alliance would not have ended either, as Mahajan would have worked out a suitable compromise between the parties. With the murder of Pramod Mahajan, the BJP lost a troubleshooter both at the national and state level.

12

Terror Returns

MUMBAI HAS OFTEN FELT THE REPERCUSSIONS OF events in other parts of the globe. Ayatollah Khomeini issues a fatwa against Salman Rushdie in Tehran, a riot happens in Bombay. Babri Masjid is demolished in Ayodhya, Bombay burns. Rohingyas are oppressed in Myanmar, violence shakes the streets of Mumbai. One aspect of the 26/11 attack was linked with the Israel–Palestine conflict, when the terrorists attacked a Jewish centre in Mumbai. Similarly, when the communal riots burnt Gujarat, Mumbai had to face the repercussions.

Riots in Gujarat, Blasts in Mumbai

On 27 February 2002, a coach of the Sabarmati Express caught fire near the Godhra railway station of Gujarat. Fifty-nine people, including a few karsevaks and pilgrims returning from Ayodhya, died in the incident. Every inquiry yielded a different cause for the fire: the state government concluded that it was an act of arson, while the Centre described it as an accident. The episode triggered unprecedented riots and violence across Gujarat from that day onwards, which continued for about a year, leading to over 1,000 killings. Cities like Ahmedabad, Vadodara and Surat were the worst affected.

Around 6.45 p.m. on 2 December the same year, the rear of a BEST bus was ripped apart by a loud explosion when passengers vacated it at a depot outside the Ghatkopar railway station. Two people died and over fifty were injured. The same evening, an unexploded bomb was discovered on another bus in Andheri.

Four days later, on 6 December 2002, another explosion took place at a McDonald's outlet in the Mumbai Central railway station and left twenty-seven people injured. This blast marked the tenth anniversary of the Babri Masjid's demolition.

The new year didn't bring any relief to the Mumbai Police. Another bomb blast at a crowded market outside the Vile Parle railway station killed one person and injured twenty-eight others on 27 January 2003. This was despite heavy security arrangements being deployed across the city, considering PM Vajpayee's visit on the following day.

Yet another bomb blast on 13 March 2003, in the first-class ladies' compartment of a local train at the Mulund railway station, killed twelve women and injured seventy-one others. The police found some leads this time, and a gang of alleged terrorists from Thane was busted. The suspects were linked with the Students Islamic Movement of India (SIMI), an outfit banned by the Indian government. Mumbai breathed a sigh of relief for a few months after the arrests, but it was short-lived. On 28 July, a bomb explosion in a BEST bus at Ghatkopar killed two and injured sixty.

Five bomb blasts in eight months! The conspirators had targeted public transportation during the evening peak hours. All the locations had an appreciable number of Gujaratis. That Gujaratis had been picked out was also confirmed by a threatening email received by a local cable news channel one day before the Ghatkopar blast from an organization called the Gujarat Muslim Revenge Force (GMRF). The media was sceptical over the arrests made from Thane, questioning whether the cops had apprehended the real culprits or the city was still at risk.

Twin Blasts

It was just another ordinary day at home on 25 August 2003. My grandmother was preparing lunch, and I was sharing some story from the underworld with my twelve-year-old cousin Ajay. At 12.40 p.m., there was a sudden and incredibly loud sound—like an enormous crash of thunder. Another bomb blast!

A cloud of black smoke and a rush of fleeing people followed. The explosion seemed to have taken place somewhere around the Mumbadevi temple, from where Ajay had just returned—he had been saved by minutes. Soon, we learnt that a powerful bomb planted in a taxi had exploded near the temple. As the police had barricaded the entire area, only ambulances and fire engines had direct passage. I walked about half a kilometre to reach the road leading to Mumbadevi.

The constantly busy junction outside the temple was devastated, with burning body parts scattered all around. Countless people had been slaughtered within seconds, and several more were injured. A man lay in a heap of bodies, crying helplessly, while clutching a picture of his wife and child. After failing to find them in hospitals and mortuaries, he had come looking for their remains at the blast spot. His grief-stricken face continues to be one of the most painful sights I've ever seen.

Panic increased in the city as the news spread. Mobile phone networks were jammed since everybody was calling their loved ones to make sure they were safe. This incident brought back memories of the serial blasts ten years ago.

There were rumours that four bombs had exploded across the city. However, just one more bomb went off half an hour later at 1.07 p.m. at the parking station of the Gateway of India. The bomb had been planted in a taxi, and it killed sixteen people and injured forty-six. The taxi was smashed, with debris falling several metres away. The glass windows of the Taj Mahal Hotel, which stands opposite the Gateway of India, were shattered. The nearby pigeon-feeding spot was covered with human body parts and pigeon carcasses.

This time, instead of mass transportation locations, the perpetrators had targeted the noteworthy landmarks of the city—Mumbadevi temple, the sacred space of the presiding deity of the city, and the Gateway of India, a monument of historic significance. Once again, the GMRF had emailed a TV channel prior to the blasts.

Shivnarayan Pande, the driver of the taxi in which the bomb was planted at the Gateway of India, survived the blast by sheer luck. Just before the bomb kept in his taxi exploded, he left to visit a bathroom. He informed the cops about a couple who had hired him from Andheri for a tour that day and asked him to take them to the Gateway of India. One link led to another, and finally, more names came to light. The man who hired the taxi to the Mumbadevi Temple was Ashrat, and the couple whom taxi driver mentioned were Hanif and Fehmida. All the suspects were arrested. The prime conspirator of the twin blasts, Nasir, was killed in a police encounter at Dadar a few days later.

Interrogation of the suspects revealed that GMRF was the brainchild of the Pakistan-based terrorist organization Lashkar-e-Taiba (LeT). Operatives of LeT scouted for skilled and semi-skilled Indian workers who went to the UAE and other Gulf countries for work. The gullible ones would be brainwashed with gruesome pictures from the Gujarat riots and the Babri mosque demolition. They would be paid an astronomical sum of money and be sent back to India as one of LeT's sleeper cells. The investigation disclosed that the GMRF had planned more blasts at the Mumbai airport, the Mumbai Police headquarters, the Bhabha Atomic Research Centre and multiple spots hosting Navratri celebrations.

I met the taxi driver whose input eventually led to cracking the case—Shivnarayan Pande—briefly outside the police commissioner's cabin, but couldn't interview him as the cops whisked him away after noticing me interacting with him. I saw him again a few years later when he appeared to testify before the court. He was kept undercover by the cops all those years in a rare case where an investigation agency undertook a witness protection programme. Pande fearlessly gave his deposition. The court awarded death sentences to Ashrat, Hamid and Fehmida in 2009.

The dawn of the new century had brought a new challenge for Mumbai Police. The underworld's grip over the city had loosened, but it was being replaced by terrorism, which was harder to deal with. The gangsters worked for money and had criminal backgrounds, but the terrorists were radicalized youngsters with minimal or no criminal records, and many of them were well educated. In Mumbai, terror attacks almost became a monthly event. Although an Anti-Terrorism Squad was established, a lot still needed to be done in terms of training and coordination with other state and central agencies.

Lifeless in Lifeline

On Tuesday, 11 July 2006, I had taken a compensatory day off from work because I had been on duty the previous Sunday and

Monday. Some miscreants had desecrated the statue of Meenatai, wife of Bal Thackeray, at Shivaji Park. This enraged the Shiv Sainiks, and they had gone on a rampage. On Monday, I was doing a follow-up story on the violence. It was only on Tuesday that I finally got a day off. I planned a relaxed evening at south Mumbai's New Excelsior Cinema where the new Hrithik Roshan movie *Krrish* was being screened.

Just as the movie began, my mobile phone rang.

'JEETU BHAI! A bomb has exploded in a train outside my building! There is chaos all around! Many people have been killed. Send a camera unit fast,' Odysteven Gomes, the operations manager at Star News, screamed over the phone.

Gomes lived in Khar, next to the railway tracks. Being an employee of a news organization, his immediate response to the event was to alert me. Back then, all mobile phones didn't have cameras, and a camera team had to be dispatched to the location to cover the incident. I hastily left the cinema hall and rang the cops to get more details. Six more bomb blasts had taken place in first-class compartments of different local trains. After informing my office and directing camera teams to reach the spots, I rushed to Matunga Road, one of the nearest blast locations.

It started raining midway, and I reached the station entirely drenched. My cameraman was already there. The metal body of the train was completely mangled, and its pieces had scattered with bone, blood and flesh. Locals gathered to help, but the intense rains hindered rescue operations.

Since all the affected trains ran on the Western Line, I could apprehend that the conspiracy was another attempt by a terrorist organization to avenge the Gujarat riots. The Western Line connects suburbs such as Khar, Santacruz, Vile Parle, Goregaon, Malad, Kandivali, Borivali, Mira Road and Bhayandar, which are densely populated by Gujaratis. The bombs exploded after

6 p.m., when the Bombay Stock Exchange shuts down and the stockbrokers, mostly Gujaratis, head to their homes along this line. The blasts' chronology showed that everything happened within eleven minutes. The first blast took place at 6.24 p.m. on the train heading towards Borivali near Khar station. It was the blast that Odysteven Gomes had witnessed.

This was followed by six others in trains near or within the premises of Matunga Road, Mahim, Bandra, Jogeshwari and Khar stations. The last bomb went off at 6.35 p.m. on a Virar-bound local train near Borivali. It took over a week to ascertain the total number of casualties, which turned out to be 209. Over 700 passengers were injured. Among the dead was my favourite Hindi poet, Shyam Jwalamukhi, famous for his humorous and satirical work. Jwalamukhi was not a regular local train traveller, but boarded one that evening to return home from Thane after some work.

The Western Line became totally dysfunctional after this, which, in turn, affected traffic. All arterial roads from south Mumbai to the north-western suburbs were choked. People pushed themselves into overcrowded BEST buses and taxis to reach home. Many clung to trucks and pickup vans. Several people stayed back in their south Mumbai offices that night.

The investigations that followed ignited a controversy, with different investigating agencies coming up with different suspects. A week after the bombings, a Hindi TV channel received an email from a new organization named Lashkar-e-Qahhar, which claimed to be behind the blasts and threatened more in the future.

The Mumbai train blasts were a close replication of the blasts in Madrid in 2004 and London in 2005. On 11 March 2004, four bombs exploded on different local trains in Madrid within ten minutes, killing 191 people and injuring 1,800. The mass transit system of the capital city of Spain was attacked in the early morning rush hour, when people left home to commute to their place of work. Next year, on 7 July 2005, three bombs exploded in London's underground trains, and a fourth one exploded in a double-decker bus. Like Madrid, the mass transport system in London was also bombed during the morning rush. The blasts claimed fifty-two lives.

The Maharashtra ATS charged twelve people a few weeks later. It stated that the conspiracy had been engineered at the behest of the Pakistani agency ISI and executed by LeT with the help of SIMI. The bombs were placed in pressure cookers at slums in Govandi and then planted on trains. However, there was a twist to the story when, in 2008, the Mumbai Crime Branch arrested Sadiq Shaikh, an alleged member of the Indian Mujahideen, claiming that this terror outfit executed the conspiracy and that Sadiq had planted the bombs along with others.

In another contradiction to the ATS's theory, the Crime Branch claimed the bombs were assembled in a flat in Sewri. This led to scepticism: did the ATS arrest the wrong people under political pressure to show results? The ATS stood by its story. In 2015, five alleged planters of the bombs arrested by the ATS were awarded the death penalty, seven were imprisoned for life and one accused named Abdul Wahid was acquitted.

The Bus Hijacking

The year 2008 can easily qualify as the most blood-soaked one witnessed in the country. Cities such as Jaipur, Bengaluru, Ahmedabad, New Delhi and Guwahati were rocked by serial bombings, which killed hundreds and injured thousands. However, Mumbai remained peaceful, as no further terrorism-related incidents were reported after the train blasts of July 2006. Although the Indian Mujahideen, which confessed to many blasts across the nation, had links in Mumbai, the city remained safe.

The popular Bollywood song '*Ye Bambai shehar haadson ka shehar hai*' calls Mumbai a city of tragedies. True to its claim, Mumbai couldn't remain peaceful for long. After a lull of a few months, a wave of fear and anxiety hit the people of Mumbai.

On 27 October 2008, at around 10.30 a.m., news trickled in that a double-decker BEST bus numbered 332 had been hijacked at Kurla. Twelve passengers were reportedly taken hostage and one was shot. My immediate apprehension was that the Indian Mujahideen was back in Mumbai. I got a call from a source in the local police that the hijacker wanted to talk to the media. I hurriedly left for the spot, which was 14 kilometres away from my office at Mahalaxmi. My colleague Umesh Kumawat rushed towards the spot as well.

I was thrilled at the thought of acting as a hostage negotiator. In my mind, I began preparing an argument to convince the hijacker to release the hostages and surrender. However, by the time I reached Kurla, after negotiating a traffic jam, everything was over. The hostages had been rescued, the area around the bus had been cordoned off, the hijacker had been killed and his body was being taken to hospital. ACP Mohammed Javed was standing near the bus, still holding the emptied service revolver in his hand. He had first fired on the hijacker and led the police team inside the bus.

'When I entered the bus, I saw him holding a passenger and pointing his gun at him. I told him to surrender, but he didn't. What should I have done to save that passenger's life? I had to fire,' Javed explained to me.[1] The policeman and his team fired over a dozen bullets at the hijacker, of which three pierced his head and one ripped his heart.

The hijacker turned out to be a twenty-five-year-old youth named Kundan Singh, aka Rahul Raj, from Patna in Bihar. That year, after MNS chief Raj Thackeray was arrested on charges of giving provocative speeches against north Indians, his party workers had attacked several people from the north. A few people were lynched by violent mobs. North Indian youngsters, who came to Mumbai to appear in a railway recruitment exam, were thrashed.

An enraged Rahul Raj reached Mumbai with a country-made pistol and boarded the BEST bus at Saki Naka. When the bus reached Kurla, he brandished the pistol, took control of the bus and held several passengers hostage on the upper deck. Seeing the police approach, he started firing randomly, and one bullet hit a passenger. The people around heard him shouting from the window that he didn't intend to harm the passengers, but wanted to kill Raj Thackeray.

A bitter war of words between the politicians of Bihar and Maharashtra ensued. Bihari politicians across party lines condemned the encounter and alleged that no efforts were made by Mumbai Police to catch Rahul Raj alive. The Maharashtra government retorted that the police behaved according to the circumstances. A chief secretary-level probe was announced by the Maharashtra government, and some petitioners also approached the Supreme Court and Patna High Court.

Although the bus hijacking incident made the citizens of Mumbai fearful, especially those using public transport, it was a minor incident when compared to what the city had endured in the past. And, at the time, Mumbaikars had no idea that exactly a month later, an incident in their city would shake the world.

13

26/11: The Lessons Not Learnt

IT WAS AROUND 10.30 A.M. ON 14 SEPTEMBER 1946. THE morning bustle at south Bombay's Kalbadevi Road had just begun when two men in army fatigues alighted from a taxi near Tanman Cap Shop and began firing indiscriminately. Seven people were left dead and over twenty injured—all innocent pedestrians and shopkeepers.

Since Kalbadevi was a prime business district in Bombay, the incident sent a tremor of fear across the city.

Within the next two months, the prime suspects, Mirza Abdul Majid and Ghulam Ahmed, were arrested. They were soldiers in the British Indian Army, who were posted in Calcutta. Interrogations revealed that Majid and Ahmed had deserted their posts, stolen arms and ammunition, and fled to the city a week before the incident. After reaching Bombay, they hired a taxi from the Byculla Station to Kalbadevi and picked up a carton from a chawl in south Mumbai en route and then fired at the crowd. Some horses attached to Victorias, the prevalent mode of transport in that locality back then, too died from bullet injuries. Following the carnage, they pulled the taxi driver out and escaped with the vehicle.

The incident was seen as an outcome of communal hatred, since a fortnight before the carnage, a terrible riot had broken out in the city. Rioters of both the Hindu and Muslim communities went on a killing spree. Just a month prior, on 16 August 1946, Mohammed Ali Jinnah had declared 'Direct Action Day' to pursue his demand for a separate homeland for Muslims. Violent riots were triggered in different parts of India, and Bombay was no exception.

Nine months after the incident, the trial began before a special judge, and Majid and Ahmed were charged with both murder and attempt to murder. The judge concluded that there could be no other punishment than the death penalty for them.[1]

This was perhaps the first terrorist attack in Bombay where firearms had been used. What Bombay saw that day was repeated sixty-two years later, but at a far larger scale.

Don't Kill Him—He Is Evidence

Inspector Hemant Bawdhankar shot at Ismail Khan's forehead. Khan was in the driver's seat of the Skoda, and Ajmal Kasab sat beside him. As Bawdhankar pointed his revolver towards Kasab, Bawdhankar's colleague, Sanjay Govilkar, screamed, 'Stop, Bawdhya! Don't kill him; he is evidence! Let us catch him alive!'[2] Govilkar had himself been hit by Kasab's bullet a few seconds earlier, but his presence of mind at such a sensitive moment proved to be a boon for Mumbai Police.

It was the night of 26 November 2008. The D.B. Marg police station received an urgent instruction from the control room to conduct a *nakabandi* (security check by barricading the junction of a road) at Girgaon Chowpatty. There were shoot-outs by terrorists reported at several locations across south Mumbai, and two of the alleged perpetrators were tracked as heading towards Girgaon in a Skoda car snatched from a hotelier near Vidhan Bhavan. Accordingly, barricades were installed at the Girgaon Chowpatty junction on Marine Drive. The car was signalled to stop at the junction by cops. However, the occupants of the car, who were later identified as Ismail Khan and Ajmal Kasab, reacted violently.

In the ensuing encounter, Tukaram Omble, a police officer, was killed, and Inspector Govilkar was injured when a bullet brushed his waist. However, the encounter proved to be a turning point in the attack. The terrorist Ajmal Kasab was arrested, and he ended up spilling the beans about the whole conspiracy, which had rocked Mumbai. Ten armed Pakistani terrorists had executed immense damage in different parts of the city. Ismail Khan, killed by Bawdhankar's bullet, was the chief of the terror team.

Around 9.40 p.m. that same night, I was informed that a group of people had fired over fifty rounds of bullets at Colaba's Leopold Cafe. I assumed it was yet another gang war, but fifty rounds were too many, as gangsters typically don't shoot over four or five bullets at their targets. This seemed unusual. When I reached the spot, it became quite clear that this was an act of terror. The eyewitnesses told me that the gunmen had fired indiscriminately on customers sitting in the cafe. The empty pellets spread all over indicated that Kalashnikovs were used. I learnt that two of the gunmen had moved towards the nearby Taj Mahal Hotel, so I rushed in that direction.

There was an eerie silence at the front gate of the hotel facing the Gateway of India. The ever-present Sikh *durbans* were not visible. I rushed through the glass door and was stunned by the sight that met me. Several dead bodies lay in the corridor beside the reception. This famous hotel, frequented by the who's who of

India and celebrities from across the world, resembled a mortuary. Suddenly, I heard a few shots fired from an upper floor and felt it would be unsafe to move further down the corridor. A team of cops rushed inside the hotel, and I was asked to leave.

Soon, the news of such shoot-outs began pouring in from varied locations. The Oberoi-Trident Hotel, the Chhatrapati Shivaji Terminus (CST), Nariman House and Cama Hospital had been attacked, and people had been indiscriminately fired upon. It was clear that the targets were the famous landmarks of Mumbai. Some of them were frequented by the elite, others by the common people. After deputing all my reporters to the different locations of the attacks, I positioned myself outside the Taj Mahal Hotel. After a few minutes, flames and smoke were seen from the sixth floor. I could hear a young woman and children crying for help. Continuous phone calls from my reporters and sources in the police updated me about the situation across Mumbai.

The terrorists at the Taj Mahal Hotel were communicating with their allies in Pakistan using a hostage's mobile phone. Soon, the intelligence agencies intercepted these calls. The terrorists were mere robots, taking commands from their handlers in a control room in Karachi. Ajmal Kasab's arrest from the encounter site and his immediate interrogation helped the security agencies join the dots, and comprehend the conspiracy.

Kasab revealed that this attack on Mumbai had been planned in Pakistan by the LeT and Jamaat-ud-Dawah. Ten Pakistani youngsters were trained and sent in a boat from the outskirts of Karachi to the India–Pakistan maritime border, where they hijacked an Indian fishing trawler named *Kuber*. By the time they reached Mumbai, all five fishers, including the trawler's captain, had been killed. The youngsters covered the last leg of their journey on a dinghy and landed at the fishermen's colony near Cuffe Parade. They separated into pairs and reached various locations in taxis.

Bombs were planted in two of the taxis, which exploded a few minutes after the terrorists disembarked from them.

Mumbai Police were the first respondents to the situation, and were unequipped, confused and overwhelmed by the prevailing chaos. The situation was so chaotic that the police couldn't strategize, and Police Commissioner Hasoon Gafoor, who should have been at the command centre, went out on the field, while his junior joint commissioner, Rakesh Maria, took charge of the control room. In this situation, the Anti-Terrorism Squad Chief Hemant Karkare went on the ground to confront the terrorists in a Qualis car with Inspector Vijay Salaskar and Additional Commissioner Ashok Kamte. The car was ambushed near Cama Hospital, and all three were killed.

That's when my reporter Mayank Bhagwat called me up. 'I was standing at the Metro Cinema junction with other mediapersons and cops when a police Qualis came and fired at us. Constable Arun Chitte has been killed. He was standing beside me. Cameraman Anil Nirmal of ETV has lost a finger after being hit by a bullet,' said Mayank, sounding panicked. Only later was it revealed that the Qualis car in which Karkare, Kamte and Salaskar had been ambushed was now occupied by Ismail and Kasab. While passing through the Metro Cinema junction, Ismail had fired on the crowd. From the Metro junction, the duo drove towards Vidhan Bhavan, where they found that one of the tyres of the Qualis was punctured. They left the Qualis and got into a Skoda after threatening its owner at gunpoint. Both then drove towards the Girgaon Chowpatty junction, where a team of the DB Marg police station intercepted them.

Another instance of the police's disorganized response was how the Quick Response Team (QRT) of commandos was deployed. The QRT was trained to combat as a team and accomplish a particular mission. But that night, the QRT was disbanded, and the commandos deployed in twos or threes like regular policemen outside different attack locations.

Outside the Taj Mahal Hotel, I saw a team of Marine Commandos (MARCOS) rushing in. A few hours later, they were replaced by the National Security Guards (NSG), who arrived from Manesar near Delhi in the morning. A team of commandos was airdropped to free the hostages held inside the Jewish Cultural Centre at Nariman House. The encounter with the terrorists continued for fifty-nine long hours, and the operation finally concluded by 8 a.m. on 29 November, when the last terrorist at the Taj Hotel was killed. All other locations were cleared a day before.

At the end, 166 people had died, including police personnel and two NSG commandos. Over 200 people were injured, and the victims were from various nationalities and religions. The continuous coverage of around sixty hours affected me psychologically. Moreover, I learnt that the cries of the woman and children that I heard coming from the sixth floor of the hotel were that of Neeti, the wife of the hotel's general manager, Karambir Kang, and their two sons Uday and Samar, aged twelve and five respectively. They were stuck on the sixth floor of the hotel and had died of asphyxiation. Over the next few days, their cries and the sound of gunshots echoed in my head whenever I tried to sleep.

There was much public outrage when Chief Minister Vilasrao Deshmukh visited the Taj Mahal Hotel to assess the damage, and was accompanied by film-maker Ram Gopal Varma. A week later, Deshmukh lost his job and was replaced by Ashok Chavan. While addressing the media, Deputy Chief Minister R.R. Patil quoted a dialogue from a Bollywood movie, '*Bade bade shehron mein chhoti chhoti batein hoti rehti hain* (Such minor events keep happening in major cities).' His words led to another row and his eventual ouster. In the Central government, Shivraj Patil was replaced by P. Chidambaram as the home minister.

David Headley and His Girlfriend

A day after the 26/11 attacks, the *Times of India* published Ajmal Kasab's photos from the scene of the crime. Everybody was intrigued to see a *raksha sutra,* or the holy thread worn only by Hindus, tied to his wrist.

In October 2009, a year after the 26/11 attacks, a Pakistan-origin American named David Headley, in his fifties, was arrested at the Chicago airport after being tracked by the Federal Bureau of Investigation (FBI) for over two months. Interrogations revealed his association with the LeT and his role in the 26/11 attacks.

The LeT assigned Headley to select and capture on video the targets. He made seven trips to Mumbai, from 2007 to 2008, for this purpose. During his visits, Headley befriended Rahul, the son of veteran film-maker Mahesh Bhatt, and a gym trainer named Vilas Varak. He travelled across the city with them and visited many places. During one such visit to the famous Siddhivinayak temple, Headley purchased a few holy threads and took them to Pakistan with him. Ajmal Kasab and his associates landed in Mumbai wearing those threads, clearly to confuse investigators.

The intelligence agencies also found that Headley had befriended a woman in her mid-twenties, who ran a sweet shop in south Mumbai—close to Hotel Outram, where Headley stayed. He met her one day when he went to buy a pastry. She fell for the handsome, chivalrous and smooth-talking Headley, and the two began meeting frequently. The woman remained oblivious to the fact that she was being used for his diabolical designs. Whenever he went to scout a target, he would take her along. Moving around as a couple prevented any suspicions from falling on him, and Headley could easily take shots of the targets and note their GPS coordinates.

After Headley's arrest in Chicago, the woman was questioned by the investigators in Mumbai, but was not required to depose before the court. Headley agreed to become an approver in the case and voluntarily accepted his role in, and prior knowledge of, the 26/11 attacks. His deposition was recorded by a special court in Mumbai through a video-conferencing facility from the US prison in which he was kept.

Ajmal Kasab and His Hanging

Twenty-one-year-old Ajmal Kasab, the only terrorist to be captured alive, became the face of the carnage. He was born in Faridkot, Pakistan, and came in contact with the LeT through its political wing, Jamaat-ud-Dawah. Out of hundreds of recruits, he was one of the ten shortlisted to execute the Mumbai attacks. During his two months in custody with the Crime Branch, Kasab grew friendly with the officers. Inspector Ramesh Mahale, the investigating officer of the case, even brought new clothes for him. When Mahale told him that his actions could attract the death penalty, Kasab is said to have laughed. He said, 'Your courts have not been able to hang Afzal Guru for the last eight years; how will they hang me?'[3]

Kasab was then shifted to Arthur Road Jail. His trial was conducted in a courtroom constructed within the premises. Swati Sathe, the then jail superintendent, recollects that Kasab was familiar with Marathi: 'Once, when I referred to him as "*gaadhav*" while talking to a subordinate outside his cell, Kasab overheard it and asked my subordinate why I was calling him a donkey.'[4] His knowledge of the language was further confirmed when during the trial, he chose to answer in Marathi. To most of the questions asked by Judge M.L. Tahaliyani, he answered in Marathi, '*Mala mahit nahi* (I don't know)', and '*Me baghitla nahi* (I did not see)'. He had apparently been taught Marathi by a handler named Zabiuddin Ansari, aka Abu Jundal, who hailed from the Beed district of Maharashtra.

While covering the trial, I always noticed Kasab smiling and enjoying the court proceedings. He often made amusing comments, making everybody in the courtroom laugh. It was hard to imagine that he was the same boy who, along with his accomplice Ismail Khan, had mercilessly killed over sixty people, including children, women and elderly people at CST. Kept in a dark solitary confinement cell, he looked forward to the court hearings. He was also an important witness against the Pakistan-based conspirators in the case. Hence, anticipating a threat to his life, the security of the Arthur Road prison was assigned to the Indo-Tibetan Border Police (ITBP).

After Kasab was sentenced to death and his mercy petitions rejected, 21 November 2012 was fixed as his execution date, undisclosed to the public. Since there are no gallows at Arthur Road Jail, he was taken to Pune's Yerawada Jail. When Inspector Ramesh Mahale went to pick him up at the Arthur Road Jail, he told Kasab, 'You thought you would never be hanged. See your time has come.'

'You were right, Mahale saab,' Kasab told him, before he succumbed to his fate.[5]

Coastal Security

The attacks exposed many chinks in Mumbai's security system and counterterrorism mechanism. The biggest question pertained to coastal security, which failed to stop the intruders.

Maharashtra has a coastline of 720 kilometres, out of which 114 kilometres surround Mumbai. It was for the second time that death came to the city via the sea. The RDX for the 12 March 1993 serial blasts had also been smuggled in season boats. The Ram Pradhan Committee, appointed by the Maharashtra government to probe into lapses in the response by security agencies during the 26/11 attacks, made damning remarks about the complacent attitude of the government towards the intelligence alerts received. In its findings, the committee noted that despite six alerts issued between August 2006 and April 2008 by the Intelligence Bureau about a seaborne terrorist attack, nothing significant was done to mitigate the threat. There was a lack of coordination between Mumbai Police and the Coast Guard.

One year after the attacks, the then Mumbai police commissioner, D. Sivanandhan, invited me for a ride on one of the newly bought speedboats at the Gateway of India. He proudly showcased the measures taken by the police to avert any further attacks. Twenty Sealeg boats, costing Rs 20 lakh each, and twenty amphibian vehicles, costing Rs 40 lakh each, had been purchased. These boats were expected to chase and intercept infiltrators, and patrol the coastline. Four-hundred-and-fifty policemen were deployed for coastal security, and four marine police stations were set up.

In 2015, I did a follow-up story to check the efficiency of the initiatives undertaken during Sivanandhan's tenure. I was shocked to find that many of the boats had gathered dust and had become dysfunctional. Some needed major repairs, while spare parts of other boats were unavailable. The maintenance contract of the Sealeg boats had ended with the company. In August 2010, a constable named Ramesh More deployed on a patrolling boat had drowned. An audit report by the Comptroller and Auditor General (CAG) revealed that 57 per cent of the staff deployed for coastal security didn't know how to swim. Dhananjay Kulkarni, the then spokesman of Mumbai Police, responded to my report saying that efforts were being made to train the cops.[6]

The CAG report also exposed a 63.97 per cent deficiency in the number of personnel assigned for coastal security in Mumbai.[7] Coastal security has three layers. The first is manned by Mumbai Police, while the next two layers are assigned to the Coast Guard and the Navy.

When I shared my observations with K.P. Raghuvanshi, former ATS chief, he was riled. 'It was a knee-jerk reaction after the 26/11 attacks. Just procuring boats is not enough. You need to arrange a support system as well to sustain it. Was adequate provision for the supply of diesel to the boats made? Were workshops set up to repair the boats? They are gathering dust due to a lack of repairs. Many policemen have seasickness. Many don't know how to swim. If they can't save their own life, how will they save others?' Raghuvanshi asked.[8]

One positive development, though, was the strengthening of the on-ground response to future attacks. Mumbai was now equipped with three sets of commando forces. The QRTs were set up under each of the five regional additional commissioners of Mumbai Police. Another commando unit named Force One reported to the state police. The NSG also opened its west India hub in Mumbai to reduce response time. In a 26/11–like situation, the QRT is expected to be the first responder, followed by the other two.

A friend working for one such agency informed me that the aftermath of 26/11 saw increased multi-agency coordination. However, concerns remain over their ability to take swift action after intelligence is received.

Bulletproof Jackets Need 'Proof'

Wearing a bulletproof vest doesn't necessarily prevent a bullet from piercing the body, because different bulletproof jackets are resistant to different kinds of bullets. One may be effective against revolver or pistol bullets, but not an automatic rifle. Minutes before the ATS chief, Hemant Karkare, was killed, he was shown on TV wearing a bulletproof jacket. A report revealed that the quality of jackets that he and other policemen wore that night was not capable of protecting against shots fired from AK-47 rifles, but only pistol or revolver bullets, that too fired from a distance of 30 feet. These vests had been in use since 2004.[9]

Many years later, an RTI application revealed that Karkare's jacket had been thrown away by a ward boy at Sir J.J. Hospital. Anil Galgali, the activist who filed the RTI, believes that if Karkare's vest had been examined, it would have exposed a scam in the procurement of the vests.[10]

Ten years later, in 2018, the Maharashtra Police received 4,600 bulletproof vests worth Rs 17 crore. However, 1,432 of these jackets failed to protect from the test bullet fired from AK-47 rifles. After the tests, the jackets were returned to the manufacturers.[11]

Nowadays, one can find door-frame metal detectors at major local railway stations and baggage-screening machines at outstation train stations—both measures seem nothing more than a mockery in the name of security. Metal detectors are seldom used to check passengers entering the railway premises, and baggage screeners are not used to check the luggage of all passengers. Are these the measures we rely on to avert any major attacks in the future?

A consolation is that most of Mumbai is now under CCTV surveillance, which can help detect crime, gather evidence and, in some cases, even prevent harm.

New Challenges: Indian Mujahideen and ISIS

Mumbai saw the very worst terrorist violence during the 26/11 attacks. The actions and official announcements that followed created a sense of safety in the city. Counterterrorism became one of the top priorities of the Central and state governments. However, three years later, Mumbaikars' faith in the city's security apparatus was again questioned.

At around 7 p.m., on 13 July 2011, three bombs exploded at Opera House, Zaveri Bazaar and Dadar—all three crowded market areas. Twenty-seven people were killed and over 100 injured. Investigations revealed that the conspiracy of the triple blasts had been hatched by the Indian Mujahideen (IM), which was accused of conducting serial blasts across several cities in India, but it was their first attack in Mumbai.

Before Mumbai Police, the ATS, Delhi Police and other security agencies could bust the various modules of the IM and make the organization defunct, another challenge emerged: the Islamic State of Iraq and Syria (ISIS), also called Daesh. Mumbai became ISIS's recruiting ground. Muslim youth were radicalized and brainwashed through the internet to join the group's global jihad for setting up an Islamic Caliphate. They were asked to join the fight in Iraq, and those who couldn't leave the country were instigated to take up arms here itself.

One of the first news of radicalized youth leaving India for Iraq came in May 2014 from Kalyan, a town neighbouring Mumbai. Shamim Tanki, Fahad Shaikh, Aman Tandel and Arib Majid allegedly joined ISIS—they left along with a group of pilgrims going to Abu Dhabi, and from there made their way to Baghdad. Majid, a civil engineering student, returned a few months later and was arrested. There is no credible news about the other three.

In 2015, the ATS booked two youngsters named Mohsin Sayyed and Rizwan Ahmed for radicalizing youngsters and sending them to Iraq as *fidayeens*. In January 2022, the two shocked everyone by pleading guilty while the trial against them was still in progress. They confessed to being influenced by videos and the propaganda circulated online by ISIS, and now regretted their acts. The court accepted their pleas and sentenced them to eight years in jail.

In 2017, the state police started a deradicalization programme to prevent more youth from joining terror outfits. This initiative included friendly but firm psychological counselling of suspects. As per a report, by 2021, around 120 youngsters, including six women, have been deterred from getting radicalized. As per the programme, each candidate is assigned a 'Friend Officer', who tracks the candidate and keeps in touch with them. The programme has great scope, and other states are also considering implementing it.[12]

14

Nature's Revenge

TO 'RAIN LIKE 26 JULY' IS TO MUMBAI WHAT 'RAINING cats and dogs' is to the world, just a lot more intense and calamitous. Every Mumbaikar will remember where they were on 26 July 2005. The deluge witnessed that day and its aftermath are both etched deeply in the collective memory of the city, and is best remembered for when nature wreaked havoc and infrastructure broke down, leaving hundreds of people dead and thousands stranded.

26 July 2005

I was at the Bombay Sessions Court in south Mumbai's Fort area to cover a hearing. Till about 3 p.m., the sky was fairly clear: the sun was shining brightly, and the roads were echoing with the regular hustle and bustle of the city.

Coming out of the courtroom, I received a frantic call from my office: 'All other coverage to be dropped! Everybody to get on the rain coverage immediately!'

'Rain? Where is it raining? There are no rains here,' I told the desk in-charge.

'All areas beyond Bandra and Sion are submerged. Phone lines are not working. There is a ten kilometre–long jam from Mahim to Mahalaxmi. Vehicles are not able to move. The situation is worsening. Leave everything and focus on this coverage,' he instructed.

It immediately struck me that if the situation in the northern suburbs was so bad, it would affect local train services, which are an important link between south Mumbai and the northern suburbs. I rushed directly to CST. The station overflowed with people, even though the evening rush hour was yet to start. All the trains had been cancelled because of flooded tracks. The people living in the suburbs desperately wanted to return home as they could not contact their families. Hours passed, and the crowd at the station surged. There was no clarity over the restoration of train services. Some social organizations made arrangements at a few nearby schools and community halls for stranded passengers.

A team of my reporters spread across the suburbs in no time and began delivering nerve-wracking stories. Considering the magnitude of the calamity, the entertainment-beat reporters were also deployed along with the regular city reporters. Disturbing visuals of the deluge began pouring in at our Mahalaxmi studio, which was as yet unaffected, being in south Mumbai.

At Kala Nagar junction in Bandra, water reached the upper floor of a double-decker bus. The distressed passengers were now trying to climb on to the roof of the bus. Several children were stuck at school, and the lack of communication added to the anguish of their parents. Bal Thackeray, whose bungalow was located in Kala Nagar, was rescued by local Shiv Sainiks and taken to a hotel nearby. Mobile phone services had been disrupted in the flooded areas. My colleague Umesh Kumawat's car, which was parked at his

Kherwadi residence, was washed away and was found a kilometre away many days later. Many people died trapped inside their cars, as the water level rose too quickly for them to get out. Several submerged cars were recovered from the Irla Nullah in the Vile Parle area. Dead bodies were seen floating in Kurla. Water levels rose over 20 feet at the Air India colony at Kalina. Buildings were submerged up to the second floor. Residents climbed on to their terraces, fearing that their buildings would soon be completely submerged.

In areas like Khar, Santacruz, Goregaon and Malad, the *tabelas*, or animal farms, got totally submerged. Over 2,500 buffaloes tied inside drowned.[1] They could have probably survived had they been untied in time, but their panicked owners abandoned them and fled to save themselves. The Western Express Highway, which connects the island city to the western suburbs and further onwards to Gujarat, resembled a river. The basement studio of a TV channel in Goregaon looked like an underground water tank.

Mumbai was marooned. Chhatrapati Shivaji International Airport was inundated, and the water level had reached above the engines of the planes parked on the tarmac. The two runways of the airport had been submerged as well. The busiest airport in India was now completely shut. Over 700 flights were cancelled, and those arriving in Mumbai were diverted to other cities. Mumbai was soon disconnected from the world. Passengers who had just landed in Mumbai were stranded at the airport. The Andheri airport colony that housed employees of the Airports Authority of India was flooded too.

The city had received a record level of rainfall that day. The Santacruz centre of the India Meteorological Department (IMD) recorded a rainfall of 944 mm in twenty-four hours and 644 mm in just twelve hours (from 8 a.m. to 8 p.m.). It was the highest ever recorded rainfall in India, beating the previous record in 1910 at

Cherrapunji in Meghalaya.[2] The devastation became clearer by the following day, although it continued to rain intermittently.

On the morning of 27 July, I went to the Disaster Management Control Room set up in the basement of the BMC headquarters of south Mumbai. Municipal Commissioner Johny Joseph and Police Commissioner Anami Roy were assessing the situation. Joseph told me that flooding in the Mithi river had added to the devastation.

It was on this day in 2005 that many Mumbaikars, including me, realized that a river flowed through the centre of the city. On the way from Dharavi to Bandra, the black water body that people mistake for an open sewer is actually a river. Close to its source, Vihar Lake, the Mithi has fish, crocodiles and other amphibians, but becomes a foul-smelling culvert further downstream. Eighteen kilometres long, it passes through Powai, Saki Naka, Kurla, Kalina, Dharavi and other areas before its confluence with the Arabian Sea at Mahim Bay. Mithi's natural flow had been choked because of large-scale encroachment on its banks, along with garbage and industrial waste being dumped into it. The deluge of 26 July overwhelmed its ability to discharge the storm water into the sea and led to the city's unprecedented devastation. Most of the highly affected areas that day were around the Mithi. '*Mithi*', in Hindi, means sweet, but that day, it left a bitter scar on Mumbai.

Joseph briefed Roy about the areas where rescue and relief operations were required. Roy's force was overworked, and the policemen faced mobility and connectivity issues. He asked for the navy's help. No aerial rescue could be conducted because of the bad weather. Motorboats were deployed to reach stranded people.

My friend Rajiv Somani, who operated a water sports complex at Girgaon Chowpatty, lent me a motorboat. I used it to access areas like Kurla and Kalina, where the water had not yet receded. I interviewed a few people to understand their suffering and the help they needed. Many burst into tears while narrating their plight. Most of the affected families belonged to the lower and middle classes. The deluge had swept away all their belongings. Electrical appliances, such as TVs, refrigerators, ACs, ceiling fans, and stored groceries, along with LPG gas cylinders, had been washed away. Many students lost their books and documents. As the weather cleared, an aerial survey of the city began, with politicians hovering around on choppers. My news channel also hired a private helicopter for aerial coverage of the calamity. From the sky, it looked like the Arabian Sea had trespassed into this coastal city.

It took about a week for the water to recede completely. In several areas, it took four to five more days for electricity to be restored. Many mobile towers had been destroyed, so services took time to return. The removal of dead animals also took a long time, and the odour of their decomposing bodies engulfed different parts of the city. Around 300 people died due to drowning, electrocutions or landslides, and the toll crossed over 1,000 in other parts of Maharashtra adjoining Mumbai.[3] Many more people died due to waterborne diseases and leptospirosis in the following days. Hospitals were overwhelmed with patients complaining of high fever. As per the Federation of Indian Chambers of Commerce & Industry (FICCI), businesses saw a loss of Rs 1,700 crore owing to the closure of industrial units. Property worth Rs 500 crore was damaged as well.[4] People had to struggle for cash as ATMs were flooded, and the machines became dysfunctional.

On 29 July, a rumour spread in the Nehru Nagar slum of Juhu that tsunami waves had hit the city. This led to a stampede, in which eighteen people died, including seven children. Forty others were injured. When I reached the spot, blood-soaked footwear lay scattered all around to tell the story. Most of the residents of the slum were natives of coastal Tamil Nadu, who had witnessed the widespread devastation caused by the Indian Ocean tsunami just seven months ago.

The Wrath of Nature

Mumbai was born by altering the natural topography of the coastline and destroying the environment. When the Portuguese settled in the islands of Bombay, they treated the archipelago merely as a good naval base, but when the British took over in the seventeenth century, they began transforming the city in a major way.

The British connected the seven islands into one major landmass and made Bombay an immense urban centre. This process of unifying the islands began in the eighteenth century and was completed in the nineteenth century, and a sizeable portion of land was reclaimed from the sea. As the city grew, mangroves were destroyed and many trees were cut. The high-profile business area, the Bandra-Kurla Complex, was constructed on one of the swampy lands which acted as a buffer between the land and sea.

The sewage and storm water disposal systems made by the British were not upgraded as the city grew in size and population. The slum mafia kept destroying Mumbai's green cover at Aarey Forest and Sanjay Gandhi National Park. Trees continue to be burnt down to construct illegal shanties. Many trees were cut to construct the car-shed of a metro rail line in the Aarey Forest.

Mumbai is surrounded by the sea and creeks from all four sides. The salt pans act as a shield between land and seawater. But these are also under threat as the Mumbai Development Plan 2034 has allowed the construction of affordable housing projects on these very lands.

The city is geographically a part of the Konkan region, which receives the maximum rainfall in Maharashtra, and is surrounded by the Arabian Sea to the west and the Sahyadri mountain range—known as the Western Ghats—towards its east. The clouds of the south-west monsoon are obstructed by the Sahyadri range, leading to heavy rains in the Konkan region. The city remains at the mercy of nature during the monsoons every year. A combination of heavy rains along with a high tide in the Arabian Sea, taller than 4.5 metres, wreaks havoc on the city. Every year, there are three to four occasions when Mumbai comes to a standstill as roads and railway tracks are flooded. The city's storm water isn't drained into the sea. Instead, the sea pushes it back into the city.

What Has Changed?

The custodians of Mumbai learnt several lessons from this tragedy, which exposed the city's vulnerabilities during the monsoons. In the years following 2005, several measures were announced to prevent such catastrophes from ever taking place again.

Weather experts suggested that to mitigate the damage, there must be an advanced flood warning system in place. Hence, the IMD was advised to install three Doppler radars in the city, which are known for their long-range and accurate weather predictions. By 2022, two Doppler radars had been installed. However, there have been frequent breakdowns, which challenge their reliability.

Efforts have also been made to revamp Mumbai's primitive storm water disposal system. In 1985, a project titled 'Brihanmumbai Storm Water Disposal System (BRIMSTOWAD)' was conceived. The project intended to construct new pumping stations, desilt drains, increase the discharge capacity of rainwater from 25 millimetres an hour to 50 millimetres an hour and rehabilitate slum dwellers. A plan was formulated in 1993, but it was put into action only after the deluge. In 2007, the Central government approved a grant of

Rs 1,200 crore for its implementation.[5] However, the project is advancing at a snail's pace. BRIMSTOWAD was to be completed in fifty-eight phases, but by 2019, only twenty-eight projects were finished.[6] Encroachments and litigations have been cited as the reasons for this delay.

Considering the role played by the Mithi river in the damage, the Maharashtra government and the BMC have focused on cleaning it. In November 2020, the BMC allocated Rs 569 crore for the Mithi River Rejuvenation Project. Widening of the river, diversion of drains, construction of retaining walls and removal of encroachments on the banks would be undertaken under this.[7] In August 2021, a pilot project was launched by the Mumbai Metropolitan Region Development Authority (MMRDA) to clean up the river. A Finland-made machine will collect floating plastic waste from the river and recycle it.[8] In February 2022, Municipal Commissioner Iqbal Singh Chahal announced that around 95 per cent of the widening and deepening work on the river had been completed. The retaining wall was almost ready. The hope is that with all these measures in place, the water-holding and carrying capacity of the river will increase.[9]

The deluge affected the public transportation system as well. The new metro rail network coming up in the city has addressed this issue. Except line number three, all the other metro lines are now elevated.

Submerged by 2050?

Mumbai has a conflicted relationship with the rains. The monsoon is both a beloved and a dreaded season for the people of the city. The water supply in Mumbai completely depends on the seasonal rains, which fills the seven lakes that store water for the rest of the year. A delay of even fifteen days in the monsoon's arrival causes anxiety in the city. The BMC announces water cuts, and prayers are held in temples to appease the rain gods.

But the monsoon also brings along a set of calamities, of which the 2005 deluge was an extreme example. Unlike Delhi and other cities of northern India, summers and winters are moderate in this city. Rarely does one need to wear sweaters or jackets during the winter. Similarly, summer is not very harsh either. All of nature's fury is concentrated on the monsoons, and results in much tragedy.

On 29 August 2017, the famous gastroenterologist Dr Deepak Amrapurkar became another victim of the rampant rains when Mumbai witnessed the second-highest rainfall after 26 July 2005, with a record of 468 mm of rain within twelve hours. The entire city came to a standstill. Train services were suspended, and the roads were choked. Dr Amrapurkar, who was returning from Bombay Hospital, got stuck in his car for several hours at Lower Parel. He decided to walk up to his home, which was just two kilometres away. However, he fell into an open sewer hole close to his house. His body was found on the beach in Worli two days later.

Another casualty was a young lawyer named Priyen Maithia, who went to help his friend who was stranded at King's Circle. The area was entirely flooded, and his car was submerged till the bonnet. The central locking system failed, and Priyen wasn't able to open the door—he died of suffocation. The deluge claimed fourteen lives that day in Mumbai. Exactly a month later, on 29 September 2017, a flash flood, combined with the rumour of a pedestrian bridge having collapsed, led to a stampede outside Elphinstone Road Railway Station, killing twenty-three people.

Global warming and climate change are causing extreme weather events across the world, and Mumbai is turning out to be one of the worst affected. In June 2020, cyclone *Nisarga* hit close to Mumbai in the Raigarh district, causing massive damage to the coastal settlements. In May 2021, cyclone *Tauktae* caused a landfall in Gujarat, affecting Mumbai on its way. The rains churned the sea waves such that, for the first time in history, the security wall surrounding the Gateway of India was broken. The waves crossed the road and touched the Taj Mahal Hotel. Cyclones, like seasons, are gradually becoming annual visitors to the city.

All such incidents portend a dark future for Mumbai. Relying on few studies, Iqbal Singh Chahal believes that by 2050 around 70 per cent of south Mumbai will be submerged due to a rise in sea levels.[10] Landmarks like the Wankhede Stadium, National Centre for Performing Arts and Marine Drive are feared to submerge. A report released by McKinsey India in February 2020 predicts that there will be a 25 per cent increase in flash floods, and the sea level will rise by 0.5 metres by 2050.[11] This will affect crores of people living within 1 kilometre from the coast. It appears that the sea is determined to recover all the space stolen from it when Bombay expanded.

It may be called a delayed awakening, but the authorities have ultimately begun preparing to tackle this imminent natural catastrophe. In March 2022, Mumbai became the first city in India to announce a climate action plan. According to it, the BMC and other governmental agencies will focus on low-carbon electricity, carbon-resilient infrastructure, zero-emission public transport, expanding the city's green cover, and a renewed focus on urban flooding and waste management.[12]

Mumbai Will Drink Seawater?

One consequence of climate change will be a scarcity of fresh water. Regions dependent on rainfall for their water requirements will face drought for some years. Many cities are likely to run out of potable water. We saw this in 2019, when the South African city of Cape Town was hit by an unprecedented water shortage.

Bengaluru in India is listed among eleven global cities that could soon run out of water.[13] In fact, in 2018–19, Bengaluru saw a glimpse of the looming danger ahead when its water crisis made national headlines. The city was about to hit 'Zero Day', which is when all water resources get exhausted. In Mumbai, there could be years of deficient rainfall over catchment areas of lakes which supply water to the city. However, at least the government has begun strategizing for ways to mitigate this problem.

In January 2022, the BMC appointed consultants to prepare a blueprint for Mumbai's first desalination plant. It will be set up at Manori Island in north-western Mumbai and will convert saline seawater to make it potable. The plant is expected to be functional by 2027 and will have the capacity to process 1,800 million litres per day. Mumbai's present water requirement is 3,800 million litres per day, which is likely to increase with the growing population. To further boost the water supply, the BMC is contemplating setting up sewage treatment plants that will convert sewage into potable water.[14] In India, there are already desalination plants functional at Minjur near Chennai and Jamnagar in Gujarat, and Mumbai needs to follow suit. However, the desalination plant proposed at Manori has come under scrutiny after change in the state government in June 2022. The new government didn't seem eager to execute the project.

15
Unglamorous Bollywood

IN MARCH 1995, AS SOON AS I WAS DONE WITH THE stressful board exams of Class X, the first thing on my wishlist was to watch the movie *Bombay*. Directed by veteran film-maker Mani Ratnam, the movie was based on the post-Babri mosque demolition riots in the city, and I was keen to see the cinematic depiction of the mayhem that I witnessed and endured. The movie ruffled the feathers of the Shiv Sena, but after a preview, the party supremo, Bal Thackeray, allowed it to be released in cinema halls. Those were the days when film-makers couldn't afford to antagonize the Shiv Sena. Although he took many creative liberties in his storytelling, Mani Ratnam was successful in connecting the events of Ayodhya and their aftermath in Bombay. The director, who hails from southern India, had just a small brush with the politicians who wield their clout over Bombay's film industry, but over the years, Bollywood has been influenced and shaped by many elements that present its unglamorous image. As a journalist, I have been a witness to some of them.

Bombay is believed to be the birthplace of the Indian film industry and is its home. Over its century-long history, it has spun thousands of stories, visually manifesting the myriad dreams held by people. It has produced several personalities who have become household names across the globe. While the communal polarization after the 1992-93 riots affected many spheres of the city, Bollywood has remained remarkably untouched and continues to attract people from different religions and backgrounds. However, the Bollywood of the 1990s and beyond has often been in the limelight for the wrong reasons. These decades have been a period of upheaval for India's Tinseltown and saw cases that attracted tremendous public attention to the otherwise glamorous Bollywood.

Glamour and Guns

One may have come across many videos being played on TV news channels where megastars of the 1980s and 1990s danced and sang praises of Dawood Ibrahim in different shows in Dubai. Dawood arranged for these performances even while he was in India. While pursuing stories around the Mumbai underworld, I spoke to many dwellers of Pakmodia Street, where Dawood lived before fleeing to Dubai in 1986. They recollect how Bollywood stars performed for the local crowds there on Sunday evenings, when a temporary stage would be erected at the street corner. These stars would also perform for every celebration held by Dawood's family. They appeared to be servile to Dawood, although he treated them with respect. All the performances were well compensated, but the fees were fixed by Dawood and not the artistes. They were expected to cancel all other engagements if they were called to Pakmodia Street, even at short notice. Some obliged him because of his fearsome reputation, while others were happy to gain proximity to such a powerful person.

Mafia dons have always wanted to hobnob with film stars. Predecessors of Dawood, such as Karim Lala, Haji Mastan and Yusuf Patel, often invited Bollywood personalities to their events and enjoyed getting photographed with them.

The underworld had a multidimensional relationship with Bollywood. One was that of predator and prey, while another was of the performer and the patron. A third was of financier and borrower. When these relationships were highlighted by the media, film personalities were vilified—although, in most cases, they were the least culpable.

Bollywood has always been an enormous source of revenue for the underworld. In the 1990s, almost every big film producer received extortion calls from the mafia, and those who refused to pay were shot dead. The underworld kept a keen eye on the box office, as discussed in an earlier chapter.

The performer–patron relationship thrived when film stars began participating in events organized by dons. After relocating to Dubai, Dawood noticed that officials in the administration there enjoyed Bollywood movies. To establish cordial relations with them, and gain favours, he flew famous Bollywood stars to Dubai and Sharjah, and arranged musical nights for his Arab friends. A few actresses developed close proximity to dons through these events, and some even had romantic relationships with them. A successful actress of the 1980s was often spotted with Dawood in Dubai. She often accompanied him to watch India–Pakistan cricket matches at the stadium in Sharjah. Another actress of the 1990s, who later joined politics, was reportedly close to Anees Ibrahim, Dawood's younger brother. Abu Salem and Monica Bedi's love story was all over the media when they were arrested in Lisbon.

This proximity between the film world and the mafia can be gauged by a conversation recorded between Chhota Shakeel and a person who sounded like Sanjay Dutt. A source had shared audiotapes of the purported conversation with me, which I played on the Aaj Tak news channel in 2002. In the clip, the two were discussing matters ranging from requesting mobile phone chips from Dubai or Karachi to complaining about actor Govinda's unpunctuality, and then further discussing the threat calls made to actress Preity Zinta.[1]

The two men appeared quite friendly with each other. The way Chhota Shakeel was discussing film scenes in the conversation showed that he had a comprehensive knowledge of film-making. A few hours before the audio clip was played on TV, I got a call from an encounter-specialist cop requesting me to desist as his 'filmi' friends would get into trouble. I told him that the matter was not in my hands and the call to play the tape was taken by my editors. Sanjay Dutt had to depose for the said conversation before the special MCOCA court, where he denied speaking to Shakeel.[2]

Thanks to Dawood's clout in Bollywood, his younger brother, who fancied himself a poet, Noor Kaskar, got opportunities to write lyrics for Bollywood numbers. One of his songs from the movie *Patthar ke Phool* simply listing road names of Mumbai, *'Kabhi Linking Road … Kabhi Warden Road … Kabhi Cadel Road …'* became a chartbuster when the film was released.

Then there is the relationship between the financier and borrower, which came to light in 2000, when Mumbai Police registered a criminal case concerning the film *Chori Chori Chupke Chupke,* starring Salman Khan, Rani Mukerji and Preity Zinta. The film was based on the delicate issue of surrogacy. However, it became more famous as a springboard for discussions about Bollywood's nexus with the underworld. Mumbai Police's investigation led to the arrests of Nazim Rizvi, the film's producer, and Bharat Shah, who was said to be Bollywood's biggest financier, under the stringent MCOCA. Relying on certain telephonic conversations, Mumbai Police believed that Bharat Shah financed Rizvi at the behest of Chhota Shakeel. It was alleged that by backing the movie, Shah helped Dawood's organized crime syndicate.

The prosecution listed Salman Khan, Sanjay Dutt, Mahesh Manjrekar, Rakesh Roshan, Preity Zinta and a few other film personalities as witnesses during the trial, which was completed within three years. Bharat Shah and Nazim Rizvi were convicted, with Rizvi sentenced to six years of rigorous imprisonment under MCOCA and Shah sentenced for one year. He was found guilty of withholding information about the Bollywood–mafia nexus from the police.

The controversy over this film also revealed a quid pro quo arrangement between the film industry and the crime syndicate. Bollywood rose as a convenient medium for gangs to launder their black money. Film producers also approved of this, as there were no formal financing facilities available for them. The underworld capitalized on Bollywood's need for money by offering its illicit income.

Former Mumbai Police Commissioner M.N. Singh, during whose tenure this case was investigated, told me, 'The underworld financing of the film industry was happening since Haji Mastan's era. Then, a time came when gangsters themselves began contemplating becoming producers. Hence, underworld money dominated Bollywood. Their influence was so great that they dictated the release date of movies. Some producers themselves approached gangsters for favours.' He added, 'I advised the Government of India to make bank finance available to the film industry. Sushma Swaraj, who was the minister of information and broadcasting, liked the idea. At her insistence, IDBI Bank started financing movies. When Bollywood started getting clean money, the underworld money stopped.'[3] The entry of multinational corporations in film finance also played a role in eventually discontinuing the flow of funds from the underworld.

Stars behind Bars

As a crime journalist, some of the major stories that I have covered during the late 1990s and early 2000s are the ones where film stars got entangled in criminal cases and were arrested. While I regularly followed up on the 1993 blasts' trial in the TADA court in which Sanjay Dutt was also an accused, I also learnt of a few more celebrities who appeared on the wrong side of the law.

One morning, in May 2001, Teepu, an informer of the Narcotics Control Bureau (NCB), asked me to rush to the NCB office in Ballard Estate, saying that a 'big fish from Bollywood has come into the net'. The big fish was actor Fardeen Khan, who acted in a few successful movies such as *Jungle* and *Pyaar Tune Kya Kiya*. Fardeen Khan was caught attempting to buy cocaine. To make a payment to the drug peddler, Khan attempted to withdraw Rs 3,500 from an ATM at Juhu, but his card got stuck in the machine. The NCB alleged that Khan had been a drug user for quite some time. However, he was bailed out within three days. Ten years later, when the trial concluded, he was granted immunity on the condition of going through a de-addiction programme.

A year after Fardeen Khan's arrest, I was busy chasing another Khan from Bollywood. On 28 September 2002, my film reporter, Manish Dube, called around 6 a.m. to inform me that superstar Salman Khan had met with an accident near his house in Bandra. I immediately rang up Bipin Kumar Singh, the zonal DCP, who confirmed the incident. I called my cameraman to the spot and reached there, riding my motorcycle at breakneck speed.

Salman Khan's damaged Land Cruiser was parked outside the Bandra police station. After taking shots of the car and interviewing DCP Bipin Kumar, I reached the accident spot. As per the initial briefing by the police, Salman Khan had driven the car there at a high speed and completely lost control around the American Express Bakery junction. He drove over workers from a neighbouring bakery who were sleeping on the pavement. They were immediately rushed to the nearby Bhabha Hospital. One of them, named Noorullah, died on the spot. Salman Khan allegedly fled the scene. I broke the news on TV around 8 a.m. with visuals of the accident spot and Salman's damaged Land Cruiser.

A case of hit-and-run was registered against Salman Khan. I tried to contact him to present his version, but he was not traceable. In the afternoon, he appeared at the Bandra police station with a lawyer in tow. He was let off in an hour, after paying a fine of Rs 950. The cameras captured an ACP-rank officer behaving in a friendly manner with Salman Khan and trying to comfort him. The officer seemed in awe of the actor's charisma. The incident led to an uproar that Salman Khan was being dealt with leniently because he was a star and that the law must be equal for everyone. This outrage finally led to him being booked under a stricter charge of 'culpable homicide not amounting to murder'. Salman Khan was rearrested within a week. The police alleged he was driving the car under the influence of alcohol. After his police custody ended, he was sent to jail.

The trial continued for twelve years. The police recorded the statements of Salman Khan's bodyguard, Ravindra Patil, and singer Kamaal Khan, who were also with him in the car at the time of the accident. Both stated that Salman was at the steering wheel. However, Kamaal Khan never appeared before the court. As the trial was about to end, there was a twist in the story. Salman's driver appeared before the court and shocked everybody by saying that he was the one driving the car when it met with the accident.

The date 7 May 2015 was fixed for the judgement. I struggled to get a space in the sessions court of judge D.W. Deshpande as it was packed with reporters, lawyers and excited staff from other courts. Sporting a white shirt and blue jeans, the movie star stood in the wooden box with a tense face. Judge Deshpande bluntly pronounced him guilty of all the charges levelled against him and declared that he was driving without a licence and under the influence of alcohol. The story that his driver was at the steering wheel was rejected. He was sentenced to five years in prison.

Salman Khan wiped his tears on the sleeves of his shirt and looked towards his two sisters, who too broke down after hearing the judgement. However, the actor and his well-wishers' anguish was short-lived as he was set free within six months. The order was challenged in the Bombay High Court, which overturned the judgement and pronounced that the prosecution had failed to prove its charges against Salman Khan.

Another actor who fell afoul of the law was Shiney Ahuja. Shiney became famous with his debut film, *Hazaaron Khwaishein Aisi*, and featured in a few other hit movies like *Gangster*, *Life in a … Metro* and *Bhool Bhulaiyaa*. However, his flourishing career came to a halt in 2009, when he was arrested on charges of raping his maid. Although the complainant withdrew her charges during the trial, the judge relied on her earlier statements and the evidence collected by the police. In March 2011, Shiney was sentenced to seven years of imprisonment.

Vindu Singh was another Bollywood name to face notoriety. The son of wrestler-turned-actor Dara Singh, Vindu had acted in a few television serials and participated in the reality show *Big Boss*. In 2013, he was jailed on the charges of being involved in a cricket spot-fixing racket. Shortly after Vindu was released on bail, I met him at the Mumbai airport, where he said that he was framed in the case at the behest of a senior Crime Branch officer.

Most of the film stars arrested in various such cases were incarcerated in central Mumbai's Arthur Road Prison. Jail Superintendent Swati Sathe, under whose tenure most of the filmi inmates were imprisoned, became famous as '*Film stars ke zamaane ki jailor*'. She was known as a strict and upright officer, who didn't allow any extra privileges to her star detainees.

The Sushant Singh Rajput Case

The film industry came to a standstill when model-turned-actor Sushant Singh Rajput died by suicide on 14 June 2020. His death not only exposed Bollywood's disreputable side, but also unveiled the sordid face of the media, investigating agencies and politics. Following the regular procedure, Mumbai Police registered an Accidental Death Report (ADR) and prima facie didn't see any foul play in the matter. However, a widely circulated social media campaign began claiming that the actor killed himself because of nepotism prevalent in Bollywood.

In no time, it was believed that the actor suffered from depression because he could not get any work. Reacting to the public outrage, Maharashtra Home Minister Anil Deshmukh asked Mumbai Police to investigate the nepotism aspect of the case as well. Soon, dozens of film personalities were called in over a month to probe this angle. The police never revealed if there was any basis for the said accusations.

Meanwhile, a small-time actor from a western suburb of Mumbai made a Facebook post linking Rajput's death with the suicide of his manager, Disha Salian, a week before. Salian jumped off the balcony of a flat where she was partying with friends. The post alleged that Salian had been killed as had Sushant, for he allegedly knew Salian's murderers. He added that some incumbent politicians of Maharashtra were also involved in the conspiracy. The post snowballed into a strong narrative, with one of Maharashtra's ministers being accused of the crime. It was reported that the case was being hushed up to save this minister.

The BJP too jumped into the fray as the narrative gave an opportunity for the party to target the Uddhav Thackeray-led triparty government of Maharashtra. Since Rajput hailed from Bihar, where Vidhan Sabha elections were due, the BJP attempted to emotionally manipulate the state's vote bank by supporting 'the justice for Sushant' social media campaign. BJP leader Narayan Rane held a press conference and made public the allegations against the government, which had been mere conspiracy theories on social media so far. Since Rane is a former CM of the state, his statements offered some credence to such theories.

On 25 July, the case took a new turn when Rajput's father registered a complaint at the Patna police station alleging that Sushant's girlfriend, Rhea Chakraborty, and her family members abetted the suicide. Chakraborty allegedly kept Sushant away from his family and took charge of his finances as well. Generally, if a complaint is registered at a police station outside the jurisdiction of where a crime has been committed, the police registers a Zero Number FIR and transfers the case to the concerned station. However, instead of transferring the case to its Mumbai counterparts, the Patna police decided to investigate the case themselves. High drama ensued when Vinay Tiwari, superintendent of the Patna police, landed in Mumbai and was immediately quarantined at a guest house by the BMC, citing Covid-19 protocols. This added fuel to the suspicion that the Maharashtra government was concealing something.

While a war of words broke out between the politicians of Bihar and Maharashtra, a TV anchor known for his loud and hysterical style began a campaign urging a CBI probe into the matter. He concluded that Sushant didn't die by suicide, but was murdered. His channel ran the story as 'Sushant Singh Murder Case'. Here, it is important to note that even Sushant's father had not alleged murder, but abetment to suicide. A few months earlier, a criminal case had been filed by Mumbai Police against the frenetic anchor for his controversial comments against Sonia Gandhi, and he had been made to sit at the police station for hours while being questioned. This case gave him an opportunity for retribution. The anchor alleged that Mumbai Police were trying to shield important people in the government.

The Bihar government recommended the case to the CBI in August. After the pleas opposing the transfer of the probe were rejected by the Supreme Court, a CBI team arrived in Mumbai and began investigating the case. Meanwhile, the Enforcement Directorate (ED) also began an inquiry into the financial aspects of the matter. The ED seized Rhea Chakraborty's phone and found some WhatsApp conversations that hinted at her alleged involvement in purchasing drugs. With this, the story got another twist, and a probe into the drugs angle was started by the NCB. Chakraborty and her brother, Showik, were arrested on charges of purchasing drugs. Many film stars were also summoned when personal mobile chats were leaked to the media, suggesting that substance abuse was rampant in India's Tinseltown.

The showbiz and glamour of Bollywood were yet again reduced to narcotic dust. How the glamour world was in the grip of the drug trade became a hot topic for TV debates.

Money Makes Movies Move

In July 2021, Rajesh Sapte, an art director in Bollywood, died by suicide at his residence in Pune. Sapte posted a video on social media and left a note in which he blamed harassment by a labour union leader for his suicide. Sapte said that the leader was not allowing him to start work on his projects under the false pretext that he was not paying his workers their dues.

In 2009, Y.P. Singh, a former IPS officer, was shooting a scene for his film, based on the book *Carnage by Angels*, at Juhu's J-49 nightclub. Suddenly, a few people barged in, claiming to be members of the Junior Artists' Association, and disrupted the shoot. They told Singh that the shoot wouldn't be allowed to continue, as the junior artists employed by him were not members of their union. An argument ensued. After Singh vociferously asserted that the artists were not legally bound to become members of any union, they left. Singh filed a criminal complaint against them.

Both cases—of Rajesh Sapte and Y.P. Singh—reflect the dark underbelly of the glitter of Bollywood. The industry is effectively under the control of unionism, and neither the producers nor the workers can afford to be at loggerheads with these unions. The labour unions emerged in Bollywood as protectors of workers' rights and as a shield against exploitation, but over the years, they have become something of a double-edged sword.

Screenwriter Sarvesh Upadhyay, who has written the web series called *Raktanchal*, explained to me how the labour unions assert their presence in Bollywood. 'Most of the cases that come before the unions are about the denial of credits and non-payment of remittances. Whenever an aggrieved writer, director, artiste, cinematographer or any other worker approaches the union for help to recover their dues, the union lays a condition before him—the complainant has to donate 5 to 10 per cent of the recovered amount to the union. This condition is levied irrespective of the fact that the complainant has been a member of the union for several years after paying a heavy membership fee. The unions charge somewhere between Rs 3,500 to 35,000 as membership fees, depending on the tenures ranging from annual to lifetime.'[4]

After receiving the complaint, the union sends a notice to the errant producer. If the producer doesn't comply, then the union leaders reach the set and announce that workers affiliated with their union must stop work at once. The shoot gets interrupted, and the producer is forced to cough up the money to resume the film. A union's power depends on the number of members it has. The unwritten rule in Bollywood is that producers can only employ union members for their projects. It was a violation of this 'rule' that disrupted Y.P. Singh's film shoot.

As of 2022, there are over forty unions of people who play different roles in a movie's production. Every union competes with the others to increase its membership. Around thirty-one of them are part of the Federation of Western India Cine Employees, an umbrella body of various unions.

To know the other side of the story, I spoke to Ashok Dubey, president of the All-India Film Employees Confederation. 'The cine workers are one of the most exploited lot, and they are subject to the whims and fancies of producers. A worker can't make rounds of courts if his dues are not cleared. In such a case, the unions step in. Earlier, if some worker died during work, his family was paid a meagre compensation of Rs 4 or 5 lakh. We insisted that the compensation must be paid according to the age of the deceased. The younger the worker, the higher the compensation to be paid. Recently, we made a producer pay over Rs 30 lakhs to the family of a youngster who died in a mishap,' said Dubey.

'Some producers,' continued Dubey, 'treat cine workers like animals. For a unit of 300 people, sometimes there are just two or three toilets. No proper arrangements for changing and eating are made. Often, the food served is not edible. If we protest against such injustice, they call it *dadagiri*.'[5] Dubey told me that after Raju Sapte's suicide, the unions were scared to address the complaints of workers.

Various political parties, too, have their wings in Bollywood, and the most powerful and oldest among them is the Shiv Sena's Bharatiya Chitrapat Sena (BCS), a film workers' union. The BCS often issues diktats for the industry, such as there should be no mimicry of veteran singer Lata Mangeshkar, no one should produce an unauthorized biopic of Bal Thackeray, and no Pakistani artiste must be employed in any movies.

Bal Thackeray had a close relation with Bollywood. During the 1980s, he often spent his evenings sipping beer by the pool at Hotel Sun and Sand at Juhu with actors like Dev Anand and Dilip Kumar. He frequently invited Amitabh Bachchan and Mithun Chakraborty for mutton parties at his farmhouse in Karjat. Thackeray was always on the list of prominent film award functions. His son Bindumadhav produced a movie starring Nana Patekar and Manisha Koirala titled *Agni Sakshi* in 1996, which was a commercial success. His other son Jaidev produced *Sapoot* in the same year, starring Akshay Kumar and Suniel Shetty; it did average business at the box office. As a film producer, Bal Thackeray's daughter-in-law and Jaidev's estranged wife, Smita Thackeray, enjoyed cordial relations in Bollywood during the late 1990s. In 1999, she delivered a hit comedy movie titled *Haseena Maan Jayegi*. After having produced only one film, she was elected as the president of the Indian Motion Pictures Producers Association (IMPPA) in 2001.

What Has Changed in Bollywood?

It was August 1997, and Ram Gopal Varma had just started shooting his film *Satya*. A couple of days into the shoot, while he was directing a scene, news broke that music baron Gulshan Kumar had been shot dead by gangsters. The shoot was stopped, and the script was rewritten to incorporate the incident in the film. A year later, the movie was released and achieved cult status.[6]

Prominent film journalist and author Mayank Shekhar observes that Bollywood has been chronicling Mumbai since its start, and *Satya* is a fine example of that. '*Black Friday* is another movie that presented the aftermath of the 1993 blasts. Movies like *Company* depict Mumbai's underworld. However, with the collapse of the Mumbai underworld, film-makers have begun telling the stories of other underworlds. Movies and web series like *Gangs of Wasseypur*, *Sehar* and *Mirzapur* are examples of such changing trends,' he told me.

In Mayank's opinion, Mumbai is no longer a muse for film-makers. 'People now focus on realism. Earlier, most of the shoots took place within studios, but to make movies more credible, they are now shot at actual locations outside studios. But shooting in Mumbai is extremely expensive. With the logistics issues and the level of extortion, it becomes a headache to shoot here. Shooting elsewhere is easy. There are films which have been shot abroad to depict the city. For the movie *Bombay Velvet*, south Bombay was recreated in Sri Lanka.'[7]

Screenwriter Sarvesh Upadhyay concurs with Mayank. 'Whenever there is a shoot at outdoor locations such as Madh or Mira Road, local politicians and shady elements create a nuisance. You can't shoot till their palms are greased. Getting permissions from various authorities is another time-consuming task. Sometimes, to avoid such hassles, a producer pays local strongmen or corporators and gets his shoot done,' he says.[8]

The question remains: is Mumbai a safe home for the Hindi film industry, or is it under threat? Developments in the last few years show that the city's monopoly might diminish in the long run. In December 2020, when Yogi Adityanath, the chief minister of Uttar Pradesh, toured Mumbai, he called a meeting of prominent Bollywood personalities at Hotel Oberoi. The meeting was attended by actor Akshay Kumar and film-makers Boney Kapoor, Subhash Ghai and Manmohan Shetty. Yogi appealed to the fraternity to make Uttar Pradesh a hub of the entertainment industry. He announced that a grand film city with modern amenities would come up in Noida. As per Film Policy 2018, the government would provide all the necessary support to film-makers. Apart from the prospect of Uttar Pradesh emerging as the new hub of film-making, an appreciable number of films are also being shot at the film city in Hyderabad.

The administration of Maharashtra is not oblivious to these developments that threaten to take Bollywood elsewhere. In June 2019, after the crew of the web series *Fixer* was brutally attacked by local goons at Thane, the then chief minister, Devendra Fadnavis, announced that the government would come up with a single-window system for the film industry. All the required permissions from different authorities for outdoor shoots would be provided promptly. After Raju Sapte's suicide, the Uddhav Thackeray–led government also swung into action. In July 2021, the labour commissioner's office issued directions that the unions couldn't compel the producers to employ only their members for shoots, and no shoot must be interfered with. If this is not followed, the producer must complain to the police. Senior officers of Mumbai Police met the producers and assured them that due action would be taken against anybody attempting extortion. A film producer has confirmed to me that such efforts are proving fruitful on the ground, but there is the fear that they could also just be temporary bubbles.

16

Lalbaugcha Raja

AS A CHILD, I EAGERLY WAITED FOR THE GANESHA festival every year, not because I was very religious, but because of the fun and frolic that characterized the celebration. Almost every street in a Hindu-dominated locality had a pandal where an idol of Lord Ganesha was installed, and, during the ten days of the festival, most of my after-school time was spent in the Ganpati pandal of a neighbouring street. In the evenings, I accompanied my friends to visit famous pandals known for their decorations, tableaus and artistic idols. One pandal I never missed visiting every year was at Keshavji Naik Chawl in Girgaon.

A visit to the chawl during the Ganesha festival is like travelling through time straight to nineteenth-century India. The shape and size of the Ganesha idol, the traditional palki in which the idol is brought, the houses surrounding the pandal and even the events organized there continue to be the same till today as they were in 1893. The Maharashtrian inhabitants of the chawl, living in over 150 small tenements, have meticulously preserved the old-world charm of the festival.

The Birthplace of Bombay's Ganesha Festival

Until 1893, the celebration of Ganeshotsav had been mostly a household affair. During their reign, till the mid-nineteenth century, the Peshwas and their Maratha confederacy organized the festivities extravagantly, but Bal Gangadhar Tilak, a pioneer of the Indian freedom struggle, came up with a completely different version of the celebration. He understood the cohesive power of religion and envisaged Ganeshotsav as an event to unite people. Ganeshotsav gradually became the mode of dissemination for his nationalist and reformist thoughts. Heeding Tilak's call, a few of his followers living in this nondescript working-class area in Bombay held the city's first public Ganeshotsav.

The festival began modestly. A two-and-a-half-foot Ganesha idol was installed in a small tent, and the residents contributed money for the rituals and the minor decorations of the pandal. Nevertheless, it adhered to Tilak's philosophy. In 1901, Tilak himself visited Keshavji Naik Chawl and participated in the celebrations. Over the years, the organizing team at the chawl began inviting prominent personalities from various walks of life, including L.K. Advani, Bal Thackeray, Sunil Gavaskar, Sachin Tendulkar, Govinda, Amit Shah and many more.

The Ganesha festival soon became popular, and within a century, thousands of Ganpati pandals proliferated in the Hindu-dominated localities of Maharashtra. Festivals make Mumbai groove with joy. They offer respite from the city's reckless pace and stressful life. Perhaps this is also why Mumbai witnesses an enthusiastic large-scale public participation during various festivals—be it Janmashtami, Navratri, Mount-Mary's Fair during Christmas or the procession on Eid-e-Milad un-Nabi, the Prophet's birthday. Ganeshotsav has, however, emerged as the prime public festival of Mumbai.

Unlike the one hosted at Keshavji Naik Chawl, Ganeshotsav has undergone a sea change everywhere else in Mumbai, and has become a festival of glitter and glamour where several crore rupees are spent. Finances flow in from various sources, including collections from local households as well as business firms. The fervour of the festival is at its peak on the first day, i.e., Ganesh Chaturthi, and on the last day, Anant Chaturdashi, when the idols are taken out in processions with people dancing to drumbeats, ending in the *visarjan*. In the 1990s, it was interesting to see people dancing to banjos that played filmi tunes such as *'Bholi soorat dil ke khote'*—in which the dance moves of actor Bhagwan Dada had become popular—and the Pakistani song, '*Jiye Bhutto Benazir*', or '*Long live, Bhutto Benazir*', which was used for the election campaign of the former Pakistani PM. Some of the revellers wore saffron bands on their foreheads, with the Shiv Sena's slogan: '*Garv se kaho hum Hindu hain*', oblivious to the party's distaste for anything Pakistani. The festival has led to the emergence of a micro-economy, ranging from idol makers to drummers and decorators. Idols as tall as thirty feet are installed at pandals.

However, among the hundreds of pandals in Mumbai, one stands out owing to the sheer number of people it attracts every year from across the globe. The Ganesha installed at this pandal is known as Lalbaugcha Raja, or 'the King of Lalbaug'.

Exponential Fame

The Ganesha pandal at Lalbaugcha Raja is the antithesis of the one at Keshavji Naik Chawl: the celebrations there are extravagant and high-profile. Interestingly, both Girgaon and Lalbaug have been known as lower- and middle-class localities, which were mostly populated by mill workers until a few decades ago. Being a prime market for Indian spices, the lane in which the pandal is located is usually filled with powerful aromas throughout the year. This setting changes as the festival approaches. The entire area gets decorated with lights and artefacts to create the effect of a king's palace.

Lalbaugcha Raja Sarvajanik Ganeshotsav, as it is officially known, is visited by well-known personalities from across India. From film stars such as Amitabh Bachchan and Salman Khan to politicians such as Amit Shah, Bal Thackeray and industrialists like Mukesh Ambani, everyone stands at the pandal equally, bowing before Lord Ganesha with folded hands. Over 1.25-crore people visit the pandal during the ten-day celebrations. At times, the queue of devotees stretches over four or five kilometres from the pandal, with an approximate waiting time of five to ten hours, to get a glimpse of the lord.

How did the stature of Lalbaugcha Raja grow over time, making him the most-visited Ganesha in Mumbai? The answer lies in his reputation of being the 'wish-fulfilling god'. Lalbaugcha Raja is known as a god of *navas*—if one takes a vow or makes a wish, he answers the prayer. As per Sudhir Salvi, the president of the pandal, the local vendors of Lalbaug lacked a sheltered marketplace to sell their wares. In 1932, they vowed to Lord Ganesha that if their wish was fulfilled, then they would install his idol every year in the market. The wish was granted within two years when a landlord named Rajab Ali Taiyab Ali offered his plot to the market. It was then, in 1934, that people started installing the Ganesha idol here. In the initial years, the idol was known as 'Market Ka Raja'.

Until the late 1990s, the idol's wish-fulfilling reputation was known only to Mumbaikars and a few people from neighbouring cities. However, the advent of satellite TV channels amplified this belief nationally, which led to lakhs of visitors and never-ending queues. People from various parts of India as well as NRIs come every year to get their wishes granted. In 2003, I covered a story for Star News, interviewing some people waiting in the long queue with their offerings for the lord. They shared at length how their desires had come true and their belief strengthened with time. This report was televised on the first day of the festival, after which the number of devotees started multiplying. Soon, all the news channels began covering the celebrations live.

Meetings at 4.30 a.m.

The police and civic administration, along with the organizers, begin making the arrangements months earlier to manage the crowds and ensure the visiting VIPs' security and convenience. CCTV cameras are set up all around to monitor the throngs of devotees who come to Lalbaug. Mumbai Police assigns 1,500 of its personnel to secure this festival venue every year. A brigade of 3,500 volunteers is tasked with various responsibilities—from regulating the queue to welcoming the celebrities.

Several rounds of rigorous meetings take place between the organizing committee and various agencies. The entry–exit route for visitors, traffic management, food and toilet arrangements for the volunteers, electricity supply, fire safety and everything else are discussed and planned to the last detail.

Sudhir Salvi once told me that in the pre-mobile phone era, the preparatory meetings were called at around 10 or 11 a.m., but by the late 1990s, the timings were changed to 4.30 in the morning. 'Whenever we sat down to have discussions with contractors or civic authorities, somebody's mobile phone would ring. Many people had to attend to important calls. The mobile phones became a nuisance. So, we decided the meetings would be called between 4.30 and 7.30 a.m., when nobody receives calls,' said Salvi.[1]

How Tension Led to Tradition

The fame of Lalbaugcha Raja culminates on the last day of the festival, when the fifteen-foot tall idol is carried out of the pandal for immersion at Girgaon Chowpatty. Lakhs of devotees participate in this seven-kilometre-long procession, which takes about twenty hours because of the swarm of people throughout. The procession passes through some of the most congested areas of south and central Mumbai, including a few communally sensitive stretches. A large number of policemen are deployed when the procession crosses Muslim-dominated localities like Byculla, Nagpada and Do Taki.

In 1946, taking note of the communal riots that preceded the festival, Bombay Police ordered the route of the procession to be changed. However, the organizers insisted on following the traditional course. Ultimately, the organizers' wishes prevailed. 'The traditional route of the procession is sacrosanct because [of the] sentiments of people are attached to it,' said Salvi.[2]

The tradition of this procession continued even during some of the most sensitive times, such as the wars with Pakistan during 1965 and 1971, and the horrifying Hindu–Muslim riots in Bhiwandi in 1984. The year 1993 was perhaps the trickiest. That year, the Ganeshotsav was celebrated in the aftermath of the deadliest communal riots of Bombay and a series of bomb blasts that shook the country.

'The situation was very tense, and we were worried about the consequences when the procession would pass through the Muslim-dominated areas. Then, a social worker named Jamdar Zariwala came to meet us with people from his community. He said, "Whatever has happened has happened. We want to welcome Lalbaugcha Raja. When the procession reaches Nagpada junction, all office-bearers are invited to our stage. We will welcome you with shahi sherbet. Let the message of Hindu–Muslim unity go to the world from Bombay." From that year, it has become a tradition,' Salvi recollected. 'Muslims welcome Lalbaugcha Raja and revellers are served shahi sherbet. Jamdar chacha died a few years ago, but his son has continued the tradition. The procession passes with no trouble through the Muslim areas.'[3]

En route to Chowpatty, Lalbaugcha Raja is welcomed at another location as well by the Muslim populace. When the procession reaches Hindustani Masjid at Byculla, the Raja is garlanded, and the Muslim residents distribute sweets to revellers.

The procession of Lalbaugcha Raja is also one of the two religious events in Mumbai in which governmental agencies also participate in an unusual way. When the procession crosses the headquarters of the Mumbai Fire Brigade at Byculla, all the fire engines blare their sirens simultaneously and switch on their beacons to salute the idol. The second tradition relates to the fifteenth-century Sufi saint Makhdoom Ali Mahimi's shrine at Mahim. During the annual urs, or fair, organized in December every year, cops from Mumbai Police sing and dance in the procession, and enjoy the first right to pay their respects at the saint's tomb. Makhdoom Ali Baba is famous as 'the saint of the police', and it is believed that policemen have been able to solve several complicated cases with his blessings.[4]

By the time Lalbaugcha Raja's procession reaches Girgaon Chowpatty, it is 6 or 7 a.m. of the following day. Colourful boats of fishers surround the idol and extend their final salutations to the lord. The idol is gently pulled into the deep waters of the Arabian Sea.

Cash, Charity and Controversies

Lalbaugcha Raja is also Mumbai's wealthiest Ganesha in terms of the number of offerings received every year. Those who feel that their wishes have been fulfilled offer jewellery and a humongous amount of cash in multiple currencies in the donation box kept at the pandal. The jewellery and other non-cash items get auctioned a few days after the festival. In 2008, the organizing committee saw a record earning of Rs 11.5 crore. In 2018, cash offerings of Rs 6.5 crore was made, while the auction of gold and silver fetched an additional Rs 1.09 crore. The total amount of offerings fluctuates from year to year.

This money is then used for charitable and social activities, like running a dialysis centre, financial help to patients with critical illnesses, computer training for underprivileged children, and donations made to yoga centres, libraries, study centres and so on. In the past, the pandal has also donated generously to the government's national fund for victims of natural calamities across the country.

In 2008, a controversy erupted when the media boycotted the coverage of the pandal after a fight with its volunteers. Some channels telecast visuals of volunteers misbehaving with devotees. Over the years, the boycott gradually faded as the high viewership that Lalbaugcha Raja yielded was just too valuable in the cut-throat media industry.

Clashes also occurred between the police and some volunteers, when the latter objected to the former showing preferential treatment to hand-picked devotees. The volunteers, on the other hand, alleged that the policemen misused their powers to help their friends and relatives jump the queue. Such clashes have now become an annual affair. Acknowledging them, Sudhir Salvi said, 'With an event at such a scale, some trifling problems are bound to happen, but they are settled immediately.'[5]

Govinda's New Avatar

While Ganeshotsav has established its stature as the grandest festival of Mumbai, Janmashtami comes a close second.

Janmashtami is the celebration of Lord Krishna's birth. Hindus across the world celebrate by fasting and visiting temples, but Mumbai has a tradition of its own. The festival, known here as Dahi Handi, is a fusion of culture and adventure. By the dawn of the twenty-first century, Dahi Handi became a super-hyped festival.

Dahi Handi is celebrated as an enactment of Lord Krishna's act of stealing butter from earthen pots. According to the narrative of several mythological texts, in Gokul village, Krishna and his friends climbed on each other's shoulders to steal the butter that had been hung at a height, out of reach. Imitating the act, members of Govinda Pathaks, or the Govinda Brigade, scout the streets for these decorated pots of turmeric water and curds on the streets, hung around 20 to 30 feet high. The members of the Pathak then form a human pyramid to reach the pot and break it open. There are cash prizes handed out to successful Pathaks, who spend many weeks practising their formations before the festival. '*Govinda aala re aala* (Govinda has arrived)' sung by Mohammed Rafi for the movie *Bluff Master* (1963) has become the anthem for this festival.

In 2001, Jitendra Awhad, an NCP legislator from the Thane district, invented a novel version of the festival. He hung the pot at an impossible height of fifty feet and announced prize money of Rs 1.11 crore to the Pathak forming the tallest human pyramid in their attempt to reach the pot. Below the hanging pot, at a street corner, a stage was erected for a ramp walk. A DJ was hired to play dance numbers, while a tanker sprinkled water on the revellers to create the atmosphere of a rain dance. Many celebrities from the Hindi and Marathi film industries were also invited on stage. The grandeur of this particular celebration kept increasing year after year, with innovative additions, such as inviting a team of Castellers from Spain, who practise a similar sport.

Awhad's idea of giving a 'modern look' to the festival was well received and imitated by others, with some dissenting voices piping up against the dilution of culture. Politicians like Sachin Ahir, Sanjay Nirupam, Pratap Sarnaik and Rajan Vichare, belonging to different parties, started organizing the Dahi Handi fest in a similar fashion. For these politicians, the festival became a medium to hog the limelight and strengthen their support base.

Another instance of this is Ram Kadam, a real estate developer who was not a familiar face to many till 2009. That year, just a few days ahead of Janmashtami, his picture was displayed on banners and posters across the city announcing a huge cash prize to the Govinda Pathak that formed the tallest human pyramid. Kadam, who was at the time a little-known man in political circles, soon became the talk of the town and bagged a ticket for the upcoming Vidhan Sabha elections from Raj Thackeray's party, MNS. In political circles, it is said that Dahi Handi served as the launch pad into politics for this real estate developer. In 2009 he was elected as a legislator from the MNS but switched to the BJP in 2014 and was appointed as the party's spokesperson.

With time, the glamour and big money that politicians added to the festival seem to have faded. The courts, acting on Public Interest Litigations, have come down heavily upon the organizers. It has ordered several security measures and barred children below fourteen years of age from participating in the sport. The court has also put in place rules about sound levels during the festival. With these restrictions, many political organizers have discontinued the celebrations.

Festivals make Mumbai move. With time, their external form might change, but they will always remain an inherent part of the city's culture. Despite judicial intervention, governmental regulations, activism and the rising cost of celebrations, Mumbai will always be a city of festivals.

17

Dance Bars: Playing Hide-and-Seek with the Law

As soon as evening descended, gigolos with their trademark red handkerchief would begin scouting for rich female clients for the night around the Gateway of India. The striptease joints in Colaba entertained sailors from across the globe. The *mujra kotha*s of Nagpada provided dance and music till dawn. The elite went to the nightclubs spread across south Bombay and the western suburbs. Large amounts of money changed hands in the gambling dens of Grant Road.

This was Bombay's nightlife till the late 1970s, before a new sort of entertainment known as the 'dance bar' made its entry and soon evolved into a major attraction. These dance bars were to Bombay what gambling clubs are to Las Vegas, casinos to Kathmandu, 'window shopping' to Amsterdam and massage parlours to Bangkok.

One of the industries most severely hit following the 1993 Bombay riots was the business of dance bars. The tension in the city led to a shutdown of these night spots for weeks to come, and the people employed here were on the verge of starvation. The industry had nothing to do with the communal conflict—in fact, it had employees as well as patrons from both the warring communities. However, it suffered in the wake of the communal tensions polarizing the city.

My First Visit

In 1999, when I was assigned the crime beat at Aaj Tak as a cub reporter, my bureau chief, Milind Khandekar, advised me to explore the city's nightlife to understand Mumbai's crime scene better. Taking his advice seriously, I decided to observe all the activities that made Mumbai's nights. My learning began by visiting a dance bar called 'Titlee' in Parel, central Mumbai.

I was entering a bar for the first time, and I felt as shy as a lamb. My naïve self trembled at the thought of being seen at what one may term a 'shady' place. I feared getting 'caught'. Thankfully, my conscience settled my hesitation—I was not here for merrymaking, but for research.

As the security guard opened the door to let me in, a blast of music hit my ears. *'Jab chhaye mera jaadu koi bach na paaye'*, a song from the 1980 Hindi film *Lootmaar* was playing at full volume. The hall shimmered with multicoloured disco lights. A few women danced on the stage. They wore shiny ghagra-cholis, saris and salwar-kameezes; their hair untied and their make-up overdone. Middle-aged men were seated with their drinks at the dozens of rectangular tables surrounding the dance floor. Many customers were dressed formally, suggesting they worked for some private firms and had come to the bar directly from office. I sat down at a corner table and ordered some beer, which was three times its regular price. Much later, I learnt that the standard of a dance bar was determined by the price it levied on the beer it served—the costlier the beer, the more elite the clientele. The beer here was served with complimentary peanuts, a salad and wafers.

The people sitting by the bar invited the dancing girls over by waving currency notes held between two fingers. The girls promptly collected the money and danced more vigorously, gazing seductively into the eyes of their patrons, compelling them to cough up more cash. Some of the men enthusiastically rose from their seats and showered money on the girl they liked. One dancer that day was garlanded with currency notes by her special patron, who asked the cashier to play a birthday song for her. Later, I learnt that a bar dancer celebrates many days in a year as her 'birthday'. The cashier at the corner supplied a bundle of notes to customers on demand. Some Marwaris in south Mumbai's Kalbadevi ran the business of fetching bundles of new currency notes of various denominations from the Reserve Bank of India and selling them to their clients on a commission basis. Dance bars were one of their customers.

I thought of speaking to a few of the girls to understand their life and profession. But it wasn't possible to talk to them during their working hours. Mediapersons in those days were hated by dance bar owners and were not allowed to enter, as they were suspected of filming what went on inside the premises and filing negative reports. This attitude, however, changed in the later years. Back then, I was sure of being thrown out if my identity as a TV reporter was revealed to the manager. I took out a ten-rupee note from my pocket and hid my visiting card within the folds of the note. Holding it between two fingers, I made eye contact with a girl who had apparently been unnoticed by the others so far. She swiftly came to my table, and I asked her for her name. 'Veronica,' she whispered, smiling. I handed her the note and told her quietly, 'I am a reporter. I want to talk to you. My card is within the note. Please call me when you are free.' I wasn't sure whether she could hear me properly because of the loud music, but she smiled, returned to the dance floor and kept gazing at me. The bar manager stared at me suspiciously.

As I was about to leave, an obese man, loaded with gold necklaces, walked up to another man sitting at a nearby table and slapped him hard. Pulling the man up by his collar, he shouted, '*Jasmine ko nahi dekhne ka* (Don't look at Jasmine)!' The music and disco lights stopped, and the girls swiftly vanished from the stage. The man freed his collar from the obese man's grip and pushed him away, saying, '*Teri biwi hai kya* (Is she your wife)*?*' Before an all-out brawl could begin, the bar manager, aka Anna, intervened. He took the man aside and explained, 'He is Guru's man. Don't mess with him.' Guru Satam, a fugitive from Chhota Rajan's gang, was feared in that locality. The man immediately backed off and prudently left. Anna appeared to be deft at handling such drunken brawls.

Ten days had elapsed since I visited Titlee, and I started losing hope of hearing from Veronica. However, after my report of a police encounter was aired on my channel, my phone rang. 'Sir, just now I saw you on TV. I had misplaced your card. But after seeing you on TV, I searched for the card again and fortunately found it.' It was Veronica.

After that first phone call, we spoke many times as she shared her story with me. Her real name was Shipra. She hailed from Uttar Pradesh's Meerut. Her father died of tuberculosis, and she was the only earning member in her family, supporting a mother and two younger brothers. Although Shipra dropped out of school after Class VI, she wanted her brothers to complete their schooling. Thousands of girls like Shipra from Uttar Pradesh, Haryana, West Bengal, Maharashtra, Madhya Pradesh and Karnataka were forced into this profession through a combination of extreme poverty and the hope for a better life. Some of them came from Nepal and Bangladesh as well. For Shipra, bar dancing was temporary. She knew her youthful appearance was her asset, which diminished with time. At the most, the women could dance only till their late thirties. Some of them were then employed as waitresses or had to find another source of livelihood.

Shipra lived in Mira Road and shared a one-room-kitchen flat with three other girls. Many other bar dancers rented flats in the same building. Every evening, fixed taxi drivers came to pick them up and dropped them back the next morning. A few of Shipra's colleagues were married and worked for the dance bars with the consent of their husbands.

How Dance Bars Ruled Bombay Nights

Dance bars were an extension of the courtesan culture in India and were preceded by houses known as kothas, or chambers, where women performed mujras, a dance form saluting the patrons, to live Indian classical music. These courtesans were known as *tawaifs*. Bacchubhai Wadi in south Bombay was particularly famous for such kothas. Certain families were traditionally part of this profession since the Mughal era. Kothas and tawaifs have long fascinated Bollywood, and have been the subject of many movies like *Umrao Jaan* (1981), *Devdas* (1955 and 2002), *Prem Rog* (1982), *Gazal* (1964) and so on.

During the late 1960s and early 1970s, many bar owners came up with lucrative add-ons to boost their customer base. Some played live music, while others employed stand-up comedians. A few went one step further and arranged for female dancers to entertain their clients. This business idea metamorphosed into the full-fledged industry of dance bars.

The history of these bars can be traced back to 1972, when an old Sindhi man started a dance bar named 'Sonia Mahal' in south

Bombay's Nariman Point.[1] The bar was not only visited by the affluent people of Bombay but also by gangsters. A member of the Pathan gang fell in love with one dancer here and proposed to marry her. When she refused, he murdered her. The bar also witnessed brawls between members of the Dawood gang and the Pathan gang, and was often in the news for the wrong reasons. It was finally shut down in the late 1970s.

But the trend picked up in the city. The Bunts from coastal Karnataka, who ran Bombay's restaurant industry, found the concept of the dance bar profitable. They had been running Udupi-style restaurants in the city serving idli, dosai, uttapam and other south Indian dishes. Soon, many of them converted their restaurants into dance bars. Wealthy Punjabis and Parsis also invested in the industry.

Manjit Singh Sethi is one such name. He entered the business when it was still in its nascent stages. Sethi came to Bombay from Amritsar in 1959, when he was just twelve years old. To make ends meet, his father began working as a field supervisor for a builder. Growing up, he was alert to the changes in the cultural landscape in the city. By the time he reached his thirties, he had noticed the growing success of dance bars. He raised funds and started a bar called 'Neelam' in the suburb of Khar in the early 1980s. Initially, he struggled as the police and civic authorities interrupted his business several times, but he soon learnt to swim in dirty waters. In 1988, he set up another bar called 'Karishma' in Dadar, where he employed thirty-five dancers, ten stewards and twelve waiters.

With his outspoken nature and leadership qualities, Sethi soon emerged as one of the most popular people in Bombay's dance bar industry. He believes everyone associated with this fraternity should engage in the business with honour, and not behave like criminals. When I asked Sethi what he thought about the stigma attached to these bars, he said, 'I never felt uncomfortable in this profession. When both my sons work with me, you can imagine what I think about this industry. No father will bring his sons into a dubious profession.'[2] Sethi went on to establish a union of dance bar owners called 'Fight for Rights of Bar Owners Association', becoming a messiah for other dance bar owners, who were often harassed by various governmental authorities. Sethi's union frequently organized demonstrations and shutdowns to protest against this intimidation.

The number mushroomed from twenty-four dance bars in 1985 to 600 by the late 1990s. This culture extended to neighbouring cities like Navi Mumbai, Thane and Mira Road as well. By 2004, there were 1,250 dance bars across Maharashtra, which employed over 75,000 bar girls and 50,000 others as waiters, stewards, cooks and security guards. These bars attracted local customers as well as visitors from across the country. Many of them arrived in Mumbai in the evening, splurged at dance bars throughout the night and returned to their home cities the next morning. Some of these visitors even began investing in dance bars.

Black and White Economy

In some dance bars, customers spent astronomical sums of money. The Topaz on Grant Road was known for employing 'ultra-beautiful' girls and lookalikes of famous actresses as its dancers. It had different sections, ranging from basic to VIP and VVIP. The younger and more 'beautiful' dancers appeared in the VIP and VVIP sections, where liquor prices were high and the number of visitors low. One night, Abdul Kareem Telgi, the fake stamp paper baron, visited Topaz's VIP section. He drank heavily and was soon captivated by one of the dancers, and showered currency notes worth Rs 90 lakh on her.

Dance bars made their owners rich, but many others richer—such as corrupt government officials, who perceived these bars as money-minting ventures. A dance bar owner had to grease many palms to run his business. From the police to local politicians and civic officials, everyone collected a fixed amount, their *hafta,* on a monthly basis. Legally, the bars were allowed to operate only till 12.30 a.m., but most of them ran till 4 in the morning thanks to these bribes.

A dance bar also had to procure around eighteen types of licences and permits from various authorities, such as the police, the excise department, the BMC and the fire brigade. The owner had to cough up more than the stipulated amount for these licences. Dance bars were a source of revenue for both the government and corrupt officials.

Gangsters, too, eyed this ever-flowing fountain of money and demanded their share of the earnings. Those who refused were gunned down and eliminated. Around ten bar owners were killed in the 1990s by the Gawli and Naik gangs. Sethi escaped two attempts on his life by Chhota Shakeel's shooters and now carries two licensed revolvers with him for protection. During the 1990s, gangsters frequently visited dance bars and spent their ill-earned money on the dancers. This proved advantageous for the police. Select dancers were roped in as informants, and they tipped off the cops when a wanted suspect visited the bar. Amar Naik was gunned down by the police in 1996 when a bar dancer leaked his whereabouts.

Some dance bars had politicians and corrupt policemen as sleeping partners who invested their ill-acquired wealth here, effectively laundering their money. Partnerships with politicians and policemen were opportune for bar owners as they mitigated troubles from various authorities.

All this money for licences, bribes and hafta came primarily from the dancers. Around 40 per cent of their earnings every night were taken by the bar owner who employed them. The income from the sale of food and liquor was secondary.

The Most Beautiful Bar Dancer

She was once referred to as the 'most beautiful' bar dancer by a tabloid, and the others quickly followed suit. The story of Tarannum Khan tells us how dance bars could take someone from rags to riches, and how fragile their quickly earned fortunes could be.

Tarannum Khan was born and brought up in Mumbai. Her father ran a small shop in the western suburb of Andheri. She was pursuing a diploma in computer education when the communal riots of 1992 occurred. The rioters attacked Tarannum's home, and her family had to flee. For a few days, the family took shelter at a relief camp. There, her father suffered a heart attack and could not earn thereafter. It became difficult for Tarannum's family to make ends meet. At eighteen, she quit her studies and joined a bar, despite her family's reluctance. She got a few assignments to participate in dance shows organized by five-star hotels in Dubai. After working in smaller bars for a while, she was then employed at Vile Parle's Deepa Bar, the most famous one in the western suburbs. Soon, she built a fortune for herself, and bought a duplex bungalow called 'Tanishq' in Versova and a sedan.

Tarannum Khan faced another setback in 2005, though, when the Income Tax Department raided her bungalow. The house was in a plush locality, where many big names of the entertainment industry lived. During the raid, the sleuths recovered Rs 22 lakh in cash, jewellery worth Rs 9 lakh and documents of other properties that she owned.

The Income Tax Department was taken aback by the amount of wealth she had accumulated from dancing every night. In the investigation, they found that she used to place bets on cricket matches through a bookie named Digjam. They passed on this information to Mumbai Police, which registered a case and began its own inquiry.

There was a twist in the story when Sri Lankan cricketer Muttiah Muralidharan's name cropped up in this case. The media reported that Muralidharan met Tarannum at Deepa Bar along with actor Aditya Pancholi. So now the story had a bookie, a cricketer, an actor and a bar girl! It was the perfect cocktail for the media. Aditya Pancholi was questioned by the cops. He admitted to visiting Deepa Bar with Muralidharan, but denied knowing Tarannum personally.[3]

All the news channels attempted to interview Tarannum to know her side of the story, but she was elusive. After considerable effort and help from a police officer friend, I succeeded in meeting her. Clad in a burkha, she spoke to me at her bungalow.

'I have seen your reports on TV about underworld dons like Dawood and Chhota Rajan. Why are you chasing a poor girl like me who earns for her family by dancing in a bar? Does this make me a criminal like them?' she asked me, her eyes pooling with tears.[4] I convinced her that giving me an interview would stop all sorts of media speculation about her.

'Yes, I placed the bets. But I was not aware that it was illegal. It was a hobby in my free time. Many people in Mumbai do that. I was not a professional gambler. I don't know any cricketers. There are many people who come to the bar and I don't know them personally,' Tarannum said.[5] She told me that her chartered accountant didn't guide her properly about filing her income tax returns, and that was why she came on the radar of the Income Tax Department.

Finally, after a week-long investigation, Tarannum Khan was arrested on the grounds of gambling. She had to spend around two months in the Byculla prison. Deepa Bar was shut. All her savings and jewellery were seized by the Income Tax Department, and her life once again spiralled into despair.

Bombay Becoming Bangkok?

By the late 1990s, there were some dance bars that went beyond dance and liquor. They facilitated prostitution. Such bars were known as pickup points. Inspired by Thailand's go-go bars, they allowed a customer to have sex with a dancer after paying an amount to the bar owner. Some bars housed small cabins for this purpose. The opponents of dance bars feared that this trend would put Mumbai on the list of destinations for sex tourism, such as Bangkok, Pattaya and Phuket.

A bar named 'Blue Nile' in Colaba differed from the others. It was south Mumbai's only cabaret-style striptease joint. In 2001, an officer friend from the State Intelligence Department (SID) told me about the bar and accompanied me there. The interior was dimly lit. There was a semi-circular seating arrangement for around fifty people with a small dance floor. When we reached, it was around 11 p.m., and the show was about to begin. Most of the patrons were middle-aged men. There were a few foreigners as well, their crew-cut hair indicating that they were sailors. We took seats in one of the back rows.

The show began with sensuous Western music. One by one, around five or six young women came to the dance floor and slowly shed their clothes while dancing. The music was drowned out by the whistles and wild shouts of the inebriated crowd. After the women finished dancing, they went to each patron and shook hands with them. Some of them got tips. The show ended with a performance of a sexual act by two women.

If Mumbai provided opportunities to earn money, it also introduced ways to spend it—overlooking the connotations of morality and legality attached to them. However, it was ironic to see that the voices advocating moral policing grew louder when India's most modern city entered the twenty-first century.

Moral Policing vs Right to Earn and Dance

The years 2003 and 2004 dented the image of Sharad Pawar's NCP, which shared power in Maharashtra with the Congress. As per the power-sharing agreement, the home ministry came within the NCP's portfolio, and Chhagan Bhujbal became the home minister. Bhujbal's tenure was marked by several controversies. The biggest one was the multi-crore Telgi Scam. Many police officers, including a former police commissioner, were arrested in connection with the scam. There was speculation that Chhagan Bhujbal and his nephew, Sameer Bhujbal, were going to be implicated in this.

To prevent further damage, Pawar removed Bhujbal from office and replaced him with R.R. Patil, who had a comparatively cleaner image. But something more had to be done to convey that the NCP was a party that worked for public welfare. The increasing notoriety of the dance bars provided the right issue for the NCP, and R.R. Patil launched a campaign against them.

In August 2005, the government announced a ban on dance bars on the grounds that they were promoting obscenity, crime and addiction. Several media reports described how some married men left their wives after falling into the 'traps' of bar girls, and how some people sold their family's land and jewellery to shower on dancers, now living a life of penury after losing all their wealth. A youngster killed his mother when she refused to give him money to visit a dance bar. Some borrowed money to spend on bar girls, and when they couldn't repay the amount, they committed suicide. Bar dancers were denounced as money-sucking demons. Some decried that addiction to dance bars was spreading like an epidemic.

The rising HIV cases in the city were attributed to these bars as well. It was alleged that they added to the cases of drunken driving and road accidents. There was also a clamour by a women's rights group to ban these because they objectified and exploited the young dancers. It was alleged that people emerging drunk from the dance bars late at night were a public nuisance and jeopardized law and order in the city.

The ban was proposed by making amendments to the Bombay Police Act. Running a dance bar was made an offence punishable with three years' imprisonment and a fine of up to Rs 2 lakh. When the amendments came before the legislature for discussion, all the parties unanimously supported the ban, as none could afford to be seen in a negative light by opposing the bill, considering the tremendous public vilification of dance bars. R.R. Patil, who became the face of the ban, issued a diktat that if any dance bar was found running within the jurisdiction of a DCP, they would be transferred at once.

The ban led to a debate between the constitutional right to livelihood and the culture of dance bars. It seemed like an attempt at moral policing. Discrimination was also alleged, as dance performances in three- and five-star hotels were kept out of the purview of the new rules. Many dancers and bar owners participated in TV debates and vociferously protested against the ban. Demonstrations were also held at Azad Maidan. Various groups associated with the dance bar industry approached the Bombay High Court against the ban.

In April 2006, the court lifted the ban by saying that the girls had the constitutional right to earn and perform. However, the Maharashtra government challenged this order in the Supreme Court. In its 2013 order, the court upheld the Bombay High Court's verdict, accepting that the ban was discriminatory as it allowed dances in certain star-graded establishments. However, the new BJP government, led by Devendra Fadnavis, was not willing to give up easily. In 2016, the government passed the Maharashtra Prohibition of Obscene Dance in Hotels, Restaurants and Bar Rooms Act and the Protection of Dignity of Women Act, which made running a dance bar impossible. The laws segregated areas where liquor would be served and where patrons could dance, mandated the installation of CCTV cameras in bar rooms and imposed a closing time of 11.30 p.m., among other restrictions. Dance bars had to be one kilometre away from educational and religious places. Only a person of 'good character' could obtain the licence to run a bar. The laws were again challenged in the Supreme Court. In January 2019, the apex court quashed most of the provisions of the laws. However, the court upheld the timings of 6.30 p.m. to 11.30 p.m. Tips to dancers were allowed, but showering notes on them was not.

Hide-and-Seek Continues

Despite this legal victory, many bar owners were fed up with the constant legal battles they faced. The government always came up with some rule or the other to circumvent the court orders. Various licence fees were hiked multiple times. Running a dance bar was no longer a profitable business. Manjit Singh Sethi, the most vocal of dance bar owners, shut down his bar Karishma and converted it into a family restaurant. Many others quit the business as well or converted their bars into eateries. Another prominent bar owner started a real estate business. Sudhakar Shetty, owner of Deepa Bar where Tarannum Khan was employed, started a Marathi news channel.[6] The dance bars that had mushroomed all over the city now began vanishing rapidly.

Some bar dancers continued their association with their old clients, who provided them with accommodation and money, whereas a few of them got jobs in nightclubs in places such as Dubai, Bangkok and Phuket. Many continued to perform at events organized by clients on private property. But not all have been as fortunate. Many bar dancers had to turn to prostitution to make a living.

'A girl who earned Rs 30,000 to 40,000 every night by dancing in a bar was now ready to sleep with a client for just Rs 2,000. The supply of girls after the ban on dance bars in the sex trade increased more than the demand, and hence, the girls got less money,' a police informer, who had a good network among bar dancers, told me.[7] A large number of bar girls had to live a life of penury. Within a month of the law banning dance bars being passed, two bar dancers, Bilkis Sahu and Meena Ramamurthy, committed suicide. Both had young children. Many such incidents followed in later years.

A few dancers resorted to crime to support the extravagant lifestyle they had become accustomed to during the heyday of dance bars. I remember covering one such case in 2009. A dancer murdered her rich client and disposed of his body at Khandala on the Mumbai–Pune Express Highway. She took his credit card and went on a shopping spree, spending over Rs 1 lakh within a few hours.

Although the dance bars of the 1980s and 1990s vanished, they have resurfaced on a smaller scale. Under the name 'Orchestra Bar' or 'Service Bar', bar owners hire women as waitresses or singers, and clandestinely make them dance for regular clients. Some bars have made secret chambers or cavities in their walls to conceal the girls in case of a police raid. However, the police often get tips from their informers about such arrangements and the bars are raided. From 2018 to 2022, four such secret chambers have been unearthed by cops at different bars. The hide-and-seek of dance bars with the law continues.

18

Heroes and Villains of the Financial Market

'SORRY TO DISTURB YOU SO LATE, BUT I HAVE INDIA'S biggest breaking news! Harshad Mehta is dead! His body is in Thane Civil Hospital. Rush there. Nobody knows about it.'

It was around 3 a.m. on 31 December 2001 when this phone call from a source in Thane Jail woke me up.

'Shit! Are you talking about the scamster Harshad Mehta?' I gasped.

'Yes ... Yes ... The share market one. You media people call him "Big Bull". He just died. The news is confirmed. You can cross-check it with the civil hospital.'

Harshad Mehta was incarcerated in Thane Jail after he was sent to judicial custody in one of the cases registered against him. A series of thoughts struck me in quick succession: had he been murdered? People accused of white-collar crimes were tortured in jail for extortion. Was there a conspiracy to kill him so that the other big fish involved in his case could be protected?

I called the civil hospital, but the number was engaged. The only way to verify the news quickly was to see Harshad Mehta's body with my own eyes. I called my cameraman and rushed to the civil hospital on my motorcycle.

At the hospital, Mehta's body was put in a hearse to be transported to Mumbai for the post-mortem. I was the only TV journalist present. The medical staff told me that prima facie it appeared that Mehta had died of a cardiac arrest.

I had seen Mehta at numerous court hearings, and while chasing him from the CBI office in Malabar Hill to the special court when he was taken into custody. He always looked calm and resigned to his fate. The same calmness was reflected in his dead face, even though imprisonment had made his physique frail.

With those visuals, I broke the news of the death of India's biggest financial scamster in a 5 a.m. bulletin for my news channel. As a crime journalist, my regular job in those days was to follow underworld killings and police encounters. But Harshad Mehta's case was different from the usual: a crime of enormous magnitude was committed without shedding a drop of blood. To understand Harshad Mehta's dramatic life story, we need to briefly return to 1991, when India witnessed an unprecedented crisis.

1991: Balance of Payment Crisis, Liberalization and Bombay

The beginning of the last decade of the twentieth century for India was marked by political and economic instability. It began with the toppling of PM Chandra Shekhar's government and the assassination of former PM Rajiv Gandhi by Sri Lankan Tamil guerrillas in May 1991. The sympathy wave that followed led to the Congress coming back into power at the Centre after a gap of two years. The foremost challenge that the new government, led by PM P.V. Narasimha Rao, had to face was the looming economic crisis. The country had money left to pay for crude oil imports only for two weeks. The erstwhile government, led by Chandra Shekhar, had mortgaged 47 tonnes of gold to the Bank of England for Rs 1,100 crore to repay its debts. The Gulf War had aggravated the situation. India's growth rate was as low as 1.06 per cent.[1]

A diagnosis of the situation by national and international agencies concluded that apart from the economy's heavy dependence on the agricultural sector, the Licence Permit Raj system was primarily responsible for the situation. The process of setting up and running factories, and then selling the products, was arduous. Wide governmental control over businesses was hampering economic growth. The International Monetary Fund (IMF) and World Bank recommended a change in the system.[2] Moreover, after the dissolution of the Soviet Union, there was a clamour across the world for privatization.

Narasimha Rao realized that radical changes in the government's economic policies were needed to rescue the nation from bankruptcy. He needed an economist and not a politician. A senior colleague in the party suggested Dr Manmohan Singh's name. Singh was a former governor of the Reserve Bank of India (RBI) and an economic advisor to the government. Rao inducted him as the finance minister in his Cabinet.

24 July 1991 proved to be a historic day for India when Singh presented his first Budget in Parliament. The face of the Indian economy was going to change forever. The Licence Permit Raj was done away with, and India opened its door to foreign investments. The new policy also implied the encouragement of privatization, disinvestment from loss-making public units, lowering import

tariffs and reduction of taxes. In his Budget speech, Singh quoted author Victor Hugo: 'No power on Earth can stop an idea whose time has come.'[3] The idea to which Singh was referring became known as 'Liberalization'.

However, the economic reforms initiated by the government had to face tough opposition from leftist parties, and various organizations of peasants and workers. Simultaneously, the Rama temple movement by the BJP was getting stronger. A minor section in the Congress that included PM Rao felt that this movement could be advantageous for the government as it would divert public attention from economic issues, which the Centre was grappling with. For Rao, the BJP's movement became a facilitator of liberalization.[4] Bombay became one of the first cities in India to reflect the impact of liberalization, which manifested in several ways and altered the lifestyle of the people. Two major private banks were established in 1994—HDFC and ICICI—and they set up their corporate offices in Bombay. Banking services became more customer-friendly, and with thousands of ATMs mushrooming across the country, the way customers interacted with their banks was forever altered. The private banks offered home loans and personal loans at competitive interest rates, which prompted public-sector banks to follow the same. All this became possible largely due to foreign investments. Foreign money was pumped into banks in the form of foreign direct investments (FDIs) and through foreign institutional investors (FII). Public-sector banks could receive foreign investment up to 20 per cent, whereas foreign investment for private banks was capped at 74 per cent.[5]

Liberalization impacted peoples' palates as well. Bombay's Parsi–Irani restaurants and Udupi restaurants, Maharashtrian eateries were now joined by American food giants like McDonald's, Domino's

Pizza, Pizza Hut and others by 1996. One of the first outlets of McDonald's to open in Bombay was outside Victoria Terminus (renamed CST) railway station. The arrival of such outlets led to the popularizing of an 'eating out' culture in Mumbai's middle class, and families thronged these joints on weekends.

It was around the mid-1990s that mobile phones were introduced in the Indian market, thereby triggering a telecom revolution. People who waited for years to get a landline connection and had to pull strings with politicians could now buy a SIM card in their local market. Maxtouch and BPL Mobile were the two initial service providers in Bombay, and Ericsson and Siemens handsets were available. Before mobile phones became accessible to the common people, there were Public Call Offices (PCOs) at every nook and corner of the city, where people could be seen queuing up to make outstation calls. But, by the dawn of the twenty-first century, such PCOs had vanished.

The monopoly of the government-owned Air India ended with the entry of private players like East–West Airlines (1992) and Damania Airways (1993), both of which were headquartered in Bombay. They were followed by Jet Airways, Air Sahara, Kingfisher Airlines, Air Deccan, SpiceJet, IndiGo, Go Air and others. These private airlines not only offered a choice but also competitive fares to travellers.

Before liberalization, Bombay's roads were mostly ruled by three brands of cars—Ambassador, Fiat and Maruti. However, as the market opened up, around forty brands of cars entered the market, including Japan's Toyota and Honda, Germany's BMW and Mercedes-Benz, South Korea's Hyundai and America's Ford.

Liberalization also broke the monopoly of Doordarshan, India's national broadcaster, and led to the advent of satellite TV channels like Star TV, Zee TV, Sony and others. Most of these channels operated from Bombay. As of 2022, there are around 1,000 TV channels available for consumption.

Harshad Mehta: The Scam and Its Aftermath

The Ayodhya episode of 1992 slowed down the economic reforms, which were launched with much vigour a year earlier. Considering the turmoil in India, especially in Bombay, many multinationals were sceptical of investing in the country.[6] In 1992, a scam rocked the financial market, which further aggravated the situation. The face of the scam was Harshad Mehta, a thirty-eight-year-old man. Mehta was born in Rajkot and came to Bombay to complete his graduate studies in commerce. After completing his education, he took up several small-time jobs—ranging from being a salesman of an insurance company to becoming the jobber of a share-broking firm. Soon, he learnt the ropes of stock trading and the functioning of the Bombay Stock Exchange (BSE). Mehta noticed loopholes in the trading and banking systems. In the mid-1980s, he opened his own asset-management company.

When Mehta started his career as a share broker, only a handful of super-rich players influenced the Sensex. However, people noticed that the prices of any scrip that Mehta bought started rising rapidly, and he booked huge profits from them. Soon, he was nicknamed the 'Big Bull of Dalal Street'. Dalal Street is the lane in south Mumbai where the BSE is located. Investors began following Mehta's buying patterns and blindly invested in shares which he bought. Mehta, too, made efforts at image building by posing with his imported luxury SUVs, sharing pictures of his plush mansion at Worli Sea Face and running ad campaigns.[7] He was often called the 'Amitabh Bachchan' of the share market. Mehta was requested to write articles in newspapers and was invited for talks on investing in the stock market.

Everything looked hunky-dory in Harshad Mehta's life and the financial market till a report appeared in the *Times of India* on 23 April 1992. It revealed that the State Bank of India (SBI) had asked a broker (Harshad Mehta) to square up irregularities of over Rs 500 crores. This report opened a Pandora's box. Many people now realized that they had seen Mehta investing big amounts and getting rich, but they had never thought about how he was getting so much money to invest in the first place and how the price of every share he bought shot up.

After a huge uproar in Parliament, PM Manmohan Singh announced a probe by the RBI into Mehta's dealings. However, considering the criminality in the case, the CBI was also roped in. Within a few days, the CBI, the committee appointed by the RBI and reports by investigative journalists revealed the sordid but daring story of a person who was about to become India's richest man by manipulating systems of banking and the equity market.

There were numerous dimensions to the scam which contributed to Harshad Mehta's phenomenal growth within a decade. One tactic that he adopted during his initial days as a share broker was to indulge in insider trading. Insider trading is buying or selling shares by obtaining confidential information about a particular business by bribing officials of that company. This was the 'secret' behind the price rise of the shares which Mehta bought. An example of this was ACC Cement. The shares were priced at Rs 200 when Mehta bought them, but the prices shot up to Rs 9,000.[8]

However, a more serious dimension of the scam was the manipulation of the banking system. As per the system prevalent then, if a small bank needed funds, it took a short-tenure loan of about fifteen days from a bigger bank by offering its securities in exchange. After the loan was repaid, the securities were returned to the borrower bank. The lending bank profited by getting interest on the lent amount. This was called the Ready Forward (RF) system. The transaction was done through brokers or intermediaries. In practice, the papers of the actual securities were not shared by the borrower bank, but a small piece of paper called a bank receipt (BR) was handed over to assure that securities would be delivered if required. The transaction was time consuming, as sophisticated technology was yet to arrive in India. To speed up the process, the lending bank gave money to the broker on behalf of the borrower bank. The broker returned the amount with interest to the lending bank on completion of the tenure.[9]

Harshad Mehta took advantage of this system with the help of a few corrupt and negligent bank officials. He got some banks to deliver cash without actually facilitating securities from any bank and used this amount to invest in shares. After booking profits, he repaid the amount on time with interest. The banks were happy as they were getting returns from the RF transactions they did with Mehta. Another tactic adopted by him was to persuade small banks like the Bank of Karad and Metropolitan Cooperative Bank to issue BRs. On the basis of these BRs, Mehta picked up cash from big banks and used it to invest in the share market.[10]

With so much money at his disposal, Mehta was able to control the stock market by creating fictitious demand.[11] When he bought a particular scrip, other investors followed suit, and the scrip's price rose exorbitantly. After booking profits, Mehta would sell off the scrips. Apart from having a network of corrupt bank officials working for him, he also made sure to be in the good books of journalists. Ajit Joshi, a journalist who covered business in 1990s, shared an anecdote with me. There was once a group of business journalists who invested in the share market. Once after meeting Mehta, some members of the group asked him for a tip on which share to buy. Mehta directed those journalists to meet one of his men. This man advised them to buy the scrip of a particular company. The next morning, when the journalists were about to trade, the upper circuit was activated at the price of Rs 14 per share. This implied that there were only buyers and no sellers of the scrip. The journalists were able to buy the scrip only a week later when the price touched Rs 169. But, three days later, the scam was unearthed. The Sensex nosedived, and the journalists lost their money.[12]

Recollecting Harshad Mehta's days in the capital market, Joshi told me many new companies approached him to promote their stocks. He raised the price of a script from Rs 10 to Rs 1,000 in no time. 'Harshad Mehta helped many bogus companies to trade. Such companies had nothing more than a table and a chair in existence. Many people became crorepatis by following Harshad Mehta. The share market became so bullish that even the boot-polish men and hawkers selling peanuts on Dalal Street thought of investing in shares,' said Joshi.[13]

On 30 May 1992, the report of the Janakiraman Committee set up by the RBI was published, and, on the basis of its findings, the CBI registered a case against the SBI officials. Four days later, Harshad Mehta, his brother Ashwin, and the deputy managing director of SBI, C.L. Khemani, were arrested. As the investigation progressed, a few more people were arrested.

After spending over three months in jail, Mehta got bail and received a hero's welcome from some investors upon his release. According to journalist Sucheta Dalal, who exposed the scam, Mehta was a unique character. Despite spending time in jail, he remained a bubbly person. He didn't hold a grudge against the journalists who wrote against him. Dalal remembers him as being easy-going and nice to talk to, and not at all self-conscious.[14] A few months after his release, Mehta once again shocked everybody—this time with his claims. In a press conference organized at

Bombay's Indian Merchants Chamber, Mehta alleged that he paid Rs 1 crore as a bribe to PM P.V. Narasimha Rao to hush up the case. In 1999, he was convicted in just one case and was sentenced to five years of rigorous imprisonment. The case pertained to the defrauding of Maruti Udyog Limited. Mehta was able to secure bail after his conviction.[15]

In November 2001, Mehta and his two brothers, Ashwin and Sudhir, were arrested again on fresh charges of fraud. They were charged with laundering shares worth Rs 250 crore by transferring them to friends and relatives, who, in turn, introduced them back into the share market. Harshad Mehta's bail was rejected this time, and he had to spend his final days behind bars. He was forty-seven years old at the time of his death.

The Harshad Mehta scam was unprecedented in the history of the BSE, which started in the late nineteenth century. Many learnt their lessons from the scam, including investors, regulators, banks and investigating agencies. Consequently, there was a systemic change in the capital market. The Securities and Exchange Board (SEBI), which had been a paper tiger so far, got more powers. It adopted several measures to regulate listed and unlisted companies, initial public offerings (IPOs) and various investment schemes.

The scam went unnoticed for so long only because the capital market was transacting in physical shares and not in electronic or demat form. The paper-based settlement system was replaced by an electronic one, and transparency in transactions was given utmost importance. It broke the dominance of a handful of people over the capital market and opened it up for any investors meeting the minimum financial requirement. The advent of the internet era in India coincided with and contributed to the capital market reforms. In 1992, the trade was executed through brokers. Now, investors can directly trade online.

But Scams Continue ...

Although there were several reforms in the capital market and banking sector after the Harshad Mehta fiasco, scamsters somehow devised ways to hack through the new system as well. A few other scams robbed investors and depositors of their money.

Ketan Parekh was a chartered accountant, who began his career in the capital market by joining a stockbroker's firm in the 1980s. While working on Dalal Street, Parekh met Harshad Mehta, who was later on regarded as his mentor. Parekh joined Mehta's firm, Growmore Investments, which was accused of playing a role in the securities scam of 1992. Unscrupulous players in the market saw Parekh as somebody who could fit into Mehta's shoes. Mehta's downfall led to Parekh's rise.

Parekh was caught on the wrong side of the law nine years after Harshad Mehta. On 28 February 2001, Yashwant Sinha, then finance minister, delivered a Budget with the aim of initiating a second wave of reforms in the economy. It focused on the reduction of taxes and surcharges, disinvestment from government-owned industries and suggested a new labour legislation.[16] The Union Budget boosted the mood of the capital market. That day, Sensex opened at 4070.37 points and gained 177 points. However, two days later, on 2 March, the market crashed heavily, losing 176 points. The date was labelled as 'Black Friday' at the BSE. One of the major causes of the fiasco was the stocks owned by Ketan Parekh. Already rumours were floating in the market that Parekh was facing problems in repaying his dues. A week later, three brokers working for Parekh at the Calcutta Stock Exchange defaulted on payments. Meanwhile, the SEBI launched an investigation to probe the stock market crash.[17]

The real trouble began for Parekh when the vigilance chief of Bank of India filed a complaint against him with the CBI. He alleged that along with two others, Parekh had defrauded the bank to the tune of Rs 137 crore. As soon as the complaint was received, Parekh's office was raided and documents seized. On 30 March 2001, he was arrested.[18] The investigation revealed that Parekh was manipulating bank pay orders to fund his stock market trade.

The epicentre of the scam was a stone's throw away from my home in Masjid Bunder. Located in an old nondescript building on crowded Qazi Sayed Street, it was the Mandvi branch of Madhavpura Mercantile Co-operative Bank (MMCB) from where Parekh got his money.[19] Pay orders worth Rs 120 crore were allegedly issued to the stockbroker, who connived with the bank's chairman and branch manager. Parekh allegedly discounted these pay orders at the stock market branch of Bank of India and got the money released into his accounts. However, later on, these pay orders bounced. In simple words, a pay order is like a demand draft. When a demand draft issued by X bank is presented by a person to Y bank for encashment, Y bank believes that X bank has debited the amount from that person's account. However, this didn't happen in Parekh's case. The MMCB issued pay orders to Parekh without debiting any money from him.[20]

Just like Harshad Mehta, Ketan Parekh too pumped the fraudulently acquired money into the stock market. His rise was concurrent with the boom in the information technology (IT) and telecommunications (telecom) sectors. He especially invested in ten companies belonging to these two sectors. These shares were known as K-10 shares, with 'K' standing for 'Ketan'.[21] However, as there was a sudden contraction in the IT industry; people began withdrawing from K-10 shares, and Parekh found himself in trouble. After the markets crashed a day after the 2001 Union Budget was presented, the SEBI and the RBI launched a probe. They concluded that Parekh had done insider trading and swindled banks. In the two decades since, Ketan Parekh has been convicted by different courts on different charges. He was also barred from trading till 2017.[22]

In 2001, when the share market was witnessing a bloodbath, another fiasco gave a fresh blow to investors. On 2 July 2001, the board of Unit Trust of India (UTI) announced that it would discontinue payments to unit holders of the US-64 scheme for the next six months, and suspended the repurchase and redemption of units. This decision shocked the entire capital market. US-64 was one of India's first mutual fund schemes and was considered a safe public-sector instrument. It was launched as a programme delivering steady income.

The UTI reached this situation due to a lack of funds. As per U.K. Sinha, former chairman of the SEBI, the root of the crisis lay in the flawed practice that had been in place since 1993-94. The UTI started distributing dividends to unit holders that exceeded the actual income of the scheme that year. In some years, the dividend offered was as high as 28 per cent. To facilitate the payment of dividends, the accounting policy of the UTI was altered to allow reserves to be used along with surplus income to make payments. Although the SEBI doesn't allow any assured returns scheme without a guarantee from some sponsor, the UTI ran an assured income scheme without any guarantor. In 2001, the UTI reached a state where it found there was no money to pay back its investors.[23]

Individual investors suffered the blow, while large institutional investors, such as SBI and ICICI Bank, were able to encash their holdings before the fiasco came to light. This was possible because these institutional investors had their nominees on the board of the UTI, and they got a whiff of the impending crisis.[24]

Political interference was also seen as one of the causes of the UTI fiasco. It is alleged that certain imprudent decisions taken by the UTI were influenced by people in power. After the

2001 Budget, the market was in bad shape, and the government was desperate to artificially boost it by forcing public financial institutions to pump money into certain favoured scrips. Instead of primarily investing in debt, the UTI invested heavily in equity with high-risk, speculative returns. The UTI made heavy investments in Ketan Parekh's K-10 shares and suffered huge losses when the IT boom abruptly ended.[25] P.S. Subramanyam, UTI's chairman, had to resign following the debacle. This fiasco is an example of the mismanagement of funds and irresponsible governance that affected the financial market at the dawn of the twenty-first century.

Despite several security measures and the upgradation of vigilance to prevent fraud, every few years, news of some scam has kept emerging from the banking sector and financial market.

In February 2022, the SEBI came across a bizarre scam in which the former CEO of the NSE, Chitra Ramakrishna, was accused of being complicit. As per the SEBI's report, issued in March 2022, Ramakrishna was appointed CEO and MD of the NSE in April 2013. She was allegedly in touch with a 'spiritual guru' who resided in the Himalayas, and apparently followed his advice on all professional and personal matters. Ramakrishna appointed Anand Subramanian as the chief strategic officer, despite him having no experience in the capital market. Later on, he was elevated to the post of group operating officer and advisor to the MD. Subramanian was given an exorbitant salary package and received frequent pay hikes. In 2013, when Subramanian was offered a job in the NSE by Ramakrishna, he drew an annual salary of less than Rs 15 lakh from a private firm. Three years later, in 2016, he was drawing a salary of Rs 4.21 crore. He was working on a consultancy basis and worked just four days a week, which was later on extended to five days.[26]

In her statement to the SEBI, Ramakrishna had confessed that she was in touch with a yogi through the email ID 'rigyajursama@outlook.com' and sought advice from him. She referred to the person as '*siddha purusha*' and '*paramhansa*'—as in one who doesn't require a physical manifestation, but can manifest physically at will. Ramakrishna told investigators that the yogi had been guiding her for the last twenty years. However, it was suspected that this spiritual guru and Subramanian were the same person, as his instructions to Ramakrishna benefitted Subramanian immensely.[27]

The SEBI, in its investigations, found that Ramakrishna not only violated several rules and regulations while appointing Subramanian and showering favours on him, but she also shared confidential information regarding the NSE pertaining to the organizational structure, dividend scenario, financial results, human resources and other related issues to an unknown person (the spiritual guru) between 2014 to 2016.[28]

On 11 February 2022, the SEBI found Chitra Ramakrishna, Anand Subramanian and the NSE guilty of various charges, and penalized them heavily. Ramakrishna and Subramanian were asked to pay a penalty of Rs 3 crore each, while the NSE was told to pay Rs 2 crore. The SEBI also restricted Ramakrishna and Subramanian from associating with any market infrastructure for the next three years.[29] A few weeks later, they were put behind bars as well when the CBI arrested them in a case known as 'co-location scam', which happened during the tenure of Ramakrishna and Subramanian. On the basis of a complaint by a whistle-blower, the case was registered in 2018. It was alleged that some stockbroking firms, in connivance with unknown officials of the SEBI and the NSE, exploited loopholes in the exchanges server system and gained preferential access to market data.[30]

In July 2022, a former police commissioner of Mumbai was arrested by the Enforcement Directorate, alleging that his company hired by the NSE had purchased certain hardware and software to illegally intercept the telephone lines of NSE employees. The company incorporated by him in 2001 was tasked with auditing cyber vulnerabilities of the exchange's server. However, he defended himself in court by saying that his arrest was caused due to political vendetta and that his company didn't record the calls but merely analysed the already recorded ones and submitted reports to the NSE.

Rakesh Jhunjhunwala's Journey: From Rs 5,000 to Rs 41,000 Crore

'Nobody is king of the market. Those who wished to become kings had to go to Arthur Road Jail,' responded Rakesh Jhunjhunwala when a veteran journalist called him 'King of the [Stock] Market'. Jhunjhunwala was apparently referring to Harshad Mehta and Ketan Parekh, who were his contemporaries in the capital market and had been hailed as 'czars of the stock exchanges'.[31]

Unlike Mehta and Parekh, a few great investors have not crossed the line to become villains and have instead become role models thanks to their extraordinary success in the capital market. Rakesh Jhunjhunwala was prominent among them.

As a commissioner of income tax in Bombay, Jhunjhunwala's father's job was to track the income of the city's affluent people and ensure that they fulfilled their tax liabilities. At home, young Jhunjhunwala often overheard his father discussing stocks, investments, income, tax and other money matters with friends and colleagues.[32] This evoked his interest in the stock market. He borrowed money from acquaintances to buy shares. Within three years, his capital multiplied, earning around Rs 25 lakh. After his graduation, Jhunjhunwala completed his education in chartered accountancy and went on to up his own stock trading firm,

RARE Enterprises.[33] Looking at his success, he was referred to by many monikers, such as 'Investor with the Midas Touch', 'Warren Buffet of India' and 'Big Bull'. Forbes has ranked him number 438 in the world's billionaires' list in 2022, and he was the thirty-sixth richest Indian of 2021, with a net worth of Rs 41,000 crore.[34] In 2022, Jhunjhunwala forayed into the aviation sector as well, by investing in a low-cost carrier called Akasa Air.

To know more about Jhunjhunwala's success story, I met his friend Hitesh Shah. Shah was Jhunjhunwala's classmate till class XI in Marine Lines Hindi Vidya Bhavan School. Later on, the two of them studied chartered accountancy together. Shah forayed into stock trading and was followed by Jhunjhunwala. As per Shah, it was he who introduced Jhunjhunwala to many key players in the stock market. Shah told me that stock trading always occupied Jhunjhunwala's mind. Even when Jhunjhunwala went out for drinks and dinner with friends, the conversation centred on the stocks he was investing in. He always did an in-depth study of the company whose stock he decided to buy. 'A sharp mind combined with luck made him successful,' said Shah.[35] Shah also noticed that Jhunjhunwala was patient with the stocks he bought. 'He started buying shares of Titan for himself and his relatives when the price was just Rs 50. Other friends and I followed suit. We sold off our shares as soon as the price doubled, but Jhunjhunwala stayed invested and his wealth multiplied in the long run.'[36]

Veteran business journalist, and my former colleague, Shishir Sinha concurs with Shah that patience has been Jhunjhunwala's key strength. 'He not only invested money in shares, but invested "patience" as well. The combination of money and patience has given him high returns. Another strategy that has worked for him is that of buying shares when the prices are low. People tend to buy those shares whose prices are rising and often face losses when the prices drop. Jhunjhunwala thoroughly studied the fundamentals of companies and invested in those which potentially had a bright future,' said Sinha.[37]

Jhunjhunwala himself had been open about how he made so much money. 'Whichever factors I considered in 1985 while investing, I consider those factors in 2020 as well. Nothing has changed. Because I was bullish, I could earn the wealth I have,' Jhunjhunwala once said in an interview with a news channel.[38]

Shishir Sinha notes that Jhunjhunwala was a highly respected name in the financial market. 'People followed him, but he never misguided people. He never manipulated. Investors trusted that if Jhunjhunwala was putting money in a particular share, it must give good returns.'[39]

Success stories of people like Rakesh Jhunjhunwala have attracted many people to the stock market. The market has expanded rapidly over the past three decades. When the Sensex or the BSE crossed the 4,000 mark in March 1992, it was considered an important milestone in the capital market's history. In 2022, the Sensex fluctuated at around 61,000 points. Since the beginning of the new century, a large chunk of investors in shares are salaried, middle-class people. With low interest rates on fixed deposits in banks and investments in real estate becoming risky, stock markets have become a promising option for them to multiply their money. Online trading has made investing in shares easy and convenient. One can find numerous wealth managers and investment advisors in middle-class neighbourhoods of Mumbai, who keep their clients abreast of the latest investment products, IPOs and mutual funds. However, veteran journalist Sucheta Dalal has an observation: 'Today, people are not doing research before investing, although we have the internet and Google. The biggest chunk of investors is the age group between eighteen–thirty-five years, but they are simply not bothered [to do their research].'[40]

Despite all its perils, the popularity of investing in shares has only soared in the new century. In the same time frame, another mode of investment appeared in the form of real estate.

19
Landscape to Skyline

'WHENEVER YOU ARE IN DELHI, STAY AT MY home.'

These words may sound common enough, but to a Mumbaikar, they appear like a warm and enticing melody. Such an earnest and hospitable offer from a Delhi resident is less likely to be reciprocated by their average Mumbaikar friend, who might live in a much smaller house, even if both earn the same amount and enjoy a similar social status.

Housing has always been expensive in Mumbai, and it is one of the costliest cities in the world in terms of real estate. A person living in a one bedroom–hall–kitchen in Mumbai could buy a much bigger house in Delhi, Lucknow, Ahmedabad, Kolkata or any other part of India, really. Often, people from other Indian cities are shocked to see their friends and relatives living in Mumbai's 'crunched homes'.

In the early sixteenth century, when the Portuguese first landed on the Bombay archipelago, they probably never even imagined that these miniature islands would transform into India's biggest urban centre in the coming centuries. It was the British who made this happen. In the late seventeenth century, Gerald Aungier, the British governor, shifted the government headquarters from Surat to Bombay, which catalysed growth in the city. Being the commercial capital of the country, Bombay emerged as a much-sought-after city over the decades. Its population grew from a mere 60,000[1] during Aungier's reign to over 2 crore in 2022.[2] Over the centuries, due to its ports, railways, industries, the stock market, Bollywood and businesses, Mumbai has attracted several migrants looking for a source of livelihood and the hope of a better life.

Emergence of Satellite Cities

As Bombay became the most populated city in India, its infrastructure and civic arrangements failed to keep up. This soon started taking a toll on its residents' quality of life. In the latter half of the twentieth century, the need to decongest the city and develop more urban centres was felt more than ever. Consequently, satellite towns and cities mushroomed over the years.

Today, most of my childhood friends and schoolmates live in neighbouring cities like Navi Mumbai, Panvel, Mira-Bhayandar, Kalyan-Dombivli or Vasai-Virar. As most of them got married and had children, the need for bigger and better homes led them to move outside the main city. Housing here was much cheaper than in Mumbai, and they were easily connected through local trains.

The closest to Mumbai is Navi Mumbai. Unlike Mumbai, Navi Mumbai is a planned urban centre. It was publicized as the 'City of the Twenty-First Century', when the Maharashtra government proposed the township in 1971. The City Industrial Development Corporation (CIDCO) was established to construct the new city. A road bridge was made over Thane Creek to link Mumbai and Navi Mumbai as early as 1973, but it was the opening of a railway bridge between Mankhurd and Vashi in 1992 that acted as a catalyst for Navi Mumbai's evolution. It facilitated travel into the heart of Mumbai via local trains. Until May 1992, local trains ran just between Victoria Terminus (now CST) and Mankhurd on the Harbour Line. Coincidentally, 1992 was the year when the first phase of communal riots broke out in Bombay, after which numerous people migrated to Navi Mumbai.

The riots led to the ghettoization of communities as people became wary of living with neighbours of different communities. Thus, Naya Nagar in Mira Road was dominated by Muslims, whereas the neighbouring Bhayandar was populated by Gujarati and Marwari Hindus. Many Muslim families shifted to places like Kausa, Mumbra and Nala Sopara. People stayed together for safety and cultural reasons. In some housing societies, where a majority of members belonged to communities practising strict vegetarianism, by-laws were made to prevent meat eaters from buying a home there. Such attempts have led to controversies and conflicts among the communities, and have been legally challenged.

As the city kept growing, many hamlets and small settlements transformed into flourishing townships with all the amenities one would expect in Mumbai. In fact, the quality of life of an average resident of Navi Mumbai is deemed better than those living in Mumbai. In the Ease of Living Index of 2018, Navi Mumbai was ranked as the second-most liveable city in India, with Pune being the first. Mumbai was number three.[3] Today, Navi Mumbai has almost everything one could expect in a modern Indian city, with state-of-the-art railway stations, institutes of higher education, high-tech healthcare facilities, regular water and power supply, a full-sized cricket stadium and an international airport. A trans-harbour link between Sewri and Nhava-Sheva has brought the two cities closer.

New Land Parcels

It seems ironic that during the1990s, people were migrating out of Mumbai while more and more land was being made available for housing in the city limits. Several government policies facilitated the emergence of new residential colonies across the city. Real estate became one of the most profitable industries.

A chunk of the northeastern parts of Mumbai—from Wadala to Anik and Mahul—composed mostly of marshy land, mangroves and salt pans, was seen as unfit for human settlement till the early 1990s. The only human presence here were a few slum pockets, so rife with criminal activity that people avoided commuting through these parts after dusk. Three decades later, the landscape and population have entirely changed. Hundreds of upper- and middle-class families have bought their homes in three residential colonies developed by prominent builders. In fact, one builder named his colony 'New Cuffe Parade' inspired by south Mumbai's plush Cuffe Parade. Another went to the extent of naming a part of his colony as 'New York'.

An amendment to the Maharashtra Slum Areas Act of 1971 led to the setting up of the Slum Rehabilitation Authority (SRA) by the state government, which proved to be a gold mine for the real estate industry. The slums, which, till then, had been considered an eyesore in the city, suddenly became valuable. The law allowed builders to erect buildings on slum lands and, after providing free houses to slum dwellers, sell the remaining flats in the open market. Any slum dweller who proved his residency in Bombay before 1995 was entitled to a free tenement under the scheme. As an incentive, the builders got Floor Space Index (FSI), also known as Floor Area Ratio (FRA) in some other parts of India, proportionate to the area of slums they developed. There are 2,397 slum clusters in Mumbai, which are gradually being developed under this scheme.[4] The slum rehabilitation scheme revolutionized the real estate market.

Dharavi, which is often referred to as one of Asia's largest slum colonies, and is a symbol of Mumbai's paradoxical nature, will change, but only gradually. In 2004, the government announced the Dharavi Redevelopment Project to transform this colony, which is spread over 2.1 square kilometres. The development was to be undertaken by government agencies along with private players. However, until 2002, out of 10 lakh slum dwellers living in 2 lakh hutments, only 350 moved to new houses constructed by Maharashtra Housing Area Development Authority (MHADA). The project has been obstructed by bureaucratic hurdles, an economic slowdown and litigations. The regular slum rehabilitation plan couldn't apply to Dharavi, which is not just a residential cluster but also houses small-scale industries of leather products and pottery. Its informal economy has to be considered as well, and this is one big reason for the delay in the project. The residents of Dharavi have united under the Dharavi Redevelopment Committee, and give voice to their issues through legal and political forums. Once the Dharavi project takes off, the real estate industry is likely to get around 600 acres of land for development.

The repeal of the Urban Land Ceiling Act by the state government in November 2007 has freed up large land parcels for development. The law was enacted to prevent the concentration of land in the hands of a few and facilitate housing for all. Under this, an individual wasn't allowed to hold vacant land of over 500 square metres. The state government was supposed to acquire the excess land and use it for the purpose of housing. However, the state failed to get hold of the land and start residential projects. The law was then criticized for being counterproductive and for holding up land in the housing market. Its repeal has made around 500 hectares of plots available for real estate projects.[5]

Frequent revisions of Development Control Rules (DCRs) have also boosted the real estate market. According to the revised rules, a builder can get an incentive FSI of around 50 per cent. This also facilitates the repair and redevelopment of old and dilapidated buildings, thus increasing their FSI. The cost is borne by the builder, who can then sell the extra FSI received as incentive.

Apart from these regulatory amendments, the city of Mumbai, which is surrounded by sea and creeks, got ample plots from mills as well. Further, the state government, in 2020, announced that it would conduct a geological survey with the help of IIT Bombay on the viability of constructing houses on salt pan land. If the project is approved, over 355 acres of land could open up for development. However, environmentalists have opposed the move, which they say will be disastrous for the city.[6]

The Reality of Realty

In 2005, I moved out from Masjid Bunder and took a loan of Rs 21 lakh to buy a 1-BHK flat in Bhakti Park, Wadala. In 2018, when I planned to shift to a bigger house, I sold the same flat for Rs 1.22 crore!

My case is a minor example of the real estate boom in Mumbai that began in 2005-06. Prices swelled rapidly, and it became tougher for middle-class people to own a house in Mumbai.

To understand this sudden boom, we need to look at the developments of the previous decade. The liberalization policy adopted by the P.V. Narasimha Rao government in 1991 impacted the real estate market favourably. By 2005, foreign direct investment was allowed in this sector up to 100 per cent, and the financial reforms attracted foreign venture capitalists.

The increase in supply led to an increase in demand as well. Senior real estate journalist Varun Singh told me, 'Earlier, people used to buy homes from their savings, by borrowing from friends or relatives, or by dipping into their retirement funds. But because of liberalization, banks made home loans easily available to the buyers.'[7] It was during the late 1990s that words like EMI (equated monthly instalment), fixed rate of interest, floating rate of interest, foreclosure, etc., began becoming a part of the middle-class lexicon. Apart from public-sector banks, private banks, like HDFC and ICICI, and housing finance companies offered low and competitive rates of interest to prospective home buyers. Home loan providers offered not only flexible repayment plans but also add-on services such as insurance during critical illness and job loss. Tax incentives to those availing of home loans further boosted the demand.

According to builder Subhash Patel, whose family has been in the real estate business for generations, the Gulf War also played a pivotal role in shaping the market. 'Many people who had invested their money in Gulf countries withdrew and reinvested in real estate in Mumbai. Several NRIs settled in the US and the UK found the real estate market lucrative, and invested heavily in various projects. Anticipating a price hike, they bought houses in bulk to be resold,' he said.[8]

With liberalization, the stock market also boomed, and investors booked rewarding profits. However, in the late 1990s, several scams in the share market were unearthed. This slowed down the returns from investment in shares. 'People were looking for alternate avenues for investment and found the real estate market convenient. Back then, there was not much taxation in this sector and surveillance by authorities was also not strict. Hence, many people parked their cash in real estate projects. This increase in demand led to skyrocketing prices,' Patel explained.[9]

Just before the 2005-06 boom, my uncle Shashikant booked a flat in an upcoming township at Dombivli. One day, he suddenly received a rude SMS: 'Your booking has been cancelled. Booking amount will be refunded.' Many others who had booked flats along with him got such messages. The builder abruptly cancelled the bookings as prices shot up and refunded the booking amount, paying no interest to the investors. A few weeks later, bookings reopened for the same project, but with much higher prices.

The salaried middle class bought houses for residential purposes, but rich investors bought them to resell and make profits, thus inflating prices. Consequently, it once again became tough to own a home in Mumbai. Varun Singh believes the builder lobby played its own game and kept the prices high using its clout in the government.

Governmental agencies like the MHADA have been tasked with providing affordable housing to people. Every year, the authority comes up with projects offering hundreds of houses suiting various income groups. MHADA homes are cheaper than the market, and hence, the demand is always more than the supply. These houses are allotted to applicants on a lottery basis.

Chimneys to Towers

In 2003, the fourth-floor canteen of Star News at Mahalaxmi offered a majestic view of central Mumbai, with tall chimneys reminding residents that the area was once known as the mill district. Today, some chimneys still survive because of their heritage value, but they are dwarfed by the numerous skyscrapers dominating the skyline. Since Mumbai is short on land, surrounded as it is by the sea and creeks, the only way the city could grow was vertically. The mill lands on which these chimneys stand have been converted into residential towers and malls. Youngsters in the city will know Lower Parel's Phoenix Mill as a shopping and entertainment destination. The neighbouring Kamala Mill too houses several fine dining restaurants, and commercial establishments like banks and TV studios.

The chimneys and the mills not only represent Mumbai's industrial history but have also played a crucial role in the evolution of the megapolis. They have given so much to the city—ranging from its character as a commercial centre to political parties, festivals and also … its underworld!

Bombay's first cotton mill was set up in 1856, shortly after the railways started and the city's port became fully functional. Soon, the number of mills multiplied, and by the end of the nineteenth century, there were over a hundred mills in Bombay. The city became such a great textile hub that it was described as the 'Manchester of the East'. By the late twentieth century, over 2.5 lakh workers were employed in various mills. Although most of the mill owners were Parsis or Gujaratis, their workers hailed from the Konkan region of Maharashtra or from north Indian states.

The blooming textile industries birthed several labour unions too. Initially, the unions belonging to the Communist parties were strong, but they were challenged by the Congress and Shiv Sena unions. In the late twentieth century, when trade unions in Bombay were undergoing an upheaval, Dr Dutta Samant emerged as the most powerful leader of mill workers, adopting a militant approach to pursue their cause. In 1982, Samant called for a strike to demand bonuses and a hike in workers' wages. All negotiations with the government and mill owners failed.

Historians of Mumbai refer to the strike that followed as 'the great Bombay textile strike', as it sounded the death knell for the city's textile industry. The strike continued for almost two years and led to the permanent closure of over eighty mills. Over 2.5 lakh workers were rendered unemployed. Many mill owners bought land in neighbouring Gujarat and shifted their businesses there.

As a result, the hustle and bustle in the mill district vanished, and the desolate buildings almost seemed haunted in their appearance. That's when they caught the attention of the real estate industry as easily accessible land for the growth of the city.

In 1991, the state government came up with new Development Control Rules for Bombay, which allowed for the sale of mill lands on the condition that a part of the parcel had to contain affordable housing and public projects. The rules were tweaked and twisted many times under the pressure of the builder lobby in later years. Ultimately, most of the defunct mills were redeveloped for commercial and residential projects. The National Textile Corporation, which owned several mills in Mumbai, also decided to sell its land for commercial use. Today, there are buildings as high as ninety floors on this parcel. Palais Royale, under construction at the time of writing this book, stands on mill land and is deemed to be one of the tallest skyscrapers in India.

The end of the mill era also changed the demography of areas in central Mumbai, such as Parel, Lalbaug, Chinchpokli, Kala Chowki and so on. These areas were inhabited by Maharashtrian mill workers who lived in British-era chawls built by the Bombay Development Department (BDD) and Bombay Improvement Trust (BIT), as well as private companies.

These chawls lacked space, and had poor sanitation and inadequate amenities. Most of them have now been replaced by tall residential towers, which house people from across India who have come to the city in search of livelihood. The BDD and BIT chawls are also being redeveloped. 'Many mill workers and their family members now work as security guards at these towers built on mill lands,' notes Varun Singh.[10]

Home Gone, EMI On!

My friend Anthony (name changed on request) booked a 2-BHK flat in an under-construction township in Kalyan for Rs 35 lakh. He paid about Rs 20 lakh to the builder, but the project soon got stuck in litigation. After waiting for around five years, Anthony cancelled his booking. He retrieved his money, but not without a struggle.

Though he didn't get any interest on his payment, Anthony was fortunate that he could recover at least the principal amount. There have been hundreds of cases in Mumbai where homebuyers neither got their flat nor their refund. Some kept paying their EMI, and those who resisted were harassed by recovery agents. In some cases, litigations stalled the projects, whereas, in others, the builders deliberately cheated their customers.

There have also been cases where builders have funnelled the money gained in one project into some other project. Some unscrupulous builders victimized homebuyers through various means, such as selling one flat to many people, giving less than the promised carpet area, not providing the promised amenities, adding hidden clauses in the agreement and so on. Such cases became so rampant that my channel, ABP News, launched a campaign titled *'Mera Ghar, Mera Haq'* to highlight the plight of the victims.

If the private security industry is the biggest recruiter of ex-servicemen in India, the real estate sector has been one of the biggest employers of retired police officers. Almost every prominent builder in Mumbai has taken former cops on board either as partners or consultants. The advantage is that policemen can help keep troublemakers at bay. If somebody threatens a builder with a police complaint, these former cops are tasked with 'managing the police station'. The officer in-charge then dismisses the complainant by saying something like, 'This is a civil matter. We can't do anything. Go to the court.' They also help in liaising with senior officials in the police and the civil administration, and are expected to deal with extortionists, who often come disguised as social workers, RTI activists, local politicians and journalists, and demand money after pointing out irregularities in their projects. Many builders willingly offer some amount to potential troublemakers calling it 'good-luck money'.

Of late, home buyers have got some respite in the form of the Real Estate Regulation and Development Act, 2016, also known as RERA. The Act safeguards the interest of homebuyers by making it mandatory for all real estate projects to get registered with the RERA authority. There are provisions of penalties and imprisonment for builders who violate the law. It also acts as a point of redressal for aggrieved homebuyers.

20

All That Glitters ... Is Going Away from Mumbai?

PEOPLE COME TO MUMBAI TO MAKE MONEY. THE CITY has traded in cotton, opium, silver, gold and diamonds over the centuries, as well as in human beings. Rags-to-riches stories sprout from every nook and corner. The city has always been beneficial for enterprising people, for risk-takers and hard workers. The city rewards people who arrive with dreams and endure the struggle. With so much upheaval in the Indian economy over the past few decades, the question now being asked is whether Mumbai is keeping up with its historical image of the country's urbs prima.

Textile Industry: Competitors of Mumbai

The closure of mills due to prolonged strikes and militant unionism led to the world-famous textile industry migrating almost entirely from the city by the mid-1990s. The production process, which was earlier completed within a single mill, was now decentralized and divided into specific sub-industries, such as yarn spinning, weaving, dyeing, printing, cutting, embroidering and packing. Since the cost of labour, electricity, water and octroi was high, such sub-industries began developing in smaller cities like Surat, Bhiwandi, Malegaon and Ichalkaranji.

Rajiv Singhal of Bharat Merchants' Chambers told me, 'Surat has now become a big ocean of the textile industry. The world's best ladies' dress materials are now available in Surat. Around forty years ago, there was a craze among the elite for imported Japanese saris that were sold mostly in south Bombay's Mohta Market and Manish Market. Now, the same quality of saris is manufactured and sold in Surat.'[1]

The flight of the textile industry from Mumbai affected its wholesale market as well. Industrialist Dhirubhai Ambani forayed into yarn exporting after quitting his business of spices and opened a small office in the nineteenth-century Mulji Jetha Market.[2] Major markets such as Mulji Jetha, Mangaldas and Swadeshi sold clothes wholesale. According to Singhal, 'Trading in these iconic markets has undergone a sea change. Due to labour issues and operating costs, many erstwhile wholesalers now deal in retail.'[3]

Singhal notes that the significance of Mumbai's ports has also diminished. Several new ports like Jawaharlal Nehru Port and Mundra Port on the western coast of India now facilitate international trade.

Gold, Silver and Diamonds

The 1978 Amitabh Bachchan–starrer *Don* had a song, '*Ee hai Bambai nagariya, tu dekh babua … Sone chandi ki dagariya tu dekh babua* (This is the city of Bombay, you see, baby … The city of gold and silver, you see, baby).'

When asked if these words still hold true, Kumar Jain replied with a firm no. Jain has continued his ancestral business of trading in gold and silver. His great-grandfather Umedmal was one of the five jewellers who opened their shop in the backyard of the Mumbadevi temple in the early twentieth century. In a few years, the area developed into Zaveri Bazaar, a prime market of gold and silver, with over 3,000 shops. 'In 1925, the price of gold was Rs 18.75 per tola [in 2022, at the time of writing this book, it was over Rs 57,000 per tola]. People visiting Mumbadevi temple used to buy gold jewellery at our shops. The merchants got to work as early as 6 a.m. But everything has changed now,' said Jain.[4]

Jain believes that shoppers at Zaveri Bazaar don't have a pleasant experience any more. The traffic jams, lack of parking space and overcrowded streets make the market unappealing. Moreover, the Zaveri Bazaar–Mumbadevi vicinity has witnessed three bomb blasts in the last thirty years, taking over a hundred lives. 'The new generation avoids coming to Zaveri Bazaar and shop at their local jewellery stores in the suburbs instead. But older customers still rely on us. There has been a drop in the number of foreign customers visiting this market as well,' says Jain.[5]

While the gold dealer Kumar Jain is unhappy with how the change has impacted the bazaar, diamond merchant Sanjay Kothari is elated with the success of his business. Kothari, the former chairman of Gems and Jewellery Export Promotion Council, says, 'India is ruling the diamond trade of the world.'[6]

The diamond trade in Bombay also began at Zaveri Bazaar, where a few diamond traders opened their shops in the by-lane known as Dhanji Street. Earlier, there were restrictions on importing raw materials, but during the 1960s, the government relaxed some of these rules. This led to the growth of the diamond industry in Bombay. From the congested and dingy lanes of Zaveri Bazaar, the diamond business stretched to the multistorey Panchratna Building at Charni Road. During Sharad Pawar's tenure as Maharashtra's chief minister in the 1980s, land was allotted for the construction of a diamond bourse in the Bandra-Kurla Complex. The bourse, spread over 20 acres and nine towers, was started in 2010. With over 4,000 members and 2,500 offices, it claims to be the world's biggest bourse.

The manufacturing of diamond products is mostly done in Surat, while marketing and trading take place in Mumbai. Many people employed in the diamond industry commute between the two cities every day, usually in the double-decker train named 'Flying Rani', operated by Indian Railways, that runs between Surat and Mumbai. However, this may end soon, as another huge diamond bourse is opening in Surat. Kothari believes that this one could lead to many businesses shifting from Mumbai to Surat, without affecting Mumbai too much. Foreigners will still come to Mumbai to shop.

'The diamond industry in India is expanding and is now worth $25 billion. It is giving tough competition to established players like Belgium and Israel,' said Kothari.[7]

Unclear Waters

'When Kasab and company landed in Mumbai, they not only killed hundreds of people but also the entire marine industry. Due to enhanced security measures, you can't take your boat out at night,' my friend Rajiv Somani said, whose business deals with water sports and beach safety.[8]

Mumbai might be perceived as the financial hub of India, but Somani's experience makes him believe that it is not easy to run a business here, especially a greenfield project. Somani is a man who dreamt of doing something different and took the risk of making it real. But the government's lack of foresight, excessive regulations, bureaucratic hassles and litigation shattered his vision.

With a coastline stretching over a hundred kilometres, Mumbai has more than a dozen beaches, but there is not a single integrated recreational water sports facility in the entire city. In 2001, when the Maharashtra Tourism Development Corporation (MTDC) issued a tender to set up a water sports facility at Girgaon Chowpatty, Rajiv Somani took the plunge.

'With conducive calm and flat water, I thought Girgaon bay has been made by god for water sports,' said Somani.[9] In partnership with film star Suniel Shetty, he started a company named 'Drishti Adventure Sports'. The company began operating H2O Water Sports Complex, a floating restaurant named Suzie Wong and a beach restaurant called Salt Water Grill. The integrated complex offered a jetty, freshwater showers and changing rooms.

However, earning a reputation for running a safe and accident-free water sports facility couldn't save him from trouble. Somani claims to have faced harassment from the bureaucracy and to being pulled into inter-agency conflicts and litigation. 'As per the tourism policy, you arrange a restaurant and a changing room, but then somebody raises a PIL and you have to stop. Coastal Regulatory Zone (CRZ) rules were cited to stop us from running the restaurant, but tell me, 400 years ago, were fishermen not cooking on the shore? One department is not aware of what the other one is doing. The tendering authority must take all clearances. The single-window clearance system will ease problems like this. But they act as mere rent collectors,' shared Somani.[10]

Local Trains: Still Mumbai's 'Lifeline'?

Anything that fails to keep up with Mumbai's pace is quickly shown the way out—be it trams in the 1960s or the iconic horse-pulled

Victorias that got banned by the Bombay High Court in 2015. Though animal cruelty was cited as the grounds for the ban on Victorias, their function had anyway been reduced to charming joyrides with the introduction of modern modes of transport.

The importance of local trains in Mumbai is often described with the clichéd phrase 'lifelines of Mumbai'. Indeed, they have become an indispensable part of the city, carrying 75 lakh passengers every day and connecting downtown Mumbai with distant suburbs. As the number of passengers rose over the years, the length of local trains also stretched from four bogies to twelve. Despite this, the local train services have been overwhelmed thanks to the ever-increasing population.

To catch a local train during the peak hours and find a place to sit (or even stand, for that matter), one has to be an adept runner, a wrestler and a gymnast. Every year, a sizeable number of passengers fall to their death due to overcrowding. Between 2005 and 2015, a total of 6,989 people left their homes to travel by local train and never returned. These were among those 25,722 passengers who fell from local trains during these ten years.[11] If you travel by local trains, you can never be certain of returning home on time (or alive!). Even an hour's disruption to the local train network during rush hours causes chaos in the city.

But Mumbai's reliance on local trains is set to change thanks to the upcoming metro network. The city got its first metro line in 2014, which runs between Versova in the western suburbs and Ghatkopar in the eastern suburbs—covering a distance of 11 km. By 2025, the network is expected to widen with fourteen lines connecting every part of the Mumbai metropolitan region. All lines are elevated, except Line 3, which is fully underground. This ensures that the network will not be affected by floods that devastate the city every monsoon.

The metro will ease overcrowding in local trains, as well. Like the local train networks, most metro lines are north–southbound, so passenger traffic from the trains can shift to the metro. Metro 3 is the longest line in the network and connects Seepz of the western suburbs with Cuffe Parade in south Mumbai. Three of the lines will provide east–west connectivity as well.

However, Rajendra Aklekar, a veteran journalist of the railway beat, doesn't see the metro as an immediate serious competitor to the existing local train network and believes that will happen only after a generation or two. 'As the new network gets completed and the level of acceptance increases, the numbers may rise. But it all depends on the algorithms of its timetabling, fare and other elements vis-à-vis the existing suburban train network. With a minimum fare of Rs 10, swanky new-tech trains, the metro network does promise to be cheaper and more appealing, but it may have its own limitations. With access control, a curated atmosphere and more sophisticated travel, the metro may, for now, become a favourite for the working class that believes in class,' he told me.[12]

In Aklekar's view, local trains still remain the cheapest and fastest mode of transport covering the vast Mumbai Metropolitan Region. 'With such free access, without any limitations, it is the crowds of commuters that have owned the Mumbai local train, moulded it in their culture and shaped it as per their aspirations, making it the lifeline, and the janta's favourite,' he quipped.[13]

Monorail: The White Elephant of Mumbai

In early 2010, a luxury resort company offered to take the crew of Star News to showcase its newly launched resort on the eastern coast of Malaysia. I convinced my superiors to send me for the junket by arguing that the tour would serve two purposes: One, we would do a short feature on Malaysian tourism since the holiday season was approaching; and second, we would be able to do a story on how the monorail system was working in Kuala Lumpur. Since the upcoming monorail network in Mumbai was being built by the same Malaysian company, Scomi, we would be able to conduct interviews with their executives as well. I was personally eager to do the story since the monorail network was planned to pass through Bhakti Park, the residential colony where I lived. The bosses were convinced, and I was off to KL.

Four years later, when the first monorail was launched in Mumbai in February 2014; long queues formed outside the stations for over a week. Families and friends thronged the station as if they were on a picnic. The crowd pushed inside the carriages like cattle to enjoy a joyride on Mumbai's newest mode of transport. In fact, it was India's first monorail project. Running on elevated concrete tracks, it was different from Patiala State Railway's monorail, whose replica can be seen at Delhi's rail museum.

Looking at the initial public response, the government was elated. But the preliminary excitement was short-lived. Once people got bored with the joyrides, their enthusiasm waned, and the monorail turned out to be a white elephant in the city. Colourful monorail carriages pass in front of my residence every day, and I often see them empty.

The project was commissioned by the Mumbai Metropolitan Region Development Authority (MMRDA) to Larsen & Toubro and the Malaysian company Scomi in 2008. During my interview in 2010, Scomi's President, Syahrunizam Samsudin, had told me enthusiastically, 'We do micro-surgeries in cities to solve the problem of traffic jams.'[14] However, the monorail project made headlines for all the wrong reasons. The total planned length of the monorail was nineteen kilometres, from Chembur in the northeastern suburbs to Jacob Circle in central Mumbai. The first phase of seven kilometres from Chembur to Wadala was to commence in 2011, but the project got delayed, leading to cost escalation. Finally, the first monorail was launched in February 2014. In the initial days, there were frequent breakdowns. There were two incidents in which passengers were stranded in the elevated monorail cars, and the fire brigade had to be called to rescue them. In another case, a train caught fire while in motion. Fortunately, there were no casualties.

Apart from mishaps, the monorail is an example of an ill-planned big-ticket project. Some stations such as Bhakti Park are far from residential colonies, while others such as Wadala Depot and GTB Nagar are barely 250 metres from each other. Another issue is frequency. While local trains or the metro arrive every three to ten minutes, often it takes thirty to forty-five minutes for one monorail train to arrive after the previous one. Due to such factors, the monorail received a poor response from Mumbaikars, and its operating cost continues to exceed its income. There were plans to construct more monorail lines, but these have been shelved.

Roads and Bridges: Work in Progress ... Always!

It seems paradoxical that the government is investing in improving public transport by coming up with metro and monorail lines while facilitating more cars on the roads of Mumbai. The development of new roads and bridges in Mumbai is primarily car-centric. This, even as the administrators are brainstorming solutions to mitigate the impact of global warming in the city.

The streak of road development in Mumbai began in 1996 after the Shiv Sena–BJP government came to power. Nitin Gadkari, the then Public Works Department minister, undertook an ambitious project of constructing fifty-five flyovers across and around Mumbai. The city witnessed chaotic traffic jams as simultaneous construction work went on at multiple locations with boards saying, 'Work in progress. Bear the inconvenience today for a better tomorrow.' Even after the Shiv Sena–BJP government was ousted in 1999, the 'work in progress' continued.

In March 2010, the Bandra–Worli Sea Link opened, which reduced the distance between the two locations from twenty minutes to five minutes. Similarly, Eastern Freeway, which opened in 2014, swiftly connects south Mumbai to the northeastern suburb of Chembur. The dawn of the new century saw the launch of long flyovers like the J.J. Flyover and Lalbaug Flyover.

Mumbai is once again experiencing the chaotic road traffic of the 1990s due to the concurrent construction of several metro lines and other infrastructure projects. In 2022, while this book was being written, both the eastern and western coasts of Mumbai were undergoing transformation. In 2018, the construction of the Mumbai Trans-Harbour Link began. The twenty-one-kilometre-long bridge will connect Sewri in central Mumbai to Nhava-Sheva near Navi Mumbai. It will reduce the travel time to Panvel, Alibaug, Pune and Goa by an hour. When completed in 2023, it will be India's longest sea bridge. An equally ambitious project is being constructed on the western coast as well by the BMC—the twenty-two-kilometre-long Mumbai Coastal Road will connect south Mumbai's Marine Drive with the northwestern suburb of Kandivali.

In February 2022, a water taxi service was started from Bhaucha Dhakka to Navi Mumbai, connecting the two cities within half an hour through speed boats and catamarans. However, due to its high cost, it has not yet become the preferred mode of transport among people who commute between the two cities, and its survival is uncertain.

Mumbai Remains Humane ...

The skyline of Mumbai can change, its infrastructure can transform, the businesses and the ways in which people conduct transactions can evolve, but there are certain elements of the city's character that have remained constant over the decades. Veteran journalist and author Shankkar Aiyar concurs with me on this observation. Aiyar has lived, observed and reported on Mumbai's politics and economy since the 1980s. When we met at a conclave organized by my channel in March 2022, he shared his observations about Mumbai's character with me.

In his view, the transformation of the landscape from postcolonial brick and mortar to flashy steel and glass conveys the transition of businesses and the economy—old industries have long since yielded to the power of globalization, the language of unions has long lost out to the pragmatic magic of moolah, and mill lands and chimneys are now props in the city's architectural framework hosting a burgeoning services economy. Without the brouhaha of Bengaluru, Mumbai is the start-up capital of business ideas, of entrepreneurship and has always epitomized the essence of the gig economy.

'Yet,' said Aiyar, 'it stands apart in solitary splendour among cities. It is still the land of opportunities. Amidst the landscape of tired aspirations, Mumbai continues to be an idea, attracting the hopefuls to the coalition of opportunities; its islands still harbour hopes and dreams which do come true. It is home to pockets of surprise and unsurprising predictability. It continues to be the city which doesn't sleep, where efficiency is valued, where time has no time, where people seem to want to be in a hurry. Yet, it is not unusual to meet human beings who reflect all that is humane.'[15]

Notes

1: Bombay before Ayodhya

1 https://byjus.com/free-ias-prep/home-states-of-ias-officers-in-india/
2 'Quarterly List of Officers of the Indian Police Services and State Police Services as on 2 August 2021', Maharashtra State Police Department, https://www.mahapolice.gov.in/uploads/posting_details/a8bc7a0f58c573b87eba9eb9367dd316.pdf.

2: The Rush+Die Riot of 1989

1 'CPDR inquiry into the police firing on Muslim Morcha' (The enquiry report was published by Committee For Protection of Democratic Rights on 13 April, 1989), http://www.unipune.ac.in/snc/cssh/humanrights/02%20STATE%20AND%20ARMY%20-%20POLICE%20REPRESSION/G%20MAHARASHTRA/2.pdf.
2 Ibid.
3 Jyoti Thottam, 'Rushdie's Mumbai', *Time*, 18 June 2009, http://content.time.com/time/specials/packages/article/0,28804,1902809_1902810_1905180,00.html.
4 Ibid.
5 Ibid.

3: 1990: The Rath Reaches Bombay

1 Meena Menon, *Riots and After in Mumbai: Chronicles of Truth and Reconciliation*, New Delhi: Sage Publications India Pvt. Ltd, 2012, pp. 22–82.
2 Ibid.
3 Ibid.
4 Ibid.
5 As told to the author by R.U. Singh.
6 As told to the author by Raghunath Kulkarni.
7 R.K. Laxman's cartoons on L.K. Advani, 21 February 2015, http://yousaidit-rklaxman.blogspot.com/2015/02/rk-laxman-about-bjp-sangh-parivar.html.

4: December 1992 Riots

1 The figures of people killed in the riots and police firings in various chapters of this book have been cited from Justice B.N. Srikrishna Commission's report, https://www.sabrang.com/srikrish/vol1.htm.
2 As told to the author by Aslam Malkani.

5: January 1993 Riots

1 Name changed on request.
2 Srikrishna Commission, 'Report of Inquiry', 16 February 1998, https://www.sabrang.com/srikrish/vol1.htm.
3 As narrated to the author by Vijayanand Gupta.
4 Meena Menon, *Riots and After in Mumbai*, pp. 91-96. She revealed that the place of the incident was Gandhi Chawl, and not Radhabai Chawl as was widely reported by the newspapers of the time.
5 Telegraph Bureau, 'Bal Thackeray Stripped of Voting Right', 28 July 1999, *Telegraph*, https://www.telegraphindia.com/india/bal-thackeray-stripped-of-voting-right/cid/918057.
6 As told to the author by Ahmed Shaikh.
7 As told to the author by Aslam Malkani.
8 Sukanya Shantha, 'With Weary Witnesses, Suleman Usman Bakery Case Goes to Trial After 26 Years', *The Wire*, 4 March 2019, https://thewire.in/communalism/suleman-usman-bakery-case-trial-witnesses.
9 As narrated to the author by Atique-ur-Rehman.

10 Srikrishna Commission, 'Report of Inquiry', 16 February 1998.
11 Sharad Pawar, *On My Terms: From the Grassroots to the Corridors of Power*, New Delhi: Speaking Tiger Publishing Pvt. Ltd, 2016, p.110.
12 Rakesh Maria, *Let Me Say It Now*, Chennai: Westland Books Pvt Ltd, 2020, p. 66.
13 As told to the author by Y.C. Pawar.
14 As told to the author by Surendrakumar Jayaswal.
15 As told to the author by Baban Jadhav.
16 Bal Thackeray's interaction with the author and other media persons at his residence.

6: 12 March 1993: A Blood-Soaked Bombay

1 Sharad Pawar, *On My Terms*, p. 112.
2 As told to the author by Kirti Ajmera.
3 B. Raman, 'Lessons from the Mumbai Blasts', Rediff.com, 14 March 2003, https://www.rediff.com/news/2003/mar/14raman.htm.
4 Rakesh Maria, *Let Me Say It Now*, p. 85.
5 This information is based on the author's interactions with the officers and prosecutors associated with the 1993 blast trial, and informers from the underworld.
6 The charge sheet of the 1993 blasts, filed by the Mumbai Police in special TADA court, https://www.hindustantimes.com/india/93-blasts-court-to-deliver-verdict/story-OaNzvfWZWbARemkkSaLenJ.html.
7 As told to the author, in the special TADA Court, by an accused in the case who wished to remain anonymous.
8 As told to the author by M.N. Singh.
9 As told to the author by Neeraj Kumar.
10 As told to the author by A.S. Samra.
11 As told to the author by M.N. Singh.
12 Lekha Rattanani, 'Bombay bomb blasts: Police ask for maximum punishment for accused', *India Today*, 30 November 1993, https://www.indiatoday.in/magazine/indiascope/story/19931130-bombay-bomb-blasts-police-ask-for-maximum-punishment-for-accused-811840-1993-11-30.
13 India Today Bureau, 'Former filmstar Parveen Babi sees plots everywhere', *India Today*, 19 August 2002, https://www.indiatoday.in/magazine/indiascope/story/20020819-former-filmstar-parveen-babi-sees-plots-everywhere-796505-2002-08-19.

14 Soniya Agrawal, 'Parveen Babi put sex-appeal in 1970s Bollywood, but constantly fought mental health issues, *The Print*, 20 January 2020, https://theprint.in/theprint-profile/parveen-babi-put-sex-appeal-in-1970s-bollywood-but-constantly-fought-mental-health-issues/180461/.

15 As told to the author by an informer of the underworld.

16 B. Raman, 'Exclusive! B Raman's unpublished 2007 article: Why Yakub Memon must not be hanged', Rediff.com, 24 July 2015, https://www.rediff.com/news/column/exclusive-b-ramans-unpublished-2007-article-why-yakub-memon-must-not-be-hanged/20150723.htm.

17 As told to the author by Justice P.D. Kode.

7: Reign of the Underworld

1 Harinder Baweja, 'I will return to India and face trial but after teaching Dawood a lesson: Chhota Rajan', *India Today*, 31 January 1996, https://www.indiatoday.in/magazine/interview/story/19960131-i-will-return-to-india-and-face-trial-but-after-teaching-dawood-a-lesson-says-chhota-rajan-833413-1996-01-31.

2 Praveen Swami, '"We are responsible for the attacks on Milind Vaidya"', *Frontline*, 27 March 1999, https://frontline.thehindu.com/other/article30159164.ece.

3 Express News Service, 'Gangster Chhota Rajan acquitted in 1993 blasts accused's murder case', *Indian Express*, 23 April 2021, https://indianexpress.com/article/india/gangster-chhota-rajan-acquitted-in-1993-blasts-accuseds-murder-case-7285610/.

4 Charul Shah, '1993 Mumbai blast accused's murder: Chhota Rajan acquitted', *Hindustan Times*, 23 April 2021, https://www.hindustantimes.com/cities/others/1993-mumbai-blast-accused-s-murder-chhota-rajan-acquitted-101619120031425.html.

5 Sumita Sarkar and Arvind Tiwari, 'Combating Organised Crime: A Case Study of Mumbai City', South Asia Terrorism Portal, https://www.satp.org/satporgtp/publication/faultlines/volume12/article5.htm.

6 As told to the author by Sunil Jain.

7 Harinder Baweja, 'I will return to India and face trial but after teaching Dawood a lesson: Chhota Rajan'.

8 As told to the author by Josy Joseph.

9 As told to the author by Faisal Wahid.

10 As told to the author over the telephone by Nadeem Saifi.

11 As told to the author by Laxman Ziman.

12 Sumita Sarkar and Arvind Tiwari, 'Combating Organised Crime: A Case Study of Mumbai City'.
13 Nazia Sayed, 'An insider's first-hand account of the mob', *Mumbai Mirror*, 17 November 2010, https://mumbaimirror.indiatimes.com/mumbai/other/an-insiders-first-hand-account-of-the-mob/articleshow/16074035.cms.
14 As told to the author by Baljit Parmar.
15 Express News Service, 'Journalist J Dey murder case verdict: Gangster Chhota Rajan, eight others sentenced to life imprisonment', *Indian Express*, 3 May 2018, https://indianexpress.com/article/cities/mumbai/journalist-j-dey-murder-case-verdict-gangster-chhota-rajan-8-others-convicted-jigna-vora-acquitted-5159738/.
16 Staff Reporter, 'Inquiry against ACP for partying with gangsters', *The Hindu*, 2 January 2010, https://www.thehindu.com/news/Inquiry-against-ACP-for-partying-with-gangsters/article16835514.ece.
17 Syed Firdaus Ashraf, 'Former judge J W Singh accused of underworld links acquitted', Rediff.com, 6 August 2002, https://www.rediff.com/news/2002/aug/06fird.htm.
18 Jayprakash S. Naidu, '360 degrees: Encounter cops too have shot into oblivion', *Deccan Chronicle*, 1 November 2015, https://www.deccanchronicle.com/151101/commentary-op-ed/article/encounter-cops-too-have-shot-oblivion-0.

8: Bitter Pill: The End of the Underworld?

1 Jayprakash S. Naidu, '360 degrees: Encounter cops too have shot into oblivion'.
2 As told to the author by late Gopinath Munde.
3 As told to the author by BJP spokesman Keshav Upadhyay.
4 As told to the author by late Vijay Salaskar.
5 Ibid.
6 Express News Service, 'Encounter probe report indicts cops', *Indian* Express, 29 September 1998, https://indianexpress.com/article/news-archive/encounter-probe-report-indicts-cops/lite/.
7 'MCOCA checks crime in state', *Times of India*, 31 August 2009, https://timesofindia.indiatimes.com/city/mumbai/mcoca-checks-crime-in-state/articleshow/4952889.cms.
8 In 2010 and 2011, the author received calls from +344 numbers from a person claiming to be Chhota Rajan. It couldn't be established whether the person was genuinely Chhota Rajan or not.

9 As told to the author by a source in Mumbai Police.
10 As told to the author by Arun Gawli.
11 As told to the author by Keshav Upadhyay.
12 As told to the author by Premkumar Bedi.
13 As told to the author by Shakuntala Bedi.
14 Raval Sheela, *Godfathers of Crime: Face to Face with India's Most Wanted*, New Delhi: Hachette, 2015, p.144, 183.
15 As told to the author by Ashwin Naik.
16 Nazia Sayed,'I tried to kill Dawood thrice: Bunty Pandey', *Mumbai Mirror*, 3 January 2011, https://mumbaimirror.indiatimes.com/mumbai/other/i-tried-to-kill-dawood-thrice-bunty-pandey/articleshow/16089282.cms.
17 Aritra Hazra, 'Santosh Shetty: A long journey from Breach Candy to Bangkok', *Hindustan Times*, 13 October 2015, https://www.hindustantimes.com/mumbai/santosh-shetty-a-long-journey-from-breach-candy-to-bangkok/story-91DasWUbKDemLjxfJaXQYP.html.
18 Arvind Ojha, 'Deepika Padukone on NCB radar in drug probe linked to Sushant death: Sources', *India Today*, 22 September 2020, https://www.indiatoday.in/movies/celebrities/story/deepika-padukone-on-ncb-radar-in-drug-probe-linked-to-sushant-death-sources-1724085-2020-09-22.

9: Tears of Khaki

1 Interview of Dr P.S.Pasricha by the author.
2 TNN, 'Relay delay: Pasricha botches baton handover', *Times of India*, 6 February 2004, https://timesofindia.indiatimes.com/city/mumbai/relay-delay-pasricha-botches-baton-handover/articleshow/478349.cms.
3 As told to the author by Daya Nayak.
4 As told to the author by ACP Avinash Dharmadhikari.
5 As told to the author by Pradeep Sharma.
6 As told to the author by J. Dey.
7 PTI, '"Sachin Waze not Osama bin Laden": Uddhav Thackeray on transferred Mumbai Cop', LiveMint, 11 March 2021, https://www.livemint.com/politics/news/sachin-vaze-is-not-osama-bin-laden-uddhav-thackeray-on-transferred-mumbai-cop-11615428746133.html.
8 https://www.dailypioneer.com/2021/india/waze-planted-bomb-for-monetary-gain--nia.html

9 ABP News Bureau, 'Anil Deshmukh Asked Vaze To Collect Rs 100 Cr For Him Per Month: Param Bir Singh Tells Uddhav Thackeray', ABP News, 21 March 2021, https://news.abplive.com/news/india/param-bir-singh-letter-uddhav-thackeray-anil-deshmukh-asked-sachin-vaze-to-collect-rs-100-cr-1449374.

10: A New Politics

1 Sujata Anandan, 'Fallouts of Babri in Bombay', *National Herald*, 19 December 2017, https://www.nationalheraldindia.com/opinion/fallouts-of-babri-in-bombay.
2 As told to the author by Nandu Satam.
3 G.R. Khairnar, *Ekanki Jhunj*, Pune: Pushp Prakashan Ltd, 1999, pp. 210, 216, 217, 218.
4 Ibid., pp. 218, 219, 220, 221, 222, 223, 224.
5 Nauzer K. Bharucha, 'The Teflon Mr Pawar', *Times of India*, 7 July 2010, https://timesofindia.indiatimes.com/blogs/nothingbutthetruth/the-teflon-mr-pawar/.
6 Smruti Koppiker, 'Suspended BMC's commissioner, G.R. Khairnar gets reinstated by majority vote', *India Today*, 15 November 1995, https://www.indiatoday.in/magazine/indiascope/story/19951115-suspended-bmcs-commissioner-g.r.-khairnar-gets-reinstated-by-majority-vote-807912-1995-11-15.
7 M. Rahman, 'Charges of underworld links jolt Pawar but he tries to ride out the crisis once again', *India Today*, 15 September 1994, https://www.indiatoday.in/magazine/special-report/story/19940915-charges-of-underworld-links-jolt-pawar-but-he-tries-to-ride-out-the-crisis-once-again-809617-1994-09-15.
8 As told to the author by Hitendra Thakur.
9 Sharad Pawar, *On My Terms*, pp. 130–131.
10 Ibid.
11 As told to the author by veteran journalist Anurag Tripathi.
12 Jitendra Dixit, 'How did remote control become a political word? Who used it for the first time?', ABP News, 5 February 2020, https://marathi.abplive.com/news/mumbai/how-did-remote-control-become-a-political-word-who-had-used-it-for-the-first-time-739075.
13 Express News Service, 'Hand over Sundew Apartment or let PMC raze it: SC to Vyas Construction', *Indian Express*, 13 October 2011, https://indianexpress.com/article/cities/pune/hand-over-sundew-apartment-or-let-pmc-raze-it-sc-to-vyas-construction/.

14 As told to the author by Vageesh Saraswat.
15 As narrated to the author by M.N. Singh.
16 Vaibhav Purandare, *Bal Thackeray & The Rise of The Shiv Sena*, Delhi: Roli Books, Lotus Collection, pp. 184-85.
17 As told to the author by M.N.Singh.
18 Express News Service, 'Bal Thackeray arrest in 2000 wrong: Ajit Pawar', *Indian Express*, 13 October 2019, https://indianexpress.com/elections/bal-thackeray-arrest-in-2000-wrong-ajit-pawar-6066454/.
19 As told to the author by M.N. Singh.
20 The author was a witness to this altercation between Commissioner Singh and Narayan Rane.
21 Narayan Rane, *No Holds Barred: My Years in Politics*, Noida: HarperCollins Publishers India, 2019, p. 68.
22 Ibid., p. 81.

11: Pramod Mahajan: The Man, His Murder and His Politics

1 As told to the author by investigating officer, Inspector Anil Mecwan. These words of Pramod Mahajan told to Gopinath Munde were included in Munde's statement to the police and were treated as Mahajan's last words.
2 As told to the author by Abhimanyu Shitole.
3 As told to the author by Kumud Sanghvi Chawre.
4 TNN, 'SC notice to CBI over Mahajan 'favouring' Reliance', *Times of India*, 3 January 2006, https://timesofindia.indiatimes.com/india/sc-notice-to-cbi-over-mahajan-favouring-reliance/articleshow/1356146.cms.
5 PTI, 'Vajpayee a statesman who asked Gujarat CM Modi to follow "rajdharma" in 2002 riots: Congress', *New Indian Express*, 17 August 2018, https://www.newindianexpress.com/nation/2018/aug/17/vajpayee-a-statesman-who-asked-gujarat-cm-modi-to-follow-rajdharma-in-2002-riots-congress-1858771.html.
6 As told to the author by Abhimanyu Shitole.
7 As told to the author by former journalist and BJP spokesperson Prem Shukla.
8 As told to the author by Nandu Satam.
9 As told to the author by Prem Shukla.
10 Ibid.

11 As told to the author by Abhimanyu Shitole.
12 As told to the author by Sanjay Nirupam.
13 As told to the author by Anil Mecwan.
14 Ibid.
15 Ibid.
16 Ibid.
17 Ibid.
18 IANS, '3 men who partied with Rahul Mahajan surrender', *Hindustan Times*, 3 June 2006, https://www.hindustantimes.com/india/3-men-who-partied-with-rahul-mahajan-surrender/story-YLlkR4PkYAGr3Rvd6LvFxL.html.

12: Terror Returns

1 As told to the author by ACP Mohammed Javed.

13: 26/11: The Lessons Not Learnt

1 'KALBADEVI SHOOTING CASE-1946', Bombay High Court Historical Cases Records, https://bombayhighcourt.nic.in/libweb/historicalcases/cases/KALBADEVI_SHOOTING_CASE-1946.html.
2 As told to the author by Inspector Sanjay Govilkar.
3 As told to the author by Inspector Ramesh Mahale.
4 As told to the author by DIG Swati Sathe.
5 As told to the author by Inspector Ramesh Mahale.
6 Newsreport telecasted on ABP News in 2016, https://www.youtube.com/watch?v=2WiK6rs4_DI
7 CAG audit report of Maharashtra, 2015, https://cag.gov.in/cag_old/content/report-2015-compliance-financial-and-performance-audit-state-finances-government-maharashtra
8 As told to the author by K.P. Raghuvanshi.
9 Shailendra Mohan, 'Bulletproof jackets used on 26/11 unsafe against AK-47s', *Hindustan Times*, 6 January 2010, https://www.hindustantimes.com/mumbai/bulletproof-jackets-used-on-26-11-unsafe-against-ak-47s/story-a0XtsdTHlMKOY2vGOSpOMP.html.
10 Based on the author's interactions with Anil Galgali.
11 PTI, '1,432 bulletproof vests for Mumbai cops failed to withstand SLR fire: Maharashtra Government', *Economic Times*, 22 March 2018, https://economictimes.indiatimes.com/news/defence/1432-bullet-proof-

vets-for-mumbai-cops-failed-test-to-withstand-slr-fire-maharashtra-government/articleshow/63419243.cms?from=mdr.

12 Sagar Rajput, Zeeshan Shaikh, 'Maharashtra Police deradicalisation project: Core curriculum step by step', *Indian Express*, 3 August 2019, https://indianexpress.com/article/india/maharashtra-police-deradicalisation-project-core-curriculum-step-by-step-5873952/.

14: Nature's Revenge

1 'Black rain claims 2,500 buffaloes', Rediff News, 29 July 2005, https://www.rediff.com/news/2005/jul/29jcm.htm.

2 Shankkar Aiyar, Malini Bhupta, Dilip Bobb, 'Mumbai floods: Unprecedented rains paralyse India's financial capital, hundreds killed', India Today, 8 August 2005, https://www.indiatoday.in/magazine/cover-story/story/20050808-monsoon-rains-flood-mumbai-thousands-evacuated-787258-2005-08-08.

3 'India: Flood: 2005/07/27', Asian Disaster Reduction Centre, https://www.adrc.asia/view_disaster_en.php?NationCode=&Lang=en&Key=857.

4 Shankkar Aiyar, Malini Bhupta, Dilip Bobb, 'Mumbai floods'.

5 'Centre grants Rs 1,200 cr for BRIMSTOWAD', *Mumbai Mirror*, 13 July 2007, https://mumbaimirror.indiatimes.com/mumbai/other/centre-grants-rs-1200-cr-for-brimstowad/articleshow/15723410.cms.

6 Dipti Singh, 'Has Mumbai's Brimstowad project gone down the drain?', Free Press Journal, 3 October 2020, https://www.freepressjournal.in/mumbai/has-mumbais-brimstowad-project-gone-down-the-drain.

7 HT Correspondent, 'Mumbai clears Rs 569 crore for much delayed Mithi river rejuvenation project', *Hindustan Times*, 27 November 2020, https://www.hindustantimes.com/mumbai-news/mumbai-clears-rs-569-crore-for-much-delayed-mithi-river-rejuvenation-project/story-HFHyPMDTNTmIBToR0c1QxI.html.

8 Express News Service, 'Mumbai: Pilot project launched to clean Mithi river', *Indian Express*, 6 August 2021, https://indianexpress.com/article/cities/mumbai/mumbai-pilot-project-launched-to-clean-mithi-river-7441485/#:~:text=The%20objective%20of%20the%20project,the%20river%20to%20clean%20it.

9 TNN, '95% Mithi river work completed: Iqbal Chahal', *Times of India*, 4 February 2021, https://timesofindia.indiatimes.com/city/mumbai/95-mithi-river-work-completed-chahal/articleshow/80677323.cms.

10 PTI, 'Mumbai: 80 pc of Nariman point, Mantralaya areas will go under water by 2050, predicts BMC chief Iqbal Singh Chahal', *Times of India*, 28 August 2021, https://timesofindia.indiatimes.com/city/mumbai/mumbai-80-pc-of-nariman-point-mantralaya-areas-will-go-under-water-by-2050-predicts-bmc-chief-iqbal-singh-chahal/articleshow/85710453.cms.

11 Sanjana Bhalerao, 'By 2050, Mumbai will see 25% increase in flash flood intensity, says study', *Indian Express*, 28 February 2020, https://indianexpress.com/article/cities/mumbai/mumbai-flash-flood-study-6290303/.

12 Ibid.

13 'The 11 cities most likely to run out of drinking water - like Cape Town', BBC, 11 February 2018, https://www.bbc.com/news/world-42982959.

14 Lyla Bhavadam, 'BMC scraps plans to build a dam to augment Mumbai's water supply, instead opts for a desalination plant', *Frontline*, 17 December 2021, https://frontline.thehindu.com/dispatches/bmc-scraps-plans-to-build-a-dam-to-augment-mumbais-supply-instead-opts-for-a-desalination-plant/article37979329.ece.

15: Unglamorous Bollywood

1 Outlook Web Desk, 'The Sanjay Dutt Tape', *Outlook*, 3 February 2022, https://www.outlookindia.com/website/story/the-sanjay-dutt-tape/216640.

2 PTI, 'Sanjay Dutt denies links with Shakeel', *Times of* India, 7 March 2003, https://timesofindia.indiatimes.com/india/sanjay-dutt-denies-links-with-shakeel/articleshow/39561574.cms.

3 As told to the author by M.N. Singh.

4 As told to the author by Sarvesh Upadhyay.

5 As told to the author by Ashok Dubey.

6 As told to the author by Mayank Shekhar.

7 Ibid.

8 As told to the author by Sarvesh Upadhyay.

16: Lalbaugcha Raja

1 As told to the author by Sudhir Salvi.

2 Ibid.

3 Ibid.
4 Mridula Chari, 'Why Mumbai police detectives are lining up at the tomb of a 14th-century Sufi saint this week', Scroll.in, 26 December 2015, https://scroll.in/article/778131/why-mumbai-police-detectives-are-lining-up-at-the-tomb-of-a-14th-century-sufi-saint-this-week.
5 As told to the author by Sudhir Salvi.

17: Dance Bars: Playing Hide-and-Seek with the Law

1 Tabassum Barnagarwala, 'Waiting in the Wings: Photographer who shot bar dancers, looks back at their life', *Indian Express*, 25 October 2015, https://indianexpress.com/article/lifestyle/life-style/waiting-in-the-wings-photographer-who-shot-bar-dancers-looks-back-at-their-life/.
2 As told to the author by Manjit Singh Sethi.
3 Mateen Hafeez, 'Tarannum case: No charges yet', *Times of India*, 1 May 2006, https://timesofindia.indiatimes.com/city/mumbai/tarannum-case-no-charges-yet/articleshow/1511070.cms.
4 As told to the author by Tarannum Khan.
5 Ibid.
6 Sagnik Chowdhury, 'Deepa Bar owner starts TV news channel, stars and politicians throng launch party', *Indian Express*, 28 April 20022, http://archive.indianexpress.com/news/deepa-bar-owner-starts-tv-news-channel-stars-and-politicians-throng-launch-party/1108686/2.
7 As told to the author by a police informer.

18: Heroes and Villains of the Financial Market

1 ABP News, 'Know how did P.V. Narasimha Rao lay the foundation of new India', YouTube Video, 24 July 2021, https://www.youtube.com/watch?v=DcR1ah0nltI.
2 Shubhomoy Bhattacharjee, 'How WB,IMF got India to adopt reforms in 1991', *Indian Express*, 17 September 2010, https://indianexpress.com/article/news-archive/web/how-wb-imf-got-india-to-adopt-reforms-in-1991/.
3 ABP News, 'Know how did P.V. Narasimha Rao lay the foundation of new India'.
4 As told to the author by journalist Rajesh Kumar.
5 C.P. Chandrashekhar, 'FDI in banking', *The Hindu*, 16 November 2012, https://www.thehindu.com/business/Economy//article56842944.ece.

6 Ibid.
7 ABP Majha, YouTube Video, 23 October 2021, https://www.youtube.com/watch?v=Ppx0qPJ1PXQ.
8 Sreekumar Ray, 'Insider Trading: A White-Collar Crime and Its Impact on the Stock Market', *International Journal of Business Ethics in Developing Economies*, Vol. 3, Issue 2, 2014, http://www.publishingindia.com/GetBrochure. aspx?query= UERGQnJvY2h1cmVzfC8yMzg1LnBkZnwvMjM4NS5wZGY=.
9 Samir K. Barua, Jayanth R. Varma, 'Securities Scam Genesis, Mechanics and Impact', *Vikalpa*, Vol. 18, Issue 1, 1 January 1993, https://web.iima.ac.in/assets/snippets/workingpaperpdf/1992-09-01jrvarma.pdf.
10 Ibid.
11 Makarand Joshi, 'Harshad Mehta scam in 1992 ushered regulatory regime in Indian capital market', *MoneyControl*, 10 October 2020, https://www.moneycontrol.com/news/business/markets/harshad-mehta-scam-in-1992-ushered-regulatory-regime-in-indian-capital-market-5944281.html.
12 As told to the author by Ajit Joshi.
13 Ibid.
14 ABP Majha, 'Investigative Journalist Sucheta Dalal in *Majha*'s discussion'.
15 Pallavi Prasad, 'Where is the Rs 24,000 Cr Lost in Harshad Mehta Securities Scam?', The Quint, 28 September 2020, https://www.thequint.com/explainers/where-is-the-rs-24000-crore-lost-in-the-harshad-mehta-securities-scam#read-more.
16 'South Asia Monitor: India Budget 2001: Can the Government Deliver?', Center for Strategic and International Studies, 1 April 2001, https://www.csis.org/analysis/south-asia-monitor-india-budget-2001-can-government-deliver-april-1-2001.
17 Debashis Basu, Sucheta Dalal, *The Scam: The Scam: From Harshad Mehta To Ketan Parekh*, Mumbai: Kensource Information Services Pvt Ltd, 2001.
18 Onkar Singh, Rediff Correspondent, 'CBI arrests stock broker Ketan Parekh', 30 March 2001, https://www.rediff.com/business/2001/mar/30ketan.htm.
19 'CBI arrests Ketan Parekh', *Times of India*, 10 August 2001, https://timesofindia.indiatimes.com/business/india-business/cbi-arrests-ketan-parekh/articleshow/1852914918.cms.
20 Jigna Shah, 'Madhavpura Bank: A Ready Reckoner', Rediff.com, 31 March 2001, https://www.rediff.com/money/2001/mar/31spec.htm.

21 Sundeep Khanna, 'BACKSTORY: Ketan Parekh and his K-10 stocks', CNBC, 20 September 2021, https://www.cnbctv18.com/business/backstory-ketan-parekh-and-his-k-10-stocks-10803981.htm.
22 Aron Almeida, 'Ketan Parekh Scam – The Infamous Stock Market Fraud', Trade Brains, 4 October 2021, https://tradebrains.in/ketan-parekh-scam/#:~:text=Ketan%20Parekh%20declared%20to%20be,15%20years%20up%20to%202017.
23 'How UTI crisis unfolded: Former Sebi chairman UK Sinha revisits the drama', *Business Standard*, 5 January 2020, https://www.business-standard.com/article/beyond-business/how-uti-crisis-unfolded-former-sebi-chairman-uk-sinha-revists-the-drama-120010400751_1.html.
24 Ibid.
25 Praful Bidwai, 'Betrayal of Public Trust. Behind the UTI Crisis', Transnational Institute, 16 July 2001, https://www.tni.org/es/node/7878.
26 'Final Order against Ms. Chitra Ramkrishna and Others', Securities and Exchange Board India, https://www.sebi.gov.in/enforcement/orders/feb-2022/final-order-against-ms-chitra-ramkrishna-and-others_56030.html.
27 Ibid.
28 Ibid.
29 Ibid.
30 Ibid.
31 Aaj Tak, 'Conversation with Rakesh Jhunjhunwala', YouTube Video, 22 May 2021, https://www.youtube.com/watch?v=Ace4mczq1Yo.
32 Kritesh Abhishek, 'Rakesh Jhunjhunwala Success Story- Rs 5,000 to Rs 41,000 Crores!', *Trade Brains*, 18 December 2021, https://tradebrains.in/rakesh-jhunjhunwala-success-story/.
33 'Who is Rakesh Jhunjhunwala?', *Business Standard,* https://www.business-standard.com/about/who-is-rakesh-jhunjhunwala.
34 'Rakesh Jhunjhunwala', *Forbes*, https://www.forbes.com/profile/rakesh-jhunjhunwala/?sh=565cc038174b.
35 As told to the author by Hitesh Shah.
36 Ibid.
37 As told to the author by Shishir Sinha.
38 Aaj Tak, 'Conversation with Rakesh Jhunjhunwala'.
39 As told to the author by Shishir Sinha.
40 ABP Majha, 'Investigative Journalist Sucheta Dalal in *Majha*'s discussion', https://www.youtube.com/watch?v=Ppx0qPJ1PXQ&t=1401s.

19: Landscape to Skyline

1 Gillian Tindall, *City of Gold: The Biography of Bombay*, Gurgaon: Penguin India, 2000.
2 World Population Review, 'Mumbai Population 2022', https://worldpopulationreview.com/world-cities/mumbai-population.
3 Scroll Staff, 'Pune ranks best among 111 cities in government's Ease of Living Index,' Scroll.in, 13 August 2018, https://scroll.in/latest/890313/pune-ranks-best-among-111-cities-in-governments-ease-of-living-index.
4 Slum Rehabilitation Authority, Mumbai, 'Department History', https://sra.gov.in/page/innerpage/department-history.php.
5 BS Reporter, 'Maharashtra repeals land ceiling Act, finally', *Business Standard*, 14 June 2013, https://www.business-standard.com/article/economy-policy/maharashtra-repeals-land-ceiling-act-finally-107113001114_1.html.
6 Faisal Malik, 'Devpt on salt pan land: IIT-B to check feasibility', *Hindustan Times*, 2 March 2020, https://www.hindustantimes.com/mumbai-news/devpt-on-salt-pan-land-iit-b-to-check-feasibility/story-ZT5WJM4CCz1LfbeK7TOosO.html.
7 As told to the author by Varun Singh.
8 As told to the author by Subhash Patel.
9 Ibid.
10 As told to the author by Varun Singh.

20: All That Glitters ... Is Going Away from Mumbai?

1 As told to the author by Rajiv Singhal.
2 'Mulji Jetha Market – A Textile Bazaar in Mumbai', Indian Bazaars Blogspot, 16 April 2010, http://indianbazaars.blogspot.com/2010/04/mulji-jetha-market-textile-bazaar-in.html.
3 As told to the author by Rajiv Singhal.
4 As told to the author by Kumar Jain.
5 Ibid.
6 As told to the author by Sanjay Kothari.
7 Ibid.
8 As told to the author by Rajiv Somani.
9 Ibid.
10 Ibid.

11 PTI, 'Deaths due to fall from overcrowded Mumbai local trains go up, reveals RTI', *Indian Express*, 13 September 2015, https://indianexpress.com/article/cities/mumbai/deaths-due-to-fall-from-overcrowded-mumbai-local-trains-go-up-reveals-rti/.

12 As told to the author by Rajendra Aklekar.

13 Ibid.

14 As told to the author by Syahrunizam Samsudin in 2010.

15 As told to the author by Shankkar Aiyar.

Index

Aarey Forest, 213
acquittals, 45, 80, 83, 95, 99, 101, 130, 140, 147, 191, *see also under separate entries*
Adityanath, Yogi, 233–34
Advani, LK, 25–31, 77, 176–78, 236; arrest of, 30; in Bombay, 27–30; rath yatra, 25, 176
Agni Sakshi, 232
Aguiar, A.S. (J), 108
Ahir, Sachin, 121, 244
Ahmed, Ghulam, 194
Ahmed, Rizwan, 206
Ahmedabad, 185, 191, 279
Ahuja, Shiney, 226
airlines, private, 264
Aiyar, Shankkar, 301
Akhand Bharat, 24
Akhand Ramayan Paath, 6
Akhil Bhartiya Sena (ABS), 117, 119–21, 123
Aklekar, Rajendra, 297
Ali, Rajab Ali Taiyab, 238
Ali Baba, Makhdoom, 241
All-India Film Employees Confederation, 231, *see also* unionism
Ambani, Dhirubhai, 9, 292
Ambani, Mukesh, 148, 238
Amrapurkar, Deepak, 216
Anand, Dev, 232
Andheri, 4, 52, 129, 185, 187, 253
Angre, Ravindranath, 107, 130, 141
Ansari, Abdul Qayoom. *See* Salam, Abu
Ansari, Zabiuddin, aka Abu Jundal, 202
Anti-Corruption Bureau, 137–38
Anti-Extortion Cell, 90, 100, 141
Antilia Conspiracy, 147–48
anti-mafia campaign, 108
Anti-Narcotics Cell, 138

anti-terrorism policy, 112
Anti-Terrorism Squad (ATS), 100, 139, 148, 188, 191, 206; ambushing Qualis care of Hemant Karkare, 198
Arif, killing of, 115
arms, 64, 67–68, 71, 206
Article 370, abrogation of, 24
Ashrat, 187–88
Assembly Elections 1995, 152
ATMs, 212, 224, 263
Aungier, Gerald, 280
Awhad, Jitendra, 243, 243–44
Ayodhya, on 6 December 1992, 32, 152, 265, *see also* Babri Masjid demolition

Babi, Parveen, 71
Babri Masjid demolition, 26, 34, 41, 55, 89, 153, 184–85, 188; carnage after, 59; Mahajan on, 28
Bachchan, Amitabh, 71, 137, 232, 238, 265, 292
Bada Rajan, 78, *see also* Chhota Rajan
Badgujar, killing of, 76
Bahujan Vikas Aaghadi, 141
Balance of Payment Crisis, 261–65
Bandra, 77, 162, 180, 190, 209, 211, 224; Kala Nagar junction in, 209; Nirmal Nagar in, 53
Bandra–Worli Sea Link, 300
Banerjee, Mamata, 176
Bapat, Shrikant, 46–47, 54
bar dancers, 106, 247, 249, 251–2, 254, 256, 258–59; suicide of, 259, *see also* dance bars
Basit, Mateen, 147
Bawdhankar, Hemant, 195
Bedi, Bobby, 124, 128
Bedi, Monica, 124, 126; arrest of, 126; love story, 221; release from jail, 129; and Salem relationship, 128; as Sana Malik Kamal, 126
Bedi, Premkumar, 127
Bedi, Shakuntala, 128
Beg, Mirza Dilshad, murder of, 115
BEST bus, 117, 168, 185, 209; blast at Ghatkopar, 185; blast attacks on, 40, 53, 146, 185, 192–93; double decker hijack, 191–95
Bhagwat, Mayank, 198
Bhaiya, Lakhan, 140
Bhakti Park, 284, 298–99
Bhandari, Sundarlal, 153
Bhandarkar, Madhur, 123
Bhandup, 39, 81; shooting incident, 88
Bhangale, A.P. (J), 109
Bharatiya Chitrapat Sena (BCS), 232
Bharatiya Janata Party (BJP), 26, 28–29, 34, 141, 150, 152, 159–61, 163, 165, 171–80, 182–83, 228; adopting Hindutva, 13; Palampur convention, 25–26; partnership with Shiv Sena, 13; using 'pseudo-secular' label, 12
Bharatiya Janata Party-Shiv Sena government, anti-incumbency sentiment, 161
Bhartiya Kamgar Sena, 119–20
Bhartiya Vidyarthi Sena, 170
Bhatnagar, Shivani, murder case, 177
Bhatt, Mahesh, 131, 200
Bhatt, Rahul, 200

Bhayandar, 189, 281
Bhendi Bazaar, 11, 34, 41, 51, 56, 68
Bhiwandi, 59, 159, 240, 292; riots 1984, 29, 46, 153, *see also under* riots
Bhosle, Praful, 107
Bhujbal, Chhagan, 29, 135, 145, 150, 164–66, 169, 256; attack on, 165–66; joining Congress Party, 29; as Lakhoba, 164; Thackeray on, 165
Bhujbal, Sameer, 145, 256
Bindumadhav, 232
Black Friday, 233
BMC elections, 120, 123, 170
Bollywood, 81, 90, 92–93, 125, 133, 199, 219–22, 224, 227, 229–34, 280; as source of revenue to underworld, 221; stars performance at Pakmodia Street, 220; unionism in, 230
Bollywood–mafia nexus, 223
Bombay: becoming Bangkok, 255–58; exporting of Gang Wars, 101–3; renaming as Mumbai, 162; seven islands of, 5
Bombay by Mani Ratnam, 219
Bombay Development Department (BDD), 288
Bombay Electricity Supply and Transport, 10
Bombay Improvement Trust (BIT), 288
Bombay Police Act, 257
Bombay Stock Exchange (BSE), 62–63, 190, 265, 269–70, 277. *See also* finance markets; share markets
Bombay textile strike, 287, *see also* unionism
Bombay Velvet, 233
bomb blasts, 47, 60–67, 69, 79–80, 156, 184–89, 191–92, 224, 233, 240, 246; 1993, 60, 156; at Bombay Stock Exchange, 62; in Madrid and London, 190; 1993, 55, 60, 75, 80, 158; on 2011 July, 206; planters, 66; in train at Mulund railway station, 185
bookies, 253–54
Borivali, 27, 189–90
box office, 91, 93, 221, 232, *see also* underworld
Brihanmumbai Storm Water Disposal System (BRIMSTOWAD), 214–15
bulletproof jackets, 204–5
Bunts, 250
businesses, 85, 90, 245, 247, 252, 258, 262, 266, 280, 287, 292–94, 300–301
Byculla, 56
Byculla Company or Daddy Company, 83

Cama Hospital, 198; terror attack at, 197
capital market, 268–70, 272–73, 275
casualties, 38, 48, 54, 63, 190, 216, 299
CBI, 68, 74, 80, 97–98, 114, 116–17, 145, 150–51, 266, 268, 270, 274; ceasing containers of Rajan, 97
central Mumbai, 81, 240, 246, 286, 288, 298, 300

Central Reserved Police Force (CRPF), 40
Century Bazaar, 63
Chahal, Iqbal Singh, 215, 217
Chakraborty, Mithun, 232
Chakraborty, Rhea, 228; arrest of, 229, *see also* Rajput, Sushant Singh case
Chakraborty, Showik arrest of, 229
Chandan Chowky, as 'Extortion Chowky,' 100
Charles, Prince, 71
Chavan, Ashok, 199
Chavan, Shankarrao, 54
Chawan, Madhu, 122
chawl, 7–9, 33, 57, 81, 83, 117, 123, 154, 194, 235–36, 288, *see also* Wadi
Chembur, 81, 99, 102, 298, 300
Chhatrapati Shivaji Terminus (CST), 197, 202, 209, 281; terror attack at, 197
Chhota Rajan, 78–81, 83, 85, 89, 93, 97–99, 101–2, 107, 110, 114–16, 131–32, 248, 254; acquittal of, 80; aka Nana, 113; arrest in Bali, 113–14; attack on, 131–32; image of 'Hindu don,' 80; operating from Newcastle, 114; Sivanandhan on, 79
Chhota Shakeel, 76–79, 84, 87–88, 90, 95–96, 98, 100, 102, 107, 109, 111, 113–15, 131–32, 222–23; hit list, 77; killing Shiv Sena office-bearers, 80
Chidambaram, P., 200
chimneys to towers. *See* mills
Chinchpokli, 81, 130, 288
Chitte, Arun, killing of, 198
Chopra, B.R., *Mahabharata* by (1988), 25
Chori Chori Chupke Chupke, 222
Chowdhary, T.K., 122
City Industrial Development Corporation (CIDCO), 280
climate action plan, 217
climate change, 216–17, *see also* monsoon
Coastal Regulatory Zone (CRZ) rules, 295
coastal security, 202–4
Coast Guard, 203–4
Colaba, terror attack at Leopold Cafe, 196–97
Committee for Protection of Democratic Rights (CPDR), 22
communal: hatred, 40, 195; polarization, 89, 152–54, 220
communal riots, 30, 62, 67, 70, 152–53, 240, 253, 281; of 1992, 253; in Gujarat, 184
company, 83, 93, 106, 115–16, 120, 294
Company, 233
Congress–NCP alliance, 121, 166–67, 169
Congress Party, 12–13, 25–26, 29, 67, 69, 152, 156–59, 161, 163, 165, 170, 172, 262–63
controversies, 56, 74, 79, 135, 141, 157, 160, 169, 177, 190, 223, 241–42, 256, 281
Cordelia Cruise Party case, 132

corruption, and underworld, 99–101
counterterrorism, 206
Crawford Market, 14, 18, 81
cricket match bets, *See* bookies
crime, fear, hatred and, 48–52; reporters, 86, 96, 135, 141, 146; reporting, 70, 116, 146
Crime Intelligence Unit (CIU), 124, 146, 148
Crime Investigation Department (CID), 147
Cuffe Parade, 144, 197, 297
cultural nationalism, 13, 26, 31
curfew, 34, 36, 39, 46, 50, 52, 54, 56, 75
cyclone Tauktae, 216–17

Dabholkar, Jitendra, 119–20; murder of, 121
Dada, Bhagwan, 237
Dadar, 29, 34, 52, 63, 65, 81, 187, 250; bomb explosion at, 206
Dagdi Chawl, 81, 83, 98, 117, 121–22
Dahi Handi, 243–44
Dalal, Sucheta, 268, 277
Dalal Street, 265, 268, 270
dance bars, 245–47, 249–53, 256–59; ban on, 256–57; Blue Nile, 255; and Bombay nights, 249–51; Deepa, 254, 258; and gangsters, 252; and *hafta*, 252; Karishma, 258; Neelam, 250; 'Orchestra Bar' or 'Service Bar,' 259; Patil campaign against, 256; and prostitution, 255; secret chambers in, 259; Sonia Mahal, 249–50; Topaz, 251; women's rights groups and, 256
D.B. Marg police station, 195
D-Company, 73, 77, 81, 83, 100, 102–3, 110–14, 116, 125, 128, 250, *see also* Ibrahim, Dawood
death sentences, 73–75, 109, 188, 191, 195, 201
December riots, 45
Delhi Police, 114, 182, 206
deluge, 208–9, 211–12, 214–16, *see also* climate change; monsoon
Deonar, 35, 56
Desai, Subhash, 162, 169
desalination, 218
Deshmukh, Anil, 150–51, 227
Deshmukh, Vilasrao, 163, 167–69, 199
Deshpande, D.W. (J), 226
Devdas (1955 and 2002), 249
Development Control Rules (DCRs), 284, 288
Dewani, Ajit, shot dead, 93
Dey, Jyotirmoy, 99, 115–17, 142; murder of, 98, 116
Dharavi, 39, 211, 283
Dharavi Redevelopment Project, 283
Dharmadhikari, Avinash, 139
diamond, 293–94
Disaster Management Control Room, 211
disinvestment, 262, 270
Dokre, Balu, 103, 115
Dombivli, 28, 58, 285
Dongri, 9, 11, 41, 45, 47–48, 60, 71, 81, 132, 155

Dosa, Mustafa, 129
Drishti Adventure Sports, 295
drugs, 132, 229; mephedrone, also codenamed MD, or 'Mummy-Daddy,' 132
D'Souza, Lawrence, 93
Dubai, 65–67, 78–79, 88, 99, 101, 103, 111, 114–15, 125, 128, 154, 157, 220–22
Dube, Manish, 224
Dubey, Ashok, 231
Duggal, Mukesh, 91, 128; murder of, 90–91
Dutt, Sanjay, 67–69, 71–72, 133, 222–24; arrest of, 69; under TADA, 68
Dutt, Sunil, 67, 69–70

Eastern Freeway, 300
East–West Airlines, 89, 264; smear campaign against, 89
Economy: black and white, 251; reforms, 263, 265, *see also* liberalization
encounter
encounters, 4, 83, 95, 100, 106–8, 137, 140, 146, 193, 196, 199; cops, 140–45; as extra-judicial killings, 107; as operations, 108; specialists, 105–6, 108, 134, 141, 167, 222
Enforcement Directorate, 151, 229, 274
English-medium schools, 11
Enron power project, 162
Escobar, Pablo, 111
Essa, 65
exodus, 51, 58
explosion/blast, 33, 47, 61–62, 146, 185–86; at Air India building, 62; crude bomb, 47; at Samuel Street, 47; in scooter bomb, 61
explosives, 62, 67, 148, 150
extortion, 79, 81, 85, 87, 90, 93, 97, 122–23, 130, 132, 137, 150–51, 233–34; by Pujari, 131; from Telgi, 144

factions, 54, 139, 159
Fadnavis, Devendra, 139, 149, 171, 173, 183, 234, 257
Fawda, Jawed, killing of, 107
Feast of Vultures, by Joseph, 89
Federal Bureau of Investigation (FBI), 200
Fehmida, 187–88
fidayeens, 206
film industry, and underworld, 90–93
Film Policy 2018, 234
financial market, 260, 263, 265–67, 277
firearms, 21, 36, 42, 195
flash floods, 216–17, *see also* deluge; monsoon
flight operations, commercial international, 5–6, *see also* airlines, private
Floor Space Index (FSI)/Floor Area Ratio, 282, 284
foreign direct investments (FDIs), 263, 284
fresh water scarcity, 217–18
funeral, 53, 116, 182

Gafoor, Hasoon, 198
Galgali, Anil, 205
Gandhi Indira, assassination, 12–13
Gandhi, Rajiv, 12
Gandhi, Sanjay, 12
Gandhi, Sonia, comments against, 229
Ganesh Utsav, 58, 235–37, 240, 242
Gangs of Wasseypur, 233
gangsters, 84–85, 87–88, 90–91, 93, 99, 101, 104–6, 108, 110, 129, 132, 223, 226, 250, 252; killing of, 106; and Bombay; 80–81
gang wars, 70, 80, 86, 101, 111, *see also* underworld
Gateway of India, 196, 217; blast at, 187
Gavaskar, Sunil, 236
Gawli, Arun, 78, 81, 83, 85–86, 88, 99, 107, 118, 130; arrest of, 98; as MLA, 117; and Naik gangs, 252; in Vidham Sabha, 118
Gawli, Asha, 83; aka Mummy, 120; in Chinchpokli seat, 122
Gawli, Geeta, 123
Gawli gang, 83, 86, 111, 118, 123; end of, 117–24
Gazal (1964), 249
Geelani, Syed Ali Shah, 131
Ghai, Subhash, 234
Ghatkopar, 29, 35, 39, 81, 107, 121, 161, 296; bomb blast case, 146, 185–86
ghettoization of communities, 281
Gholap, Babanrao, 160
Ghule, Datta, 107, 141
Girgaon, 81, 196, 235, 237
Girgaon Chowpatty, 195, 211, 241, 295; immersion at, 240
global jihad, 206
Goa, 5, 171, 300
Godhra railway station, 184
gold, 291–94; auction in pandals, 242; market, 62; mortgaged to Bank of England, 262; smuggling, 90
Gomes, Odysteven, 189–90
Goregaon, 189, 210
Govandi, 81, 191
Govari community demand march, 159–60
Govilkar, Sanjay, 195–96
Govinda, 222, 236
Govinda Pathaks, 243–44
Gowariker, Ashutosh, 93
Grant Road, 245, 251
Growmore Investments, 270
Gujarat, 5, 85, 171, 177, 184–85, 210, 217–18; riots in 2002, 177, 188–89
Gujaratis, 8, 11, 185, 189–90, 287
Gujarat Muslim Revenge Force (GMRF), 186–88
Gujrathi, Arun, 168
Gulf War, 262, 285
guns, 108, 116, 192, 220; demand for, 49
Gupta, Ramnarayan, aka Lakhan Bhaiya, 140
Gupta, Shekhar on 'Walk the Talk' on NDTV, 107
Gupta, Vijayanand, 46
Guru, Afzal, 201
Guru Satam, 248

H2O Water Sports Complex, 295
Haldankar, Shailesh, 78, 158
Hamid, 39, 188
Hanif, killing of, 187
Haseena Maan Jayegi, 232
Hazare, Anna, 160
HDFC, 263, 285
Headley David, 201; arrest of, 200
headlines, 76, 86–87, 104, 106, 218; on monorail, 298
Hindu–Muslim riots, 26–27, 240
Hindu Rashtra, 24
Hindutva ideology, 13, 25, 29, 46–47, 153, 173, 176
Hingora, Samir, 68
Hiran, Mansukh, 148–50
hitlist, 100
homebuyers and EMIs, 289–90
home loans, 263, 285
Hugo, Victor, 263
human rights, 109, 118
Human rights activists, 107, 109

Ibrahim, Anees, 66–68, 78–79, 81, 125, 221
Ibrahim, Dawood, 42, 65–68, 76–81, 85, 89, 96, 100–102, 110–18, 125, 132, 141, 154–58, 220–23; attachment of properties, 112; escape to Dubai, 99; operating from Dubai, 65; as Specially Designated Global Terrorist, 112; surrender offer of, 111; UNSC list as terrorist, 112
Ibrahim, Haseena Parker, 111; killing of, 78, 158
Ibrahim, Iqbal Kaskar, 110; arrest of, 141; attack on, 111
Ibrahim, Mehazbeen, 115, 154
Ibrahim, Noor Kaskar, 111, 222
Ibrahim, Qadri Building of, 154
Ibrahim, Sabir, 111
ICICI, 263, 285
identities, 48, 51–52, 94, 104; for survival, 37–38
Igwe, Rajesh, 100
Imamwada, 11, 34
India Meteorological Department (IMD), 210; for Doppler radars, 214
Indian Motion Pictures Producers Association (IMPPA), 232
Indian Mujahideen (IM), and ISIS, 191–92, 205–7
India–Pakistan cricket, 221
India Security Press, 143
informers, 106, 124, 138–41, 259; zero numbers, 106
insider trading, 266, 271
International Monetary Fund (IMF), 262
Inter Service Intelligence (ISI), 65–66, 71, 113, 191; and blasts in India, 65
Islamic State of Iraq and Syria (ISIS), 205–7; as Desh, 206

Jacob Circle, 95, 298
Jadhav, Jayant, 119
Jadhavji, Keshavji, 7
Jagtap, Devendra, 129
Jaideo, 162

jail/prison, Amravati, 119; Arthur Road, 69–70, 201–2, 227, 275; Aurangabad, 119; Taloja, 129; Thane, 260; Tihar, 94, 117; Yerawada, 202
Jain, Kumar, 293
Jain, Pradeep/Pradip, murder of, 88, 105, 129
Jain, Preeti, arrest of, 123
Jaish-ul-Hind, 148, 150
Jaitley, Arun, 176, 178
Jamaat-ud-Dawah, 197, 201
Jamsandekar, Kamlakar, murder case, 123
Janakiraman Committee set, 268
Janata Dal, 13, 26
Janata Dal (Secular) JDS, 168
Janmabhoomi, 8, 62
Janmashtami, 236, 242–44
Jan Sangh, 28
Javed, Mohammed, 192
Jawaharlal Nehru Port, 292
Jayalalithaa, 176
Jayaswal, Subodh, 144–45
Jayaswal, Surendrakumar, 56
Jet Airways, 179, 264
Jethmalani, Ram, 111, 158
Jhunjhunwala, Rakesh, 275–78; Sushir Sinha on, 277
Jinnah, Mohammed Ali 'Direct Day Action' by, 195
Jitendra, birth of, 10
J.J. Hospital, 19, 21, 46, 78, 205; Dawood shooters attacking, 158
Jogeshwari, 35, 53, 167, 190; Gandhi Chawl incident, 46
Joseph, Johny, 211
Joseph, Josy, 89
Joshi, Ajit, 267–68
Joshi, Manohar, 29, 69, 105, 108, 153, 160–62, 165, 169, 176
Joshi, Sudhir, 162
journalists on target, 95–99
Jumani, Samira. *See* Salem, Samira
Juni Masjid, 9
Jwalamukhi, Shyam, 190

Kadam, Laxman, death of, 45
Kadam, Rajaram, death of, 45
Kadam, Ram, 244
Kadawala, Hanif, 68, 80
Kaho Na … Pyaar Hai (KNPH), 92–93
Kala Chowki, 288
Kalbadevi, 24
Kalbadevi Road, 11, 51, 194
Kalyan, 206, 288
Kalyan-Dombivli, 280
Kamte, Ashok, 198
Kandivali, 189, 300
Kang, Karambir, and sons, 199
Kapoor, Boney, 234
Karkare, Hemant, 95, 198, 205; martyred, 97
karsevaks, 26, 34, 184; demolishing Babri masjid, 33
Kasab, Ajmal, 195–97, 200; arrest of, 196; hanging of, 201–2
Katha Bazaar Street, 61, 71
Kausa, 281
Keshavji Naik Chawl, 235–37

Khairnar, Govind Raghav, 154–56; anti-corruption crusade by, 156; as Demolition Man of Bombay, 155; *Ekanki Jhuj* of, 155; suspension of, 156
Khalnayak, 67–68
Khan, Aamir, 93
Khan, Fardeen, 133, 224; arrest of, 224
Khan, Ismail, 195–96, 202; chief of terror team, 196
Khan, Kader, 100
Khan, Kamaal, 225
Khan, Salman, 222–23, 225–26, 238; hit and run case, 224–26
Khan, Tarannum, 254, 258; IT raid on, 253
Khandekar, Milind, 96, 246
Khar, 189, 210, 250; blast near stations, 190
Khatau, Sunit, killing of, 88–89
Khemani, C.L., arrest of, 268
Khetwadi, 29, 50, 52, 77
Khomeini, Ayatollah, 16, 184; fatwa against Rushdie, 17
killings/ murders, 45, 86, 111: of gang members, 119; high-profile, 86; of shooters, 115
kill-one-scare-all policy, 90
Kini, Ramesh, murder case, 161, 170
Kode, P.D. (J), 70–71, 74
Koirala, Manisha, 91, 93, 232
Konkani, Firoze, escape of, 45
Koshyari, Bhagat Singh, 150, 171
Kothari, Sanjay, 293
Kulkarni, Dhananjay, 203
Kulkarni, Raghunath, 28, 30
Kumar, Akshay, 232, 234
Kumar, Bipin, 225
Kumar, Dilip, 232
Kumar, Gulshan, murder of, 92, 125, 129, 233; as 'Cassette King,' 81, 91
Kumar, Neeraj, 68
Kumawat, Umesh, 192, 209
Kurla, 81, 192, 210–11
Kurup brothers, killing of, 88

Lakdawala, Ejaz/ Ijaz, 80, 93, 115
Lala, Karim, 11
Lalbaug, 237–39, 288
Lalbaugcha Raja, 235, 237–38, 240–43
Lalbaugcha Raja Sarvajanik Ganeshotsav, 238
Lashkar-e-Qahhar, 190
Lashkar-e-Taiba (LeT), 112, 187, 191, 197
Latur earthquake, 159
Laxman, R.K., 31
Laybhari, mobile app by Waze, 147
legal reform activists, 110
liberalization, 261, 263–64, 284–85; and Bombay, 261–65
'Liberation of Goa,' 126
Licence Permit Raj system, 262
lobbies, 139. *see also* factions
local trains, 4, 37, 185, 189–90, 280–81, 295–97, 299, *see also* trains; metro network; monorail
Lok Sabha elections: 1984, 29; 1989, 13, 25, 29; 1998, 76, 161; 2004, 173, 179
lootings, 42, 51

Lootmaar, 246
Lower Parel, 81, 216

Madhavpura Mercantile Co-operative Bank (MMCB), 271
Madrid, 190–91; bomb explosion in local trains, 190
mafia dons, 85–90, 221
Maha-artis, 43, 51, 53, 54, *see also under* Shiv Sena
Mahajan, Pramod, 28–29, 166, 174–78, 180–82; as in charge of Lok Sabha election campaign In 2004, 177; joining Advani rath yatra, 176; murder of, 174, 176, 182–83; as RSS member, 30; relationship with Shiv Sena, 178–82; Shitole on, 178; and Uddhav, 179
Mahajan, Pravin, 175, 177, 180–82; conviction of murder, 181; death of, 182; *Majha Album* by, 177, 181; shooting Pramod, 175
Mahajan, Poonam, 181
Mahajan, Prakash, 182
Mahajan, Rahul, 182
Mahajan, Rekha, 175
Mahalaxmi, 192, 209, 286
Mahale, Ramesh, 201–2
Maharashtra Administrative Tribunal (MAT), 140
Maharashtra Control of Organized Crime Act (MCOCA) (1999), 108–12, 129, 223
Maharashtra Housing Area Development Authority (MHADA), 283, 286
Maharashtra Navnirman Sena (MNS), 171, 244; 'son of the soil' agenda of, 171
Maharashtra Prohibition of Obscene Dance in Hotels, Restaurants and Bar Rooms Act (2016), 257–58
Maharashtra Slum Areas Act (1971) 282
Maharashtra Tourism Development Corporation (MTDC), 295
Maharashtra Vidhan Sabha elections, 122
Maha Vikas Aghadi, 172, 183
Mahim, 39, 45, 63, 66, 75, 190, 209, 241
Maithia, Priyen, 216
Majid, Mirza Abdul, 194
Makhdoom Ali Mahimi's shrine at Mahim, 241
Malad, 189, 210
Malhotra, Vicky, 115
Manchekar, Suresh, 107
Mandal Commission's recommendations, 165
Manjrekar, Mahesh, 223
Mankhurd, 281
Maria, Rakesh, 65, 75, 97, 100, 139, 198; *Let Me Say It Now* by, 54
Marine Commandos (MARCOS), 199
Mark, Rebecca, 161
Masjid Bunder, 7–8, 46, 62, 81, 271, 284
Masjid railway station, 9, 40, 61
Masjid to Mandir, road connecting, 9

Mateen, Hafeez, Gawli thrashing of, 98
Mathadi workers, murder of, 44–45
Mathadi workers Union, 44–45
Matunga, 37, 81
Matunga Road, 189–90
McDonald's outlet bomb explosion, 185
McKinsey India report, 217
Mecwan, Anil, 180–81
Meenatai statue, desecration of, 189
Mehazbeen Tower, demolition of, 155
Mehta, Ashwin: arrest of, 268; death of, 261
Mehta, Harshad, scam of, 260–61, 265–71
Mehta, Sudhir, arrest of, 269
Memon, Ayub, 65
Memon, Majeed, 92, 131
Memon, Mushtaque (Tiger), 65
Memon, Suleman, 65, 75
Memon, Tiger, 65–67, 73
Memon, Yakub, 65, 72–73, 113; hanging of, 75; and last-minute mercy petition, 74–75
Memon, Yusuf, 65
Metro Cinema junction, 51, 198
metro network, 296–97, *see also* monorail
middle classes, 23, 117, 212
Midnight's Children, Booker Prize for, 16
migrants, 4, 4–7, 280
mills: cotton, 287; Kamala, 286; Phoenix, 286; workers, 3, 7, 27, 85, 88, 237, 287–88
mill workers union, 85
Minara Masjid, incident, 30, 34, 48
Mira-Bhayandar, 58, 173, 280
Mira Road, 59, 189, 233, 249, 251, 281
Mirzapur, 233
Mithi River Rejuvenation Project, 215
mobile phones, introduction of, 189, 239, 264
mob lynchings, 46–47
mobsters, 94
Modi, Narendra, 177
Mohammed Ali Road, 14, 18, 20, 34, 50, 57
Mohite, Bhujangrao, 146
Moitra, Vivek, 181–82
monorail, 297–99
monsoon, 8, 36, 208–16, 296; submerge in, 209–10, 215–17
moral policing, 255–57
More, Ramesh, 203
Mukerji, Rani, 222
Mukti Foundation, 162
Mulji Jetha Market, 292
Mulund, 17, 35, 81, 118
Mumbadevi temple, 9, 40, 62, 186–87, 293
Mumbai Central, 81, 97, 185
Mumbaikars, 193, 206, 208, 211, 238, 279, 299
Mumbai Metropolitan Region Development Authority (MMRDA), 215, 298
Mumbai/Bombay Police, 14, 17–18, 22, 30–31, 55, 65–67, 70, 86–87, 90, 92–93, 106–8, 114–15, 117, 129–30, 137–40, 144–48,

166–67, 188, 203–4, 222–23, 227, 229
Mumbai–Pune Expressway, 162
Mumbai Samachar, 8
Mumbra, 59, 281
Munde, Gopinath, 105–6, 161, 163, 165–66, 169, 175–76, 181–83; death by accident, 182; and 'to protect the law, break the law,' 105
Mundra Port, 292
Muralidharan, Muttiah, 254
Mushrif, S.M., 142
Muslim Integration Council, 17

Nadeem–Shravan, 92
Nagpada, 45, 77, 81, 100, 240, 245; Jairajbhai Lane, 112
Naidu, Chandrababu, 176
Naik, Amar aka Ravan, 81–82, 85–86, 88, 94, 107, 129, 252; arrest and acquittal of, 130; Amar, encounter killing of, 129
Naik, Ashwin, 94–95, 129, 269; from engineer to Gangster and builder, 129–30; acquittal of, 95, 130; meeting Thackerays, 130
Naik, Neeta, murder of, 94
Naik, Ram, 28
Naik, Sudhakarrao, 38, 54–56, 62, 155, 159
Nala Sopara, 141, 281
Nalwalla, Yusuf, 68
Nana Company, 83; disintegration of, 113–17
Nanjiani, Ali, killing of, 111
'Nara e Takbeer,' 48
Narasimha Rao, P.V., PM., 54–55, 262–63, 269, 284
narcotics abuse, 132, *see also* drugs
Narcotics Control Bureau (NCB), 132, 224, 229
Nariman House, 199; terror attack at, 197
Narvekar, Milind, 169
Nasir, killing of, 187
National Investigation Agency (NIA), 148–50
Nationalist Congress Party (NCP), 57, 121, 135, 163, 166–68, 172, 183, 256
Nationalist Congress Party-Congress alliance, 163
National Security Guards (NSG), 199, 204
National Textile Corporation, 288
Navalkar, Pramod, 162
Navi Mumbai, 58, 129, 131, 173, 251, 280–81, 300
Nayak, Daya, 106–7, 134, 137–38
Nayak, Ramdas, 77; assassination, 77
Naya Nagar, 59, 281
Nepali, Bharat, 115
New Cuffe Parade, 282
Nhava-Sheva, 281, 300
nightclubs, 245, 258, *see also* dance bars
Nikalje, Rajan. *See* Chhota Rajan
Nikam, Ujjwal, 71–72
Nirmal, Cameraman Anil, 198
Nirupam, Sanjay, 179–80, 244

Oberoi-Trident Hotel, terror attack at, 197
Omble, Tukaram, killing of, 196

Opera House, bomb explosion at, 206
organized crime syndicates, 84, 140, 223

Pakistan, 66–67, 102, 112, 125, 132, 157, 197, 200–201, 240; ISI, 66; wars, 240
Palais Royale, 288
Pancholi, Aditya, 254
Pande, Bunty, 115
Pande, Shivnarayan, 187–88
Panvel, 280, 300
Parab, Anil, 80
Pardeshi, Naresh, 123
Parekh, Ketan, 270–71, 275; K-10 shares of, 273
Parel, 81, 246, 288
Parker, Haseena, 77, 100, 111–12
Parmar, Baljit, 97
Parsee–Muslim clashes, 27
Pashte, Pramukh Kishore, 82
Pasricha, P.S., 134–36
Patekar, Nana, 232
Patel, J.N. (J), 70
Patel, Subhash, 285
Pathan, Chinku, arrest of, 132
Pathan gang, 42, 78, 250
Patil, Ravindra, 225
Patil, R.R., aka Aabaa, 135, 199, 256–57
Patil, Shivraj, 200
Patwa, Sundarlal, 28
Pawar, 55–56, 62, 101, 156, 158–59, 166, 256
Pawar, JCP, 56
Pawar, Sharad, 29, 54–57, 62, 69, 101, 105, 136, 155–59, 162, 165–69, 256; anti-incumbency wave against, 160; as Chief Minister for fourth time, 55; defeat of, 160; establishing NCP, 163; *On My Terms* of, 54, 158; ousted of power, 105
Pawar, Y.C., 56
Pawle, Sada, aka Mama, 107, 120; killing of, 121
Peasants and Workers Party (PWP), 167
petitioners, 75, 107–8, 193
petrol bombs, 33, 38, 42, 47, 50
Philip, Raju, 83
police/cops, 14–15, 18–20, 30, 33–35, 39, 41, 99, 106, 118, 122–23, 145–46, 186–89, 196–98, 252, 254;, (*see also* Mumbai/Bombay Police); attacks on, 42, 48, 56; encounters, 82, 110, 130, 132, 146, 187, 248, 261; firing, 16, 33, 37–38, 41, 47–49, 87, 199; to jail, 135; killing of, 45; and Muslims hostility, 57; and politics, 38–39; suspensions of, 100
political killings, 76
politics, criminalizing, 156–58
Portuguese, 4–5, 126, 213; landing in Bombay, 279
Prakash, aka Bunty Pandey, arrest of, 132
Prem Rog (1982), 249
privatization, 262
prostitution, 255, 259, *see also* dance bars
Protection of Dignity of Women Act 2016, 258

Public Call Offices (PCOs), 264
public study centre, 60–61, 71
Pujari, Ravi, 99, 115, 130–31: as Anthony Fernandes, 131; arrest of, 131; end of gangs, 130–33
Pujari, Hemant, 115;
Puri, S.S., 144
PWP members, 168
Pydhonie, 11, 34, 45, 50, 81

Al-Qaeda, 112
Quick Response Team (QRT), 198, 204

Raghuvanshi, K.P., 57–58, 204
Rai, Rajiv, 91
railway recruitment exam, attack on candidates of, 193
rain coverage. *See* monsoon
Rajput, Sushant Singh Case, 132, 227–32
Raktanchal, Upadhyay in, 230
Ramabai Nagar, 120, 161
Ramakant, 61
Ramakrishna, Chitra, 273–74
Raman, B., 74
Ramaswamy, Anandita, 98
Rama temple campaign, 25–26, 152, 178, 263, *see also* Ayodhya, on 6th December; Babri Masjid demolition
Ramkumar, 4, 7
rampage, 27, 41, 48, 166, 189
Ram Pradhan Committee, 203
Rane, Narayan, 94, 162–63, 167–70, 228; kidnaping, Congress– NCP MLAs, 166–69; rebellion of, 170; *No Holds Barred* by, 169
Rao, Anand, 181
Rao, D.K., 99
RARE Enterprises, 276
Rashtriya Swayamsevak Sangh (RSS), 11–12, 24, 51, 176; blackboards in Bombay, 24, *see also* rath yatra
Rathod, Shravan, 92
rath yatra, 24–26, 28, 30, (*see also under* Advani, L.K.; Mahajan, Pramod); in Bombay, 27, 29; commenced at Gujarat's Somnath temple, 26
Ratnam, Mani, 219
Raut, Sanjay, 43
Raval, Sheela, 128
Rawale, Mohan, 76, 121
RDX, 66–67, 203
Ready Forward (RF) system, 267
real estate market, 277–80, 282–86
Real Estate Regulation and Development Act (RERA), 2016, 290
Red Corner notice, 114, 125
relief camp, 35, 41, 253
Research and Analysis Wing (R&AW), 74
resettling, 58. *See also* exodus
restaurants, 250, 257, 263–64, 286; after liberalization, 263; Salt Water Grill, 295; Suzie Wong, 295
rioters, 33, 35–36, 38–40, 42, 46–47, 49–53, 56–57, 168, 195, 253; with firearms, 36–38; Hindu, 48; killing of police, 35; killings by, 39; Muslim, 56; shooting at, 56; torching slums, 53

riots, 20, 22, 26–27, 30, 32–34, 37–40, 42, 50, 52–56, 58–59, 64–67, 182, 184; 1936 in Byculla, 27; 1937, 27; 1941, 27; 1983 January, 44–48; 1984 in Bhiwandi, 29, 46, 153, 240; 1992 December, 45, 55, 64; 1993 January, 44, 64; 1997 in Ramabai Nagar, 161; affected areas, 47, 54, 56; anti-Rushdie, 57; escalation of, 33; killings, 54; post-Babri Masjid demolition, 22
Rizvi, Nazim, arrest of, 223
Road Safety Patrol (RSP), 11
roads and bridges, 299–300
Rohingyas, 184
Roopam, case of, 86–87
Roshan, Rakesh, 92, 223: attack on, 93
Roshan, Hrithik, 92
Roy, Anami, 135, 211
rumours, 21, 26, 48, 88, 145, 212, 216
Rushdie, Salman, 14, 16–17, 184, (*see also* riots, anti-Rushdie); book *The Satanic Verses*, 12; born in Bombay, 16; letter to Rajiv Gandhi, 16

Saamana, 43, 63, 166, 171, 179; and arrest of policemen, 145; editorials, 47; on Joshi, 162; and murder of Pashte, 82; on Sanjay Dutt, 69
Sabarmati Express, fire of, 184, *see also* Godhra railway station
saffron alliance. *See* Shiv Sena-BJP alliance
Sagar, Ramanand, *Ramayan*, by (1987), 25
Sagvekar, Shashikant aka Chikna Babu, 82
Saifi, Nadeem, 92
Saki Naka, 98, 123, 193, 211
Salaskar, Vijay, aka Maharaj, 105–7, 121, 129–30, 138–39, 198
Salem, Abu, 67, 81, 84–85, 88, 92–93, 105, 107, 124–28, 221; as Arsalan Mohammed Ali, 125–26;; arrest of, 125–26, 129; end of his gang and love story, 124–29; escaping to UAE, 125; real name as Abdul Qayoom Ansari, 125
Salem, Samira, 125, 128
Salian, Disha, suicide of, 227
Salvi, Sudhir, 238–39, 242
Samant, Dutta, 287
Samra, A.S., 62, 68
Samsudin, Syahrunizam, 298
Samuel Street, 11, 47
Santacruz, 35, 189, 210
Sapte, Rajesh, 229–30
Sapte, Raju, 232; suicide of, 234
Saraf, Vasant, 22, 84, 94
Saraswat, Vageesh, 162, 177
Sarnaik, Pratap, 244
Sarpotdar, Madhukar, 70
Satam, Nandu, 153, 178
Satanic Verses, The, by Salman Rushdie, 12, 14, 16, 59; politics over, 14, *see also* Khomeini, Ayatollah, 16, 184; fatwa against Rushdie, *see also* riots
Satellite Cities, 280–84
satellite TV channels, 238, 264

Sathe, Swati, 69, 201, 227
Satya, by Ram Gopal Varma, 232–33
Sawant, Pradip, Best Detection Officer Award for, 109
Sawant, Sunil aka Sawtya, 80, 101
Sayyed, Mohsin, 206
Securities and Exchange Board (SEBI), 269–74
Sehar, 233
serial blasts, 63–64, 66, 68, 71, 75, 79–80, 99, 158, 187, 203, 206; across cities in 2008, 191
Sethi, Manjit Singh, 250–52, 258
sewage and storm water disposal systems, 213
sex trade, 259, *see also* prostitution
Shah, Amit, 172, 236, 238
Shah, Bharat, 87–88, 91, 223; arrest of, 222; shot dead by Shakeel, 87
Shah, Hitesh, 276
Shah, Viren, 88
Shah Bano case, 12
Shaikh, Azizuddin, 109
Shaikh, Mohammed Zuber, 109
Shaikh, Sadiq, arrest of, 191
Shaikh, Shakeel Ahmed. *See* Chhota Shakeel
share market, 260, 265, 267–69, 272, 285
Sharjah, 125–26, 221
Sharma, Pradeep, 106–7, 137–38, 149; aka Bawa, 138; arrest of, 140–41; dismissal of, 140; joining Shiv Sena, 141
Sharma, Prem Kumar, 77
Shashikant, 61
Sheena Bora murder case, 117
Sheikh, Fazal, 109
Shekhar, Chandra, PM, 262
Shekhar, Mayank, 198, 233
Shetty, Manmohan, 93, 234;
Shetty, Santosh, 115, 132; arrest and deportation of, 132
Shetty, Sharad, 80, 102–3; aka Bada Idli, 78
Shetty, Sudhakar, 258
Shetty, Suniel, 137, 232, 295
Shinde, Eknath, camp/coup, by 171–73
Shitole, Abhimanyu, 176, 178–79
Shivankar, Mahadeo, 160
Shivdasani, Aftab, 137
Shiv Sainiks, 46–47, 50, 52, 58, 66, 153–54, 162, 165–67; attacking Muslim colony, 45; rampage of, 189
Shiv Sena, 1–2, 29, 43, 69–70, 76–77, 119–20, 141, 152–53, 156, 159–66, 169–70, 172, 178, 219, 299; adopting Hindutva, 29, 172; bicycle rally by, 34; as cadre-based organization, 1; campaign against namaaz on road, 43; joining with NCP and Congress, 183; Maha-artis by, 43, 51, 53–54; revolts in, 169–73; *Saamana* of, 43, 63, 69–70, 82, 145, 162, 166, 171, 179; 'sons of the soil,' 46
Shiv Sena–BJP government, 55, 57, 118, 121, 152, 154, 156, 160, 163, 166, 169, 178, 299
Shivshahi, 159–63

shooters, 78, 80, 83–85, 87–88, 92, 94–95, 102–3, 129, 158; arrest of, 99; killing of, 130
shopkeepers, 1, 24, 44, 61, 194
Shrivastava, Ajay, 112–13
Shukla, Prem, 98, 179
Singh, Bipin Kumar, 224
Singh, Kundan, aka Rahul Raj, 193
Singh, Manmohan, as Finance Minister, 262; as Prime Minister, 266
Singh, M.N., 67, 69–70, 100, 107, 163, 168, 223
Singh, Parambir, 148, 150–51
Singh, Rajnath, 176, 178
Singh, R.U., 28
Singh, Sanjay, 144
Singh, Varun, 284, 286
Singh, Vindu, and cricket spot-fixing racket, 226, *see also* bookies
Singh, V.P., 13
Singh, Y.P., 230–31
Singhal, Rajiv, 292
single-window clearance system, 234, 295
Sinha, Shatrughan, 30
Sinha, Shishir, 276
Sinha, U.K., 272
Sinha, Yashwant, 270
SIT investigations, 144
Sivanandhan, D., 79, 99, 108, 110, 203
skyline, 279–89, 300
skyscrapers, 286, 288
Slum Rehabilitation Authority (SRA), 282–83
slums, 53, 57, 117, 161, 191, 212, 282; mafias, 213
Somani, Rajiv, 211, 295
south Bombay, 2, 29, 233, 245, 249; Altamount Road, 148; Azad Maidan, 39; Bacchubhai Wadi in, 249; Ballard Estate, 107, 224; Byculla, 35, 81, 88, 240–41; Colaba, 81, 245, 255; Dongri area, 132; Kalbadevi, 4, 25, 50, 194; Khetwadi, 29; Marine Drive, 300; Mastan Talao, 17–18; Nagpada, 17; , Pakmodia Street, 96, 110–11, 115, 154–55, 220; Victoria Terminus, 4; Zaveri Bazaar, 2, 8, 10, 40, 62, 66, 81, 155, 293
Soviet Union, 12; dissolution of, 262
Special Investigation Team (SIT), 134
Special Task Force (STF), 57–58, 74
Srikrishna Commission Report, 54–55, 57
stabbings, 39, 42, 46–47
stamp paper scam, multi-crore fake. *See* Telgi scam
stars behind bars, 224–27
State Intelligence Department (SID), 255
State Reserved Police (SRP), 39–40, 42
State Reserved Police Force, 18
stone pelters, 36–37, 47
Students' Islamic Movement of India (SIMI), 146, 185, 191
Subramanian, Anand, 273–74

Subramanyam, P.S., 273
suburbs, 4, 35, 50, 81, 189, 209, 250, 293
Sujata, wife of Rajan, arrest of, 115
Suleman Bakery firing, 48, 57, 65, 75
Surat, 45, 185, 280, 294; textile industries in, 292
Suresh, aka Pappu Kalani, 157, 159; joining Congress, 158
Suryarao, Jaywant, 159
Sutar, Shashikant, 160
Swaraj, Sushma, 176, 178, 223

Tahaliyani, M.L. (J), 202
Taj Mahal Hotel, 187, 196, 199, 217; terror attack at, 197
Taliban, 112
Tanasha, Farid, 80, 99, 115
Tandel, Vijay, 107, 121
Tanki, Shamim, 206
Tanzeem-e-Allah-Ho-Akbar, 17
Tata–Singapore Airlines joint venture, 179
Taurani, Ramesh, 92
Tawde, Vinod, 174
taxi bombs, 186–87, 198
taxi drivers: Abu Salem as, 125; and bar dancers, 249; as guardian angel, 64; getting lead from, 187–88; as informers, 106; and terror attack, 195; as victims 46
telecom revolution, 264
Telgi, Abdul Karim, 134, 142, 251; arrest of, 142
Telgi, Ladsaab, 142
Telgi scam, 134, 142–45, 147, 150, 256
Tendulkar, Sachin, 236
terror attacks, 26/11. *See* 26/11 terror attacks
terrorism, 188, 191
Terrorist and Disruptive Activities (Prevention) Act (TADA), 66, 68–71, 74, 105, 108–9, 157, 159, 224
terrorists, 48–49, 68, 112, 184–85, 188, 196–99, 201
textile industries, 287, 291–92, *see also* mills
Thackeray, Raj, 162, 170–71; attack on railway exam candidates, 171
Thackeray, Aditya, 172
Thackeray, Bal, 29, 43, 47, 69, 71, 100, 118–19, 159–64, 166, 169–70, 178–79, 232, 236; arrest of, 164; and Bollywood, 232; arrest of, 166; as 'Hindu Hriday Samrat,' 47; inflammatory speeches, 153; on Sainiks and Ayodhya demolition, 153; and Satam on, 178
Thackeray, Matoshri of, 58, 162, 166, 169, 178
Thackeray, Raj, 130, 161, 170–71, 193, 244; arrest of, 193
Thackeray, Smita, 162, 232
Thackeray, Uddhav, 130, 140, 149–50, 162, 169–72, 178–79, 183, 228, 234; and Rane, hostility, 169; and Mahajan, 179
Thadani, Anil, 93
Thakur, Hitendra, arrest of, 157
Thakur, Jayendra, aka Bhai Thakur, 141, 157, 159

Thakur, Kshitij, 141
Thakur, Subhash Singh, 78
Thane, 29, 46, 107, 131, 148, 173, 185–86, 190, 234, 251
Tilak, Bal Gangadhar, 236
Tiwari, Vinay, 228
torching shops, 49, 53
trains, 4–5, 50, 142, 153, 189–91, 203, 209, 297, 299, (*see also* Sabarmati Express, fire of); blasts, 189–90; blasts of July 2006, 188, 192; Flying Rani, 294; outstation, 51; Trans-Harbour Link, 300; Western Line, 189–90
trials, 66, 70, 73–75, 99, 109, 130, 158, 195, 201–2, 206, 223–26; of 1993 serial blasts, 71; in 2002, 71
Tulsidas, Goswami, 6
26/11 terror attacks, 97, 147, 184, 194-207
twin blasts in August 2003, 186–88
Tyagi, Ramdev, 48, 57

Udayshanker, 124
Ulhasnagar, 156–57
Umadutt, 1–4, 7–8, 10
Umarkhadi area, 41
Umrao Jaan (1981), 249
underworld, 76–117, 121, 123, 125, 127, 130–31, 133, 141, 145, 221–24, 233; and box office, 221; financing of film industry, 223; killings, 86, 261
unionism, 230–31, 291
union of dance bar owners, 'Fight for Rights of Bar Owners Association,' 251
unions, 45, 85, 230–32, 234, 287, 301
United Arab Emirates (UAE), 65, 101, 125–26, 187
Upadhyay, Keshav, 118
Upadhyay, Sarvesh, 230, 233
Urban Land Ceiling Act, repeal of, 283

Vadgadi, 9–10, 36
Vaidya, Milind, 80; attack on, 109
Vajpayee, Atal Bihari, 55, 77, 176–78; Mahajan as advisor to, 177
Valvi, Padmakar, 167; escape of, 168
Varak, Vilas, 200
Varma, Ram Gopal, 199, 232
Vasai, 156–57
Vasai-Virar, 280
Vashi, 281
Vichare, Rajan, 244
victims, 33, 39, 41–42, 46, 48, 64, 68, 86, 91, 93, 95, 107–8, 138–39; of natural calamities, 242, *see also* monsoon
Victoria Terminus, 50–51, 264, 281
Vidhan Sabha elections, 118, 141, 157, 165–66, 169, 171, 182, 228, 244; 1985, 165; 1990, 29; 1995, 118; 1999, 166–67; 2009, 171; 2019, 182
Vile Parle, 35, 189; bomb blast at railway station, 185; Irla Nullah in, 210
violence, 16, 19, 21–22, 26–27, 29, 34, 37–39, 42, 46–49, 52, 55, 75–76, 184, (*see also* killings; rampages; riots); in 1893, 26;

in 1929, 26; in 1932, 27; across Gujarat, 185; between Shias and Sunnis, 27
Virar, 156
Vishwa Hindu Parishad (VHP), 25, 34, 51, 152
Vora, Jigna, 99
Vora, Ravi Mallesh aka D.K. Rao, 115
V.P. Road, 45
Vyas, Girish, 161

Wadala, 81, 282, 284, 298
Wadi, 8, 10, 20, 33, 35, 38–40, 48–50, 58; first attack on, 50
Wahid, Abdul, acquittal of, 191
Wahid, Faisal, 89
Wahid, Thakiyuddin, murder of, 89–90
water sports, 211, 294–95
water taxi service, 300
Waze, Sachin, 107, 141, 145–50: *Jinkun Harleli Ladhai* of, 147
We' and 'They, 42–43
weapons, 49, 52, 66–68, 84, 88, 94, 106
women, in dance bars 246, 249, 255, 259; killed in CST station terror attack, 202; killed in train bomb blast, 185; and radicalization, 207; stripping and burning alive, 53; underworld and, 95, 125; as victims, 160
World Bank, 262
Worli, 63, 81, 83, 175, 216

Yeshwant, 1–4
Yunus, Khwaja, 131, 145–47; case, 149; disappearance of, 145
Yusuf Meherali Road, 9, 40; as Masjid Bunder Road, 9

Zakariya Masjid, 9, 39
Zaveri Bazaar, 2, 4, 8, 10, 40, 62, 66, 81, 155, 206, 293; bomb explosion at, 206
Ziman, Laxman, 94–95
Zinta, Preity, 222–23

Acknowledgements

It took me around three years to complete this book, but it took thirty years to live it. My teenage years had just begun when Bombay was rocked by communal strife in 1992–93. Being exposed to bloodshed, experiencing the sharp fear of death and hurriedly abandoning home to escape mobs blinded by communal hatred at that young age has left an indelible mark on me. The report by the Justice Srikrishna Commission, fact-finding committees by non-governmental organizations and journalists have all chronicled the horrors that the city endured, but I always wanted to tell my story—a story from the perspective of a person who not only closely witnessed the riots that ripped apart the social fabric of the city, but was also impacted by them. This book tells the story of the worst communal riots that the city suffered and looks at the circumstances foreshadowing the unprecedented violence. It narrates how those riots, in later years, affected various spheres of life in Mumbai, including its politics, its underworld, its social fabric, its businesses, its real estate and so on. I am a witness to this transformation as a Mumbaikar and a journalist, who has covered the city for more than two and a half decades.

When D. Sivanandhan was chief of the Mumbai Crime Branch, he was busy supervising the teams of 'encounter cops'. I used to meet him almost every day to get stories on his mission 'Finish Underworld'. After he retired as director general of police (Maharashtra), our meetings became less frequent. However, whenever we still meet, he always has words of motivation to share. Sivanandhan not only encouraged me to write, but also shared interesting anecdotes from his policing career for my works. He has read all my books and has offered me valuable feedback. I am thankful to him for his support and encouragement.

My interest in writing introduced me to a wonderful person, fellow journalist and author, Dhaval Kulkarni. My gratitude to him for not only guiding me and helping me with resources for the book, but also for acquainting me with Anish Chandy of the Labyrinth Literary Agency. Anish's desire for quality seemed insatiable, and I found his professionalism and love for books inspiring. He has played a huge role in refining my writing and I am grateful to him for representing my work.

I am thankful to veteran journalist and author Meena Menon for gifting me her book *Riots and after in Mumbai: Chronicles of Truth and Reconciliation*, which helped me understand the causes behind the recurring communal conflicts in the city. My gratitude to Atique-ur-Rehman, who taught me political science in the Wilson College and lent valuable research material for this book.

Jehanara Wasi and Shruti Bhushan helped in editing the first draft of the book and I am grateful to them for their inputs.

I have deep regard for Swati Chopra, associate publisher at HarperCollins India, who gave me the opportunity to write my first book in English, *35 Days*. It was a pleasure to collaborate with her for this project as well. I am immensely grateful to Swati and her team at HarperCollins, who worked hard to ensure that the book got published on time. I'd like to thank Jyotsna Raman and Ujjaini Dasgupta for expertly copy-editing the text.

I have met and interviewed several people to gather content for this book. I am grateful to all of them for their time and support.

And I am thankful to my wife, Rimpi, and son, Vedaanta, for their support and for sacrificing their claims on my post-office hours so I could devote time to writing this book.

About the Author

Jitendra Dixit is an author and the west India editor of the ABP Network, based in Mumbai. During his childhood, he closely witnessed acts of violence associated with gang wars and experienced the horror of communal clashes. It is this experience that led him to pursue his career in journalism and specialize in covering crime and conflicts. From the 2002 Gujarat riots to the gang wars of the Mumbai underworld and the 26/11 Mumbai terrorist attacks, Dixit has reported from the ground in his career spanning two and a half decades. His documentary on the Kashmir elections 2014 won the RedInk Award. In 2011, he participated in the Combat International Organised Crime Conference, organized by the FBI in New York City, USA. His previous books are *35 Days*, *Bombay 3* and *Valley of Red Snow*. He is a bibliophile, an itinerant and a certified ocean diver.

30 Years *of*

HarperCollins *Publishers* India

At HarperCollins, we believe in telling the best stories and finding the widest possible readership for our books in every format possible. We started publishing 30 years ago; a great deal has changed since then, but what has remained constant is the passion with which our authors write their books, the love with which readers receive them, and the sheer joy and excitement that we as publishers feel in being a part of the publishing process.

Over the years, we've had the pleasure of publishing some of the finest writing from the subcontinent and around the world, and some of the biggest bestsellers in India's publishing history. Our books and authors have won a phenomenal range of awards, and we ourselves have been named Publisher of the Year the greatest number of times. But nothing has meant more to us than the fact that millions of people have read the books we published, and somewhere, a book of ours might have made a difference.

As we step into our fourth decade, we go back to that one word – a word which has been a driving force for us all these years.

Read.